BRIGID DELANEY has worked as a lawyer, journalist, travel writer and screenwriter and, most recently, as a speechwriter for two federal cabinet ministers.

She is co-creator and associate producer of the Netflix smash hit *Wellmania* and wrote the long-running and popular *Guardian Australia* column 'Brigid Delaney's Diary'.

Her previous books include *This Restless Life*, *Wild Things*, *Wellmania* and *Reasons Not to Worry*, which has been published in North America and the United Kingdom and translated into nineteen languages.

She writes 'The Chaos Era with Brigid Delaney' Substack, and lives in Sydney.

Praise for

REASONS NOT TO WORRY

'Brigid has the most incredible gift of taking seemingly complex and esoteric concepts and explaining them to the reader in a way that is generous and clear, but above all, relatable. Reading this book is like having a long walk with your cool big sister while she just happens to be giving you the skinny on Greco-Roman philosophy.'

BEN LEE, actor and musician

'*Reasons Not to Worry* is both an introduction and an interrogation of Stoicism. With acute thoughtfulness and a genial lightness, Delaney convinces us that this ancient philosophy is still relevant and necessary. I appreciated the kindness in this book, and I was grateful for the care and commitment and joy of the writing and argument.'

CHRISTOS TSIOLKAS, bestselling author of *The Slap*

'A real eye-opener . . . Stoicism is the way I've been trying to live my life.'

RICHARD HARRIS, on ABC Radio National

'This the perfect book for the times. I've been loving it. I found it really fantastic . . . this is going to be a reference book for me. She's also bloody funny.'

ZAN ROWE, Bang On podcast

'It's the book I'm going to be giving everyone I love this Christmas. It's so good!'

MYF WARHURST, Bang On podcast

THE SEEKER AND THE SAGE

A Stoic conversation to hold you together in a fractured world

BRIGID DELANEY

First published in 2025

Allen & Unwin
Cammeraygal Country
83 Alexander Street
Crows Nest NSW 2065
Australia
Phone: (61 2) 8425 0100
Email: info@allenandunwin.com
Web: www.allenandunwin.com

Allen & Unwin acknowledges the Traditional Owners of the Country on which we live and work. We pay our respects to all Aboriginal and Torres Strait Islander Elders, past and present.

EU Authorised Representative: Easy Access System Europe, Mustamäe tee 50, 10621 Tallinn, Estonia, gpsr.requests@easproject.com

A catalogue record for this book is available from the National Library of Australia

ISBN 978 1 76147 077 6

Set in 13/16 pt Garamond Premier Pro by Bookhouse, Sydney
Printed and bound in Australia by the Opus Group

10 9 8 7 6 5 4 3 2

The paper in this book is FSC® certified. FSC® promotes environmentally responsible, socially beneficial and economically viable management of the world's forests.

TO JO BEATTIE—

A STOIC, AND A FRIEND
SINCE WE WERE SEVEN

'The melancholy of the antique world seems to me more profound than that of the moderns, all of whom more or less imply that beyond the dark void lies immortality. But for the ancients that "black hole" is infinity itself; their dreams loom and vanish against a background of immutable ebony. No crying out, no convulsions—nothing but the fixity of the pensive gaze.

With the gods gone, and Christ not yet come, there was a unique moment, from Cicero to Marcus Aurelius, when man stood alone. Nowhere else do I find that particular grandeur.'

—GUSTAVE FLAUBERT

'What should young people do with their lives today? Many things, obviously. But the most daring thing is to create stable communities in which the terrible disease of loneliness can be cured.'

—KURT VONNEGUT

'Think of yourself as dead. You have lived your life. Now take what's left and live properly.'

—MARCUS AURELIUS

THE JOURNEY

Once upon a time, I was shot in the head. It was the side of my head—the skull above the ear, a whisker away from the brain. I was lucky, I suppose, but it was my head, nonetheless. And I was unhappy it had happened.

If there was an upside it was philosophical only. I was suddenly able to appreciate the shortness of life, how it can end at any time.

For me, the reckoning happened on an ordinary day. At work, seated at my terminal with my three monitors, one hand on the mouse, the other half-raised to my mouth—a corn chip between my fingers—eating, typing, eyes constantly flicking to the clock on thc wall where the seconds ticked down to the 4 pm print deadline.

I'd been out all day with the staff photographer, Pete, who was clocking up his sixth job for the day and waiting for the right light. We were investigating a school classroom asbestos scandal and now, back in the newsroom, on deadline, I was hastily transcribing interviews and inserting the best quotes into my piece.

After I'd put in months of legwork—making calls, getting samples tested in labs—the piece was shaping up well and was now a contender for page one. I'd briefed my editor, Lou, on our return from the school and he said, 'Good story, kid,' which is strong praise from him. As the deadline approached, I could see his cursor moving swiftly through the shared doc, editing almost as quickly as I was writing.

A newsroom on deadline is hushed and focused except for the sound of fingers tapping on keys, and the occasional exhale from someone trying to work a tricky sentence. It was in this hush that a sudden carnage erupted, a thicket of bullets ploughing through everything in their way.

I looked up.

Have you ever heard all your colleagues scream? It's like nothing I had ever heard: primal, strange, horrific, bizarre. I almost started laughing.

Later I was told that a man with a gun had managed to get through security (to be fair there was very little security, just Mel downstairs with his bad leg that made standing quickly difficult) and by the time I could clock there was a gunman, a bullet was whizzing past my head.

More screams and the sound of Joe, the paper's sportswriter, hitting the floor.

The clocks on the wall, each with a different time zone, were splintered into shards.

Daryl hid under a desk. Pete fell to the floor, head slumped back at an unnatural angle, glasses smashed up against his eyes, blood pouring from the sockets. And Julie frighteningly exposed—seemingly frozen in terror—a pen midair, as if correcting the trajectory of a flying bullet instead of one of our sentences.

It is as all shooting survivors describe it: time slows down; there's even room to think, reflect and experience a range of emotions. Fear, panic, terror, anger, sadness, grief, rage, regret coursed through me all at once, like these things do in a dream.

In the lengthening moment, there was so much to register: my colleagues falling from their chairs, the bullets moving fast like bees from a disturbed hive, the spraying of blood and shattering of bone, the now lone clock on the wall showing Greenwich Mean Time (United Kingdom, Republic of Ireland, Portugal) and the blinking green light of the gunman's GoPro attached to his helmet.

So much going on that I didn't have time to duck.

However, this story is not about that—it's about what happened in the aftermath, and how it changed me.

—

In the hospital, I regressed to a state that felt infantile, and even, at certain times, embryonic. With little awareness of what was happening around me, there was just a strange sensation of being underwater and close to the source of all things. I was comforted by the presence of my mother, who most nights slept curled in the chair beside me, her arm across my bed, touching my hand. I wish I could have talked to her—told her how strange things were in my head right now. (And how I wish I could have comforted her when I heard her cry.)

Day brought fractals of light, filtered through a curtain of hospital green, motes of dust tumbling through the air, long corridors of sunlight across the bed, the pressure of the bandage on my head, a feeling of fathomless exhaustion.

A parade of doctors and friends and relatives filed past my bed. There was Lou, my sister Caroline with Hannie, her new baby, sleeping in her arms. Old friends from school swept in with arms full of flowers. People I had thought were long lost. A colleague from a long-ago internship on the other side of the country arrived with a vial of holy water from Lourdes and glass rosary beads. I was touched to see so many former co-workers from the deep past, Noel, my regular barista, and even Mr Patch, my grumpy neighbour. They said they missed my dry, often dark sense of humour, or the time I made for them when they needed a friendly ear, or my idealism and strong sense of justice; my barista even said he missed making my elaborate coffee order (triple shot latte with soy milk). All reassured me that I was loved, looked after, and would be home soon.

I waited for my father, but just when I thought I sensed him near, I would be gone again into a dark and dreamless place that was entirely without content or sensation. It was not unpleasant; it was just nothing.

It was in this timeless other realm that sometimes I saw Mel—the security guard—leg healed, charging down the corridors, strong and purposeful. I saw Pete, with his head thrown back at that unnatural angle (just an hour before he had been photographing schoolchildren in the golden hour), Julie correcting a page proof, and then the gunman himself—walking towards me, this time—as if through a mist.

'Why did you do it?' I asked him, genuinely curious. 'You ruined everything.'

'You can read my manifesto on the internet,' he replied.

I turned away.

If I had emotions, they were faint. I felt detached.

The phrase 'life is cheap' seemed to hang in the air, like a billboard advertising an interest-free period on a credit card.

My colleagues Joe, Rachel, Sonya, Mel, Pat, Alex, Vin, Pete and Julie were killed.

'It's not cheap—it's more precious than . . . more precious than . . .' I struggled to find the words.

From my hospital bed, it felt as if to be here, in the world, with all its suffering, pain, problems and violence—well, I could take it or leave it. How easy would it be just to slip away, with my ticket to board the Crystal Ship? At the 2 am shift change between nurses or at the midpoint in the afternoon when my mother would go to the vending machine, or my drowsy sister would stir to nurse the baby, I could slip out, ghosting everyone.

But at other times to die seemed unbearable, impossible, an intolerable notion. Beauty, mystery and a miraculous sort of order seemed to coexist everywhere, even in the coloured bulbs of the machines attached to me and keeping me alive. In their flashing sequence, I could see music.

For a long time, I hovered in this strange, liminal space.

At night, my mother's body close to mine, the radio harmonies tender and sad, I was back there—in the town where I grew up. It was cold, by the sea, and our apartment was too small, and the stairwell smelt of sweet, rotting garbage, and our neighbours were mostly misfits—but now I only recalled sunny days. It may have been the drugs they gave me in hospital or it may have been my near-death experience, but everything that had once seemed mean, shabby, harshly lit and unromantic was transformed into memories that unfurled elegiacally, infused with sacredness. Still a child, I was barefoot and walking on the soft grass with my sister, her plump baby hand in mine, the light in columns of pale gold shining through the slats of the fences we walked past, the air scented with brine. Then older—in our best dresses, walking through the seagrass, and beyond, the trees a vivid green, deep and alive, humming with birds, insects, cicadas . . . life . . . And it all seemed so achingly beautiful that to depart would be unbearable—and I would do anything, make any promise, to stay for just a little bit longer. One more day, please. Just one more day.

In that time, as orderlies turned me over and I was sponged and changed (hoisted and lowered, rising and falling, like a Mayan princess on a throne), I could hear fragments of human voices.

'Attach a line . . . Just there . . . schedule for tomorrow . . . the team is ready . . . Okay, yes . . .'

Look around, look around, the radio told me. I saw the linoleum floor sliding nightmarishly through my unstable vision, nurses' hands moving about my body, my sister on one side of the bed, my mother on the other—their faces marked by fatigue and anxiety.

Then one morning Lou's voice cut through my aquatic world. He was sitting by my bed, just talking, as if time wasn't important and he didn't have a newspaper to edit.

'I'm sad you didn't get to travel much. You always worked too hard,' he said, moving his chair closer to the bed.

'You need to have a life outside work. I know you love what you do, but what about boyfriends? What about friends? I worry about you. You seem so alone sometimes . . . When I was young, we didn't work so hard. There were years and years of just hanging out.

They were the best years. That's the secret you never hear. That time doing nothing with your friends is the best time. That, and travelling. Did I ever tell you about Silver Springs? It's paradise.'

He sighed. His voice softened, and he leaned back in his chair as if settling in to tell a long story. It was fine—I wasn't going anywhere.

'It was 1970 and in those days there was just so much freedom. I left home at sixteen and became a stevedore down at the wharfs and that was it—I was gone for three years. I went everywhere—Hawaii, Rhodesia, Australia. Indonesia, the Philippines, Nepal, India. The Vietnam War was still raging, I didn't really want to come back home. God, it was good. I felt so free. I was furious that I had missed the sixties, free love and the hippie trail, the ashrams and the gurus and the bearded men who could teach you how to live for a thousand years. Strange to think but in the 1970s I thought it was all over, that all nirvanas of what we called the East had been discovered and what was left was discarded and exhausted. Little did I know then that the world was still quiet and pristine compared with now. It only becomes paradise when you realise it has been lost.

'But there was this one place, one last holdout. I heard rumours of it from other travellers. The local people, Jinghpaw I think, called it San Ai, meaning "crystal waters". The English gave it a more romantic name—Silver Springs. Gertrude Bell was said to have visited just before the Great War and fell in love with the landscape—the high green cliffs and azure lakes below, the shaded woodlands, the sense of being enclosed, held by the surrounding mountains. Bell described it to friends as a lost Eden, with a night sky famous for its brightness and clarity, galaxies that could be seen with the naked eye. Hanging gardens, shaded verandahs on the jungle's edge, a broad and handsome town square lined with civic buildings devoted to justice, education, governance and town meetings. A sophisticated—even enlightened—self-governing, self-sustaining region that existed halfway between the democratic world and the celestial realm. A peaceful place—according to Bell's diaries—where pacts with neighbours were respected.

'The Nazi-hunters arrived in the late 1940s and had to be cajoled to continue their journeys. They found it so delightful they wanted to stay. In the fifties, Jack Kerouac was said to have passed through, again staying for months longer than anticipated. He called it "an enchantment" that kept him there so long. Aldous Huxley visited with his wife and recorded several entries in his journal marvelling at the assorted people that called Silver Springs home—Jinghpaw, Naga, urban Burmese, exiled Indian gurus, English hippies, wandering shepherds, travelling monks, runaways, rebel aristocrats, writers and astronomers.

'But for all the legend surrounding the town, it was a very difficult place to get to. So many tried and didn't make it. You needed to walk for at least a week up steep mountains, where sometimes the tracks just disappeared. Then through jungle, crossing a river, a lake, dodging landmines and suspicious villagers and armed militia. The drug trade operated via the alternative Southern Silk Road, and all the way to China was bandit country. Get through all that and if you made a wrong turn then it was all for nothing.

'No one would tell me straight up where exactly Silver Springs was. Somewhere on the Indian side of Burma, high up in the mountains. Close to inaccessible. There were maps but they were tightly held. Not shared. Not copied. Travellers are a secretive bunch, sensitive to the magic of a place and how fragile it can be. There was a pact—unspoken but understood—that the location of this town should be kept secret. It's spectacularly beautiful, built into the side of a cliff—looking down into a fertile valley, a string of turquoise lakes and hot springs like jewels placed around the stone neck of the mountains.

'Aside from beauty, this town was also extremely unusual. It was run according to Ancient Greek principles found in the philosophy of Stoicism and had been for many generations. Travellers came back saying they had found the secret to happiness—and if only this model of community would spread, then there would be no wars, no divisions, no separations between different types of people.

'I think I got close to finding it but there was a landslide. The road was closed, monsoons were forecast. To try to cross the affected area meant risking my life. My motorbike needed repairs. The snow started early that year. And my guides got spooked. They didn't want to chance going higher. I was devastated to be leaving without having visited paradise. I had made it so close . . . But I was young and I was sure I'd come back some day.'

Lou was quiet for a long time—like he was going back there in his mind.

'But life got in the way and I never returned. Later I wondered if it was dreamt up by all those travellers. That if instead of visiting Silver Springs they had some sort of inner experience, a collective sartori. That all of us were chasing a fantasy.'

Our newspaper tried to recover as best it could after the mass shooting—but, truth is, we were on our last legs even before the events of 22 April. *The Sentinel* had gone from fat and thriving in the twentieth century to something that limped along with the support of small donations and classifieds. When private equity made an offer on *The Sentinel* and twenty other regional and suburban newspapers just like us, it was the end of the thing I had loved. My role as an investigative reporter would be merged to create a mega cities desk, serving the twenty different regions. But even without the private equity mergers, the aftermath was going to suck.

Traumatised *Sentinel* staff not only had to adjust to returning to a crime scene (one that had been cleaned up, but the violence never totally erased: the stubborn bloodstains on the walls and floor, the bullet holes, a smell too, that was hard to place but impossible to forget), but also had to carry on without some key colleagues. Rachel, Sonya, Mel, Pat, Alex, Vin, Pete and Julie were killed, Joe died in the ambulance and I was in hospital.

The gunman's motives were depressingly banal. We had published an editorial the week before on some culture war topic that had unreasonably and overwhelmingly provoked him to homicidal madness.

I won't repeat the topic here. It does the dead no service.

Lou—who penned the editorial—had been in a separate office down the hall at the time of the shooting, editing my story. He was unscathed, except for the fact that he would probably never stop blaming himself.

Lou delivered the bad news in person. Still in hospital, I was well enough to sit up by then and hold brief conversations before the fatigue floored me. But I had been hoping to return to work. That was what was keeping me going. Lou could barely look me in the eye when he gave me the bad news. There was enough money in the bank for another six months, but the private equity offer was the only way the paper could continue, albeit in a skeletal form. My position was being made redundant in the merger. This news devastated me more than I had expected. That newspaper had been my life, my colleagues like family. What was I going to do now?

'I want you to do one last story for me,' said Lou, his voice cracking.

I hesitated. I was still recovering. Some days the fatigue knocked me out so badly that it was all I could do to have a shower and watch something short on my phone. But other days I felt I could take on the world, go back to journalism and write a killer page one story. I was still angry that the asbestos story hadn't got a run (the shooting meant that nothing was sent to the printers that afternoon). The gunman had taken so much from me—but he also took away my page one.

'It's just one more time on the road,' said Lou.

'Look at me, I'm in no fit state to be writing stories,' I said, turning away because there were tears in my eyes. 'Particularly not from the road.'

'I wouldn't ask if I didn't think you could do it.'

'What's the brief?'

Lou smiled. 'It's a good one, I promise. I want you to travel to Silver Springs and write a story about it,' he said.

'The hippie town you were telling me about?'

'You remember that conversation?'

'I could hear things—I just couldn't respond. But it sounded like paradise.'

'Yes! It is. It's more than just a hippie town. It's a great story! No one's reported on it for decades. It's more secretive than North Korea. As far as I'm aware, there's not even the internet there. It's like it just vanished from the map. Yes, it's hard to get to but not impossible. What's become of it? Is it a utopia? Or is it a cult? Is it still an autonomous kingdom or did it get swallowed up in the junta? Does it even exist and, if so, do they have anything to teach us? Or did they fuck things up there too?'

Lou was getting excited and talking a mile a minute. His enthusiasm was infectious—I wanted to see this place for myself—but I wondered if Lou was also delusional. How did he think I could go back on the road in my current state?

'It sounds like a tough journey. You said so yourself. I don't know if I'm strong enough,' I said. 'I mean—look at me!'

My arms were sticks, skin translucent, the right side of my head bandaged. And then there were the things he couldn't see:

the night terrors, cold sweats and flashbacks, the fear that washed through me like a transfusion of icy blood every day at 4 pm.

But Lou pushed on. 'I spoke to your doctors. I spoke to your mother and sister. Everyone agrees you're strong enough. You're made of steel, the bravest reporter I know. And the most dedicated. I saved this one for you because you're special and because this is it, kid. What a great last piece to do before *The Sentinel*, as we know it, dies,' said Lou.

I was sad, but also speechless for a moment—the unflappable Lou actually sounded emotional.

Yet, despite the promise of a great story, the risks overshadowed the reward.

'A long time—decades!—have passed since you first tried to get to Silver Springs. It's not even called Burma anymore. No one can get in without great difficulty. Everything will have changed,' I said.

'Silver Springs would definitely have changed,' said Lou. 'Everything is always changing. I just want to know *how*. It'll make a great story. C'mon, you're always saying I never send you away.'

That was true. There was never enough money to go anywhere. But still, I hadn't fully recovered. At least, not mentally. Some mornings after a terrible night's sleep, I would go to the bathroom and in the overhead light, haloed as though I was under interrogation, I didn't recognise my own face. I had to touch it just to make sure I was real.

Lou put a warm hand on my shoulder. 'Just think about it, okay?'

I nodded, believing it probably wouldn't happen, but the reporter part of me hoped it might.

Decades on from Lou's expedition, finding the exact location of Silver Springs—or San Ai—was harder than I had anticipated. Was this the last obscure place in the world? More mysterious than Mars? It seemed so, with very little written about the town—and evidently so few visitors due to its relative distance from civilisation and an airport.

Nothing on Instagram. Nothing on TripAdvisor or Facebook. Even when I managed to track down an old paper copy of the Lonely Planet guide, there was no mention of it under either name. Some places were too lonely, even for the Lonely Planet.

I cobbled some notes from Lou's memory. Arriving overland via India and crossing the border near Davantown. Then three days climbing past the jungle lowlands, before milder climate and mountains. Part of the journey was to be taken by river, but that's where it was easy to get lost, and where lawlessness reigned.

In an old digitised encyclopedia I found some photos and a short description, but it was stuff that seemed abstract and pointless. *Elevation—5000 ft. Population—2000. Industry—Farming.*

Of note—the colonial hill station architecture, the blue-green lakes, cool climate and the clear night skies that had drawn astronomers for hundreds of years. Nominally a kingdom, but smaller than any of the hundreds of principalities that cooperated with the central administration. There were no details of a royal family, and no mention of the philosophy.

'Yes, that's it!' said Lou when I showed him the entry. He was off on his reminiscences, but it all sounded unsure and vague about how to *actually* get there.

'Well, I had come the roundabout way, overland from India and Afghanistan. When you could still cross Afghanistan . . .'

'Well, that's not much help to me.'

'You could cross from China, if you can get in there, and go via the old smugglers' route, the alternative Southern Silk Road—'

'Where the bandits and drug runners are? No thanks.'

'You need to contact the Mayor,' he texted one day. 'That's the key.'

The Mayor? Who even was that? Did this far-flung place really have this layer of government? Doubt started creeping in that Silver Springs even existed. But if Lou taught me anything about reporting it was that you don't stop looking; just spend another hour after you've decided to give up.

He was right.

Finally, deep into a Google search on page 54 (scrolling past all the Silver Springs that were rehab centres, hot springs resorts or wellness facilities and planned suburbs, and all the San Ai's that were Korean AI start-ups), I found some more references to a Silver Springs in old travel blog posts, made using ancient HTML code and sans serif fonts. They described the town's beauty, built snug in a valley, surrounded by high mountains, verdant farmland, turquoise lakes and hot springs.

Legendary traveller and writer Michel Chan Jana called it 'The world's last true paradise' and said 'The only hardship of arriving is having to leave.' How did he get there? But he had died later that year, and his estate did not return my emails.

After some difficulty, I managed to reach some of the other travellers via ancient Yahoo and AOL addresses.

One of the old hippies (he of the sans serif font) called me back when I was halfway through changing my bandages. I scrambled for a pen. He said he met the Mayor of Silver Springs on a pilgrimage he took in the early 1980s.

'He was a mixture of a conventional mayor and the town's spiritual director. We sat on the ground, and he talked about death. It was . . . heavy.'

'Can you remember what he said?' I asked.

'That when we die we are returned to the Earth. That was the word he used—"returned". Death is nature. And that the town had these macabre burial rites. The bodies would be driven on a road out of town—a real no-man's-land—and placed on a mountain to be devoured by wild animals. Eyes pecked out by vultures. Heart ripped from your chest by a hungry leopard. No thanks! What a place to die!'

He warned me about travelling to such a backward and 'medieval' place (in fact, he explicitly said, 'Don't go there'), told me about the airstrip that had become overgrown and was no longer operational, and the military junta to the east.

But he also put me in touch with a woman who had grown up in Silver Springs and was now working as a psychologist in London.

She had an unusual accent, but her English was perfect. She told me she had good memories of her childhood, but ultimately left Silver Springs due to its small size, isolation and limited prospects.

'It was a happy community—not an Eden, it wasn't perfect. But at least people tried. A lot of people in the town were philosophically inclined, to the extent that I would call it an intentional community. Everyone knew each other, everyone helped each other. There were lots of feast days and festivals. It was a party town, too—people got together a lot to play music, sing, talk. It was a very happy childhood. But please don't write about it. The publicity would not be good for the town. I've seen what happens when people flock to so-called utopias. They kill the thing that drew them there in the first place. And it's so fragile, and rare.'

'Can you at least give me the details of the Mayor—'

She hesitated.

'The current mayor is quite old now. Might even be in an old folks' home. I'm sorry—but I don't think he'd like it if I just handed out his address,' she replied.

'Okay, you said they were philosophically inclined. What philosophy?' I asked.

'Stoicism—the classical Greek and Roman philosophy. It was big in pre-Christian times and was generally viewed as a philosophy most integrated with the world as it is, rather than an idealistic view of the world that you might see in the romanticism of Epicureanism or in the radicalism of the Cynic school.'

'Why that philosophy—and not religion?'

'That was the tradition of the town; I never thought to question it. I didn't know any other way.'

'Was this philosophy useful? Or was it too conceptual?'

'It was useful. I still use it every day—both in my work and in my life,' she said.

Another old link took me to a Benedictine monastery in Spain where one of the monks had also visited the Mayor of Silver Springs as part of a PhD program and had written about the encounter in a parish newsletter.

'I even wrote the town's Wikipedia entry—under its Anglicised name Silver Springs—until the Mayor convinced me not to publish it,' he told me. 'Said the town wanted to be private. That's the word he used, which I thought was strange. What's he got to hide?'

I was intrigued.

The monk said although the Mayor was wise, I should be careful not to single him out as special, as the one with all the answers.

'He is just a man,' said the monk. 'He's not a god. And he's not a sage.'

'What's a sage?' I asked.

'It's a philosophical thing. Kind of like a Stoic version of a saint. The highest practitioner of Stoicism—someone supremely virtuous, who sees everything that happens to him as part of nature's plan. The sage delivers a "joyful yes!" to all that occurs to him or her, and all that occurs in the universe.'

'A joyful yes?'

'Yes.'

'I love that!'

'Good luck finding a real-life sage. As far as I know, no one alive today is claiming to be a sage. And if he—'

'Or she—' I interrupted, sure that there were women sages as well as men.

'If he or she existed, they wouldn't be going around saying they're a sage,' he said.

'Does this Mayor call himself a sage?'

'No, not as far as I'm aware. He is actually quite unapproachable; I would even say unfriendly.'

'Hmm. Where can I find him? Do you have a phone number or an email address?'

The monk laughed.

'He's not on email. He's extremely offline.'

'No one's offline.'

'You'd be surprised,' said the monk. 'And a warning: if you travel there, be prepared. It's beautiful. An absolutely stunning place, but the philosophy will challenge you. Not for nothing is Silver Springs known as the dread realm of absolute truth.'

My reporter's sixth sense fired up and I started to see the shape of a really good story. Had this place found some sort of secret to happiness that they were jealously guarding from the rest of us? Or had it all gone to shit? Was the town even still there? Or had it been destroyed by climate change or war, or modernised, the way so many other special places had been destroyed? With so few mysteries left in the world, with everything mapped by Google, and at our fingertips, I sensed this could be a genuinely new discovery. I wanted to go.

In pain before my evening meds, I allowed myself the delicious and seductive anaesthesia of fantasy. My fantasy was this: my story would crack open the secret to happiness, go viral and change lives. I imagined awards. I imagined a podcast series and being number one on Spotify. I imagined job offers from the big media companies. I imagined a Netflix deal. I imagined the Emmys. I imagined fame and money—posting selfies from the red carpet, the envy of my peers.

And maybe it didn't have to be a fantasy. I could make it real. After my pleading, in the case of public interest journalism, the Benedictine monk reluctantly offered to act as an intermediary between myself and the Mayor of San Ai or Silver Springs or whatever this place was called, and post a letter on my behalf.

After my urging verged on harassment, the monk also relented and sent me the draft Wikipedia entry.

'Not for publication!' he said. 'I promised the Mayor.'

Silver Springs/San Ai

Independent principality on the border between north Myanmar and north-east India.

Silver Springs, also known as San Ai, is a small independent principality located in the Myanmar–India highlands near the Indian region of Nagaland. Colonial records state the land area of the Silver Springs concession as 38 square miles (just under 100 square kilometres), although no survey has been undertaken for more than a century. Land borders with neighbouring tribal areas are customary.

Silver Springs is unusual in that there are no records of war or even violence with neighbours: skilful diplomacy, remoteness, and a philosophy of non-violence has allowed the tiny 'kingdom' to maintain independence at least going back 200 years, and possibly further. The principality is ruled by a council, with the Mayor having the status of a monarch. The political system—municipal elections, courts etc.—and much else about Silver Springs is obscure because the community restricts tourism or immigration and discourages communications with the outside world.

HISTORY

The first Europeans in the area, approaching Silver Springs from the south-west, noted a reluctance from Nagaland tribal guides to enter the foothills beneath the Silver Springs plateau. Whether this was a form of taboo or a more practical fear is not known. What is certain is that a handful of adventurers nevertheless managed to make it to the town, and there discovered a people 'quite unlike both the Naga and Burmese in aspect'.

The sources state that several Europeans did not return, with an implication they settled in the town. As with almost all Silver Springs history, this is unclear because residents apparently refuse to correspond with the outside world. In the mid-nineteenth century, many European-style houses and buildings were constructed after an influx of European colonial administrators, seeking relief from the heat of either Burma or the north-east lowland Indian frontier. Although never a formal colonial property, it was at this time that Silver Springs took on the appearance of a more typical colonial hill station.

At the beginning of the Second World War, it is noted that the Silver Springs Mayor decided to further isolate the already remote community from the world. The British were asked to leave and, to the surprise of outsiders, complied. We have very few verified facts about the principality from this time. Silver Springs henceforth becomes a kind of obscure Shangri-la for idealistic travellers.

The town is famed for its clear skies. It is the clearest vantage point to see the Milky Way and has long attracted the interest of stargazers and serious students of the cosmos.

Now I was even more intrigued. I put my request for an audience with the Mayor in the most flattering terms. I thought if I appealed to his vanity, he'd grant me an interview; after all, don't all old men think they know how to fix the world—if only everybody would listen?

I wrote, *I want to write something giving people a model of how to live. And I want to give people hope. Among people my age, there is a level of cynicism and hopelessness about the future that is close to despair. We often ask ourselves—what is the point of it all? If you meet with me, and agree to be interviewed, this could be your chance to put it all down—create a legacy.*

The Mayor wrote back (what a strange thrill to get a letter in a soft-blue airmail envelope, with stamps!!, almost six weeks after I had posted mine) and said, '*Look at how soon we're all forgotten. The abyss of endless time that swallows it all. The emptiness of those applauding hands. The people who praise us: how capricious they are, how arbitrary. And the tiny region in which it takes place. The whole Earth a point in space—and most of it uninhabited.*'

What? Interesting—the Mayor was not to be flattered with talk of a legacy. But his objection didn't worry me. We had started talking; he was real. It was a start—and now I had his address.

I wrote back, *Maybe a free-flowing conversation that I could record could be of use to others? People have abandoned religion; work no longer provides meaning; family is not necessarily stable; friendships are conducted virtually; young people are depressed; mental health is at an all-time low—our society and its people feel exhausted.*

No answer.

I wrote a third letter—more personal this time and more truthful: *It was an ordinary working day when the shooter came into the newsroom. A Tuesday . . .*

I told him the ugly truth—that I was traumatised by a random act of violence, but even if I hadn't been, even if I had kept on going, was everything *really* that great? I lacked a rudder. Internally I cycled between confused, depressed, anxious and numb. What did I believe in? What outside cause or passion was I truly engaged in? There had to be more to life than this. Maybe he could enlighten me?

This letter must have got me over the line.

A very short reply came inquiring if I was well enough to travel, but there it was: a cautious 'yes'. Not a 'joyful yes'. But a yes, nonetheless. In the same letter, the Mayor warned me of Silver Springs' remoteness and the hard roads I would need to travel to get there.

After I obtained the correct visa from the nearest regional centre—Davantown—he would speak to me over the course of three days and three nights, and in that time I could ask him anything.

—

The night before I left, Lou came to see me in my studio apartment. It was the first time he'd visited and I was feeling well enough to be self-conscious about how small and cluttered it was. There was only one chair, so I offered him that and sat on the bed.

'I'm scared, Lou. I'm not used to being scared—but I think it's because of what happened to us. I get nervous even leaving the apartment,' I said, feeling anxious even alluding to the shooting.

'You need to take this step,' he said.

'I don't think I'm ready.' I tried to stop my voice from shaking.

'I think you're ready. And if you don't do it now, you'll never do it.' He was firm. I knew not to argue when he used that tone.

He reached into his bag and pulled out a dictaphone.

'It's okay—I can record on my phone,' I told him.

'Kid, always assume technology will fail. This little machine will survive everything you can throw at it, as long as you have batteries.' It was surprisingly weighty and solid.

Then he took out a book: *Meditations* by Marcus Aurelius. 'You need to read this before you meet the Mayor. This book is foundational, and will make even more sense when you get to Silver Springs.'

'This is a self-help guy?'

Lou rolled his eyes. 'This is a Roman emperor. The Philosopher-King.'

I flipped the book open—you know, how you do to be polite—and a phrase jumped out and grabbed me.

'Be neither vexed at the present, nor afraid of the future.'

Then to my surprise, Lou unclipped the watch from his wrist. It was his trademark. He never took it off and refused to pull out his phone whenever he needed to know the time. A chunky and faded Casio—nothing special or expensive but for the fact that he wore it every day. The back case was smooth from decades on his arm, his wrist paler and softer where the watch had been. He clipped it around my narrow wrist but it was so loose, it was more like a bracelet.

'Lou—no. Not your watch! How will you tell the time?'

'You have it for luck. It gave me luck when I first went looking for Silver Springs.'

'But you didn't get there in the end.'

'Yeah,' he said ominously. 'But also—I didn't die.'

Next challenge. How to get to Silver Springs?

It had been easier back in Lou's day—a socialist government had negotiated a ceasefire between two warring villages.

But the old regime had long fallen, and much of the region was now broken up into small fiefdoms, controlled by distant corporations—sometimes based as far away as Russia. They did deals with local thugs who enforced ownership of land and resources. The resources included large crops of opium to the west (one of the largest in the world, it was rumoured) that was guarded by the Davan State army.

The other big industry was bauxite mining, with pristine jungle rapidly receding in the race to clear land.

The capital itself—Davantown—named after some old colonial ruler, Lord Davan or some such, was run-down but maybe not for much longer. A Russian company had started drilling just before Covid; it was looking destined to be another petro-state, controlled by a distant oligarch.

After a sleepless night flying north-east, I changed planes in Singapore and got a flight to India, then another flight from New Delhi to Davantown. I went through it all as if I was a zombie, among all the other zombie travellers. Sitting at gate lounges, feet on my backpack, drowsy, waiting for flight calls. An overpriced airport burrito sitting like a brick in my guts. Trudging through bleak corridors. Waiting in line. Showing my passport. Waiting in line.

Red wine and valium. Changing my bandages in the plane toilet, avoiding looking at my reflection under those harsh fluorescent lights. Knowing it will be bad, and that I have aged *hard* since that last day at work. Back in my seat, time not moving, even as I tracked the plane's journey across the screen.

Davantown's airport was a few shipping containers next to a strip of concrete. Bags were left on the tarmac and I tried not to feel unsafe. But Dav did not feel like a safe place. It felt like I'd fallen off the map, and everyone else there was similarly adrift, and somehow unaccounted for. Every person I met seemed exhausted—spiritually and physically.

The consulate only took visa applications to San Ai every Monday, and I'd just missed my window, so I took a room at a faded grand hotel that had long ago gone to seed. The wood was rotting in the stairs leading to the lobby, and seemed likely to collapse under the weight of a heavy footfall. Mould climbed the walls, the water from the taps smelt fetid, and the electricity supply was unreliable. I spent frustrating hours trying to contact Lou and my mother by phone, but the signal made several long, eerie beeps before cutting out.

As for email, the clerk on the front desk shrugged and said, 'Sometimes', but it was as if the lack of energy in Dav itself had infected its communications system, and emails that looked like they might send (albeit slowly and sluggishly) ran out of power before taking flight.

Sleep came with the help of the sweet, strong rum they sold in the bar, but then I'd wake up hours later, thirsty and afraid. In dreams—more vivid and real than any I'd ever had—it all came back (Lou, confused, walking down the hall; Vin, slumped in his brain-soaked chair; my hand to my bleeding head, still not comprehending; the smell of iron in the air from all the blood).

At night, I sat at the bar—prospectors, oil executives, financiers, sex workers, geologists coming and going, and a crooner singing James Taylor and the Eagles (and how I came to dread that line from 'Hotel California' about never being able to leave). 'One day soon it will be richer than Qatar,' said an Indian prospector, gleeful to be here before the hordes. The scene was as weird as the *Star Wars* cantina. The men mostly left me alone when they found out I wasn't for sale. Even the missionaries avoided me when they saw my eyes, and the deep pain in them. I felt exiled here or, even worse, like once here, away from all who knew me, I had ceased to exist. There was just one man who seemed to clock me. Tall, handlebar moustache, tremor in his right hand that he kept hidden behind his back, drink in his left hand, cigarette smouldering in the ashtray. He held me in his gaze—eyes flickering to my face then away. Over and over again. You can never leave. One night I swear he said, 'Come with me,' as he passed me on the stairs. Come with me? *Where?*

On the Monday morning I woke up (still exhausted, in a tangle of sweat-soaked sheets, the fan cutting the hot air too slowly) to find dried blood on my sheets, my hand bleeding and my phone violently smashed. Its screen was shattered to bits, its insides hanging out, as though it had been thrown across the room with great force. I panicked—had someone come in and done this? But the door was locked from the inside. Was it me? No! Glass shards were stuck in the charging port—even when I forced the cord in, it wouldn't fire up. I was able to bandage my hand and stem the flow of blood with gauze. But I was fucked without my phone. Hand throbbing, I fell into despair and contemplated turning back. A bad hand I could live with—but how could I do anything without my phone? I tried to call Lou from the public phone in the lobby but just kept getting the long beeps, and an operator in a foreign language coming at me fast.

It was with a paper map I found my way to an administrative building in downtown Dav, its doors protected by chicken wire and a scared, skinny security guard with a machine gun thicker than his torso.

I grumbled at the administrative headache (paperwork! forms!), and cursed Lou for pressuring me to take this assignment. The delay in Dav was beginning to worry me. And for what? Essentially a long weekend in Silver Springs?

Even now, a visitor's visa wasn't guaranteed, and it might take days for them to grant it. The Mayor had written a letter in support and I had to present for an interview at the consulate. Tiny Silver Springs had a consulate! I showed up in my creased dress, with my shiny, wet face—so sweaty that any make-up just slid off. My smashed and broken phone was the ghost limb in my pocket. I kept feeling it vibrate but it was just my leg shaking.

My injured hand, I kept behind my back. By the time my name was called, I was ready to beg, plead, do just about anything to get out of Dav. I had been there for six days and was delirious, swimming in a soup of rum, sweat, fear, paranoia and lack of sleep. The man with the tremor was now keeping my hours in the bar, and once or twice, in the pretty coal-burning haze of dusk, when I took my walk, I swear he was right behind me. When I wasn't in my room, bent over maps, planning my journey into the highlands, I was gripped by the gaps in my memory—gaps that seemed horrifically large and gaping. Was the gunman still alive? In jail? Or was he shot or did he turn the gun on himself? I couldn't recall but this seemed like a fatally ignorant position to be in. If I didn't know if my would-be killer was killed or locked up, how could I feel safe?

And so, in the darkest hours of day and night, I sensed he was hunting me still, that he had followed me all the way to this hot, uncomfortable place. Ice melting fast in my drink, hard-faced children at the bar, bandages dirty on my mangled hand, mind disturbed and losing track of all time.

Just when I thought I would be in Dav forever, in the grip of some sort of psychic spiral, word came via the hotel that my papers were in order and a visa would be granted.

'No extensions,' said the man at the consulate. 'And prison if you overstay, even by an hour. Good luck getting there. It's not a trip for the faint-hearted. Many die trying to get to San Ai.'

Before he stamped my passport, he looked at me closely.

'Are you sure you're healthy enough to take the trip? You don't look . . .'—he let the word hang in the air—*well*.

'It looks worse than it is,' I reassured him quickly, something that he didn't seem to believe, but exhausted—like all the others—and not really caring, he stamped my passport anyway.

—

Finding a vehicle was harder, and very costly, but eventually I paid over-the-odds for a lift with a group of prospectors going north, right up into the jungle 'where it's still pure', said one, with a mercenary glint in his eyes.

We drove from the capital on laterite roads, through noisy rainforests to Sawlinn, a bauxite mining town. 'You've got to pray it doesn't rain, otherwise you'll get stuck,' said a prospector. 'Gullies develop in the rain—that's where you can get up-ended.'

After two days on the road, we stopped abruptly—a great big river met us at the end of the track.

It was magnificent. It felt like the end of the world. Or maybe the beginning. The river teemed like a living thing—its caramel waters rushing past, smelling sweet and clean. The dankness of Dav receded like waking after a bad dream.

The boat waiting for us was little more than a floating pontoon, with two planks that we carefully rolled the former military jeep onto. We waited all day until the ferry was full (it was all men bar me, going to prospect), then we made our crossing.

An old man stood with me at the edge of the barge. 'Best rum in the world is made from the river water. The silt comes down from the rainforest—"sweet water" they call it—and once you taste the rum, you can never get enough.'

He gave an exaggerated wink then passed me his flask, which I took reluctantly. I passed it under my nose before taking a sip. It was heaven—just as he promised. I wanted more.

After a smooth crossing, we rolled the jeep off the barge but this side of the river seemed wilder and stranger than Dav.

There followed more humid days, driving slowly with the windows down, the air thick as a blanket, and nights sleeping draped in mosquito nets in hammocks on the terraces behind the roadhouses, fuel purchased in drink bottles, hard biscuits, packet ramen noodles and bananas for dinner.

We crossed an abandoned military checkpoint and, from there, the towns thinned out; we went further and further from bolded place names on the map, and deeper into the jungle. Away from the river, there were unprosperous places where there was little food, the water was bad and all the shops, temples and churches had been abandoned. There had once been missionaries along this stretch of land they called Fever Valley but they were driven out by the opium trade. The opium traders murdered everyone, even their friends in the church.

Then came a sector known for being particularly treacherous. The old jeep climbed high into the mountains before abruptly sputtering to a stop at a cliff edge. I looked down and far below were the rusting shapes of other buses and trucks that had missed the turn. I gasped and my guts turned to sludge. I'd survived being shot in the head and now I was going to die forgotten at the bottom of a ravine, food for maggots, thousands of kilometres from home?

The fear was replaced by a sudden and piercing loneliness, and I felt irrevocably cut off from all that I had known, all that gave me weight, solidity and identity. Here I was as light and as insubstantial as air, with nothing but a broken phone, a backpack, clothes turned to rags by sweat and mud, and the company of a few sorry humans who'd come here out of greed and god knows what else.

They knew nothing of philosophy—nothing of Silver Springs—though I had learnt to trust them over the last five days. But there were far too many wrecks of far too many fallen vehicles for me to feel safe to keep driving. After a sleepless night summoning up the courage to go the next leg alone, I bid goodbye to my prospector friends.

It turned out I was okay on my own—and that the worst thing I could face was my own thoughts. 'My mind is fucked,' I thought more than once, as it veered wildly between extreme anxiety and murderous rage. With great effort, I tried to keep my mind blank to stop from thinking about the shooting but sometimes I wondered if this whole complex and dangerous assignment was just a tactic by Lou to stop me ruminating about that day in the newsroom.

At night I had the stars for company and my copy of Marcus Aurelius's *Meditations*, the one Lou had pressed on me before I left. I opened it and saw a passage underlined. I imagined Lou's surprisingly delicate fingers holding the pencil.

'Dwell on the beauty of life. Watch the stars, and see yourself running with them . . .'

Sitting there in the dirt, tired and frightened, I spoke out loud. 'This town better be worth it, Lou.'

The jungle grew less dense the higher I climbed, allowing in light and air—and my spirits lifted slightly. On the outskirts of one small settlement, I was startled by a young boy carrying a large machine gun. On closer inspection he was guarding a small opium patch.

'Don't go that way—landmines,' he said.

I was sceptical until he pointed to another small boy in a neighbouring field—a boy with one leg, and a stump where the other should have been, not far from the hip. He was leaning on a crutch.

'Landmine,' he said again, satisfied with his exhibit. Then he pointed at my watch.

Or rather Lou's watch.

I touched it protectively. This was my talisman, my good luck charm.

'No.'

He pointed to the maimed boy again, then to my legs.

'You want legs?'

I agreed I wanted my legs.

I handed the Casio to him with a heavy sense of guilt. This watch was a physical reminder of Lou every time I looked down. It was his parting gift. But Lou was a pragmatic man. I could imagine him saying—'what better use for it than to trade that old chunk of mental for your safety—or even your life?'

My wrist felt light and bare without it.

In exchange for the watch, the boy guided me away from the landmines and the checkpoints with their corrupt soldiers and threat of violence.

Climbing ever higher, he brought me to a large lake, and removing a canoe from behind a tree, he rowed us along an expanse of light pink water, past lily pads the size of satellite dishes, with fuchsia- and coral-coloured blossoms on top. I had been told of this place in Davantown—not by a prospector but by an ecologist who had just returned, excited and dazed as if back from another planet.

'*Nymphaea lotus* lily pads! They're made of fibres I've not seen before—you could stump a house on them, they're so strong! And then there's the animals—giant squirrel, crested porcupine, various civets or bears . . .'

It was as he promised.

Up this high, I saw things I could scarcely believe. Things I had never seen before. The pink lake, the birds of bright and strange colours so large they looked like relics of the Jurassic age. There were butterflies as big as my hand, shafts of sun where the mountain's head appeared to glow gold and purple.

I was dazzled and distracted from my pain and hunger by things that had to be seen to be believed. But who would believe me if I had no record? The only thing spoiling the beauty was the sorrow that I was without a phone, so couldn't Instagram it.

Leaving the lake, we travelled by foot for the next six hours, the boy walking slightly ahead, cigarette dangling from his fingers, gold watch glistening under the sun, higher up into the hill country—where the jungle had receded and there was a pleasing cool breeze. When he turned and said I was safe now, pointing out a narrow hill track, I gave him the last of my local currency. He had kept his word.

The next morning, energised, nervous even—I walked for several hours up the track until I reached a Buddhist monastery, feeling a further shift in the atmosphere as I moved higher and my legs ached with the effort of the climb. The air was sweet and cool, and from time to time I heard an enticing birdsong—a haunting, regular call that I couldn't quite place.

—

The Mayor had promised an escort for the final part of the journey. 'Once we hear word that you have obtained the visa, we'll make plans to send someone to meet you at the gates of the abandoned monastery. The path up the mountain is no better than a goat track—high and tight. All forty-two kilometres of it. Don't look down. Your driver will get you here safely. They'll have a motorbike.'

The monastery gates were chained shut and, before I could shake them or try to find a way in, a young man on a motorbike pulled up. He had dark tousled hair, a scowl and a soft black leather jacket.

He said my name like a query, but didn't return my smile.

Arms around his back, the leather of his jacket hot and buttery against my cheek, my eyes to the left staring at the rockface, away from the drop to the right, I was tugged by a sense of deja vu.

Something about him was familiar.

Grass under the tyres turned to rock. The track was so steep, narrow and winding that there was no way a car could have made the climb. At some places, due to tricky bends, we got off the bike to walk single file. Clouds were within touching distance. Peaks of other mountains spread out as far as the eye could see, the green grass of distant hills glowing a rich emerald in the sun. We stopped at a lake for a brief rest. It was the most beautiful place I had ever seen. I could barely take in such beauty. As we skipped stones, I tried to find out more about my driver and Silver Springs but he just shrugged off my curiosity and replied, 'You'll see.'

So he spoke English . . .

'What's your name at least?'

'Dominic.'

'Dominic. That's nice.'

Back on the bike, we passed through a forest, not the jungle tangle of the lower parts of the journey but something more delicate and soft. Light filtered through the trees, giving everything a kind, golden filter, and the air smelt of pine. I saw from outside myself how romantic we must have looked riding through this forest, like a couple in a commercial selling deodorant.

Then I remembered, I realised that *he* was the familiar thing. Cleaved to his back, I felt the pull of some distant memory.

Paul. He reminded me of Paul.

It was a long time ago. Fourteen or fifteen, a sleepover, in someone's house when the parents were away. It was fun without parents—sleeping in the day, dozing in front of porn someone's brother had running in a continuous loop on the large screen in the basement, waking in a tangle of blankets, a tangle of limbs, to the sound coming from the computer of an ass being slapped or a groan or the cheap sound of royalty-free hip-hop that you hear in low-budget movies. What else? Pop Tarts for dinner and cylinders of Pringles for breakfast, the sweet smell of pot burning in a glass pipe, someone playing Korn over and over from an upstairs room—and this guy.

Paul. Older than the rest of us—someone's cousin. Black leather jacket that he didn't take off all weekend (except the once) and shiny hair that flopped across his eyes like a boy-band star. Beautiful and stoned—here but not here. I watched him throughout those strange, looping days and nights, inching closer each hour until our legs were touching, the leather of his jacket smooth and wet-looking, like dolphin skin, impossible to resist stroking.

Some of the kids had cylinders of gas and bags of glue, and took turns inhaling hard, falling back into the carpet in a kind of dissolving glee. And it was easy then to just start touching his jacket, and kissing him—even when the drugs had worn off. By inches we made ourselves a couple for the weekend, and my happiness was pure, and everything, even the Pop Tarts, was enhanced.

Nothing bad happened; everything felt good. I told my mother later there was consent. And she raged—*you're too young to consent. You don't even know what consent is!* But I did. I promise I did.

It was an upstairs bedroom where she found us. He was undressing and I was pantless under him—ready for this moment, wanting it. Someone's parents must have rung. The house was full of them now, angry adults, pulling kids off each other, and off the floor, away from their cans of vodka premix and bags of glue.

Paul and me, we never technically did it. It happened later with a boy my age who had half his beauty and charisma and when it was happening it felt as rough as sandpaper, not as smooth as leather—and I thought that, in my heart, it was Paul who was truly my first time.

That's what I answer when asked, who was it with? I say Paul.

Paul. I hadn't thought of him for years—but now it was all coming back. This boy—Dominic—same hair, same jacket, strong jaw, sad eyes. He even smelt like him. Cheek against leather, pine trees and a soapy, sandalwood smell.

It was so good. This was Paul—come back to me in a different incarnation. I relaxed against him. Just when I could feel myself nodding off, half asleep on his shoulder, we arrived.

Was this it? Silver Springs? It was dusk, and although I was exhausted, everything seemed suspended and beautiful, as if trapped in a snow dome: fir trees and mountain glades, with houses nestled in snugly among the trees; a clocktower, silver in the night; a deeper valley with a river running through it; houses lit up along a ridge, with fires going and smoke curling from chimneys. The hoot of an animal. The call of that bird again. A slight chill in the air—an immediate sensory contrast to the swampiness of the lowlands. I immediately felt I was somewhere enchanted.

'I made it, Lou, I actually made it,' I said to myself in wonder.

The Mayor had booked me a room at an inn at the outskirts of town, and Dominic saw me to the gate, before turning back to say goodbye. 'I hope to see you around,' he said. My heart lurched.

I had no expectations of my accommodation. Most places I stayed on assignment were total shitholes, one step above caravan parks, owing to the paper's tiny budget. On this occasion, I was just happy to be inside, away from the mosquitoes that swarmed me in the lowlands.

But this place was gorgeous—a jewellery box of a room. The walls were dull gold, and the teak bed was made up with stiff, clean white sheets and puffed-up pillows, under satin cases and a pale-yellow bedspread. There was a fireplace, a comfortable armchair, a small desk by the window overlooking a meadow, twilit and dusky. Lamps glowed warmly in the corners. It was a windless late summer evening, and as the sky darkened, the moon spilled silver all over the fields and through the window, which I kept open, letting in air that smelt unusually sweet.

The innkeeper, Thida, had warned of the cool nights and prepared a steaming bowl of plain noodles, which I ate so quickly my stomach ached, and a hot water bottle, which soothed the ache.

Before bed, exhausted (and, I must admit, a little nervous) I checked I had enough fresh notebooks, the dictaphone, spare batteries and my copy of *Meditations*.

Despite thinking I had no use for it, I had started reading it during those insomniac nights in Davantown, sweating under the ceiling fan, and later on the road by the light of my headtorch. If only I could talk to Lou about what he saw in it! It puzzled me, as though there was some sort of key I was missing. There were lots of repetitions and instructions about how to behave. Lots of emphasis on self-discipline. Lots of edicts on how to treat others. Lots of reminders about how short life was.

'Your days are numbered. Use them to throw open the windows of your soul to the sun. If you do not, the sun will soon set, and you with it,' Aurelius wrote.

It had been, said Lou, a man's diary to himself, and not intended to be published.

I washed and rebandaged my hand, crawled into bed and sighed with contentment.

That night, I slept soundly. It was the first time since the shooting I wasn't woken by a nightmare. Without having set an alarm, the next morning I was shocked to discover that it was well after nine, the sun was full and ample in the sky—and if I didn't hurry up, I'd be late for my first interview with the Mayor.

The Mayor lived on a small acreage on the outskirts of town, not far from the inn. Assisted by the high altitude, he grew grapes, he had told me in his letter, although he was old now and relied on friends to help with the harvest. His advanced age was part of the urgency in getting to Silver Springs, Lou had said. No reporter likes it when their main source for a story has one foot in the grave. Every day counts.

After a quick shower, I self-consciously put on my creased, sweat-marked dress.

I met Thida downstairs, who would escort me to the Mayor's house, and noticed her looking me up and down.

'It's all I have.'

'I can lend you some of my clothes.'

Now it was my turn to check Thida out—a big, baggy shirt and a longyi of bright green and red cotton, her hair in a topknot.

Sometimes the best lines in a story come from chance interactions, people you meet who *aren't* the main character. I tried to pump Thida for information about the town and the Mayor, who, as it turned out, was her father, as we walked along a dirt track.

'Was he a good dad?'

'Of course. The best.'

She looked at me sideways, still assessing me. 'I was surprised when my father said he had invited a journalist here. It's not like him to seek any kind of publicity.'

'He's shy?'

'I wouldn't say that. I would more say that he doesn't think any type of attention, particularly media attention, has merit.'

We walked for a while in uncomfortable silence.

The sun was bright and the air cold. Birds sounded from the nearby trees—and I heard again the call I heard yesterday—a shrill cry.

'Can you hear that? What is it?'

Incredibly, Thida didn't notice it.

We came closer. Shh—listen . . .

'Oh that—I didn't hear it until now—it's a highland koel. It's such a regular sound around here that we often don't register it. But the bird is precious to us, it's a kind of mascot of the area. Small, jet black, with a red eye. But hard to find. You go looking for it, and the call seems to be coming from the wrong place,' she said.

'What else can you tell me about Silver Springs?' I asked, hungry for information.

'You'll learn everything you need to know from my father,' she replied curtly—and left it at that.

THE MIND

IS THIS THE HAPPIEST PLACE ON EARTH?

SILVER SPRINGS, The Mayor's house, Thursday, 10 am—No photo existed of the Mayor on the internet, but I had created a picture of him in my mind. Someone very old and feeble—like Yoda but dressed like the mayors we wrote about in *The Sentinel*. These local mayors were usually spivvy, shiny-suited men and women, always getting exposed in dodgy deals, accepting kickbacks for developments, and having long, alcoholic lunches in the private rooms of strip-mall Chinese restaurants.

But, as it turns out, this mayor was different. For a start, he didn't look as frail as I had expected. Nor as sleazy.

Overlooking a garden that was a riot of green, he sat on a hard, high-backed chair on the verandah, his posture rigid. At first glance, his race was ambiguous. He could have been from almost anywhere. His eyes were closed when I arrived, but they snapped open when he heard me approach. His gaze was sharp and appraising. The sunlight fell full on his face, giving him a harsh, almost severe appearance—like a golden bust you'd find in a museum. He had high cheekbones and a wide, angular face with a sallow complexion, lightly lined with age. His thick grey hair caught the light, but his expression didn't soften. His eyes were pale green, piercing and utterly indifferent.

I glanced around, half-expecting to see minions or a PR person at least. But he was alone, except for a dog—an Irish wolfhound by the looks of it—that sat alert and straight on the ground nearby. The air was still and fragrant, and all was quiet.

Without preamble, he gestured towards a nearby chair. 'Sit.'

MAYOR: How was your journey?

JOURNALIST: It was rough, long, tiring, terrifying in parts—but I made it. Davantown sends its regards.

MAYOR: Hmm. Davantown.

JOURNALIST: Good ol' Dav. What a shithole.

MAYOR: Correct. An absolute shithole.

Despite myself, I laughed. He didn't. So much for breaking the tension. So he was going to be a tough customer? I groaned on the inside, but I had dealt with the type before and could handle the challenge.

MAYOR: Well, you got here—congratulations. It's not an easy trip. I don't think it's a stretch to call us one of the most isolated communities on Earth. And getting even more remote as the years go by. The army base in the next town shut down, and we lost our airport. The runway is overgrown, returned to the forest, and the only way to get here, as you know, is overland. It's a difficult journey.

JOURNALIST: It does feel very cut off. But do you have the internet? You're never totally isolated if you're online.

MAYOR: No. That would defeat the purpose of being isolated, wouldn't it?

He said this with a faint curl of his lip, as if the question annoyed him. But surely he didn't *want* to be so isolated? I changed the subject.

JOURNALIST: How have you managed to stay out of the various armed conflicts?

MAYOR: Old peace pacts, respected by those who understand their value. And the fact that we don't meddle with the junta. Even warlords appreciate the wisdom of leaving us alone. Meddling breeds conflict. But the junta also breeds landmines and rogue militias. So it's not uncommon for our people to stay put. We do not want for anything here. We're not a rich place but we have all the produce and goods we need. Anyway, very few people here have the means to travel. Three times in fifty years I've taken a big trip out, as long as it's safe enough on the roads. I've been to where you are from. And I intend to never go back.

I felt moved to defend a place that I spent my life railing against.

JOURNALIST: It's not all bad. We have the most incredible comforts that you probably don't have here. Most people have air conditioning, for example; there are electric cars, and whatever you want you can buy online and it gets delivered to your house. You don't have to go anywhere or struggle to get anything.

I was rambling out of nerves. Was Amazon delivery really a high point of modernity? The Mayor seemed unimpressed with my list, and, when he rose, I thought for a moment he might say something conciliatory or offer coffee—I was craving my usual triple shot latte with soy. Instead, he disappeared inside without a word, the dog following at his heels. I sat in silence, wondering if I'd made a terrible mistake coming here. The vibes were off. But when he returned, it was with a tray laden with a pot of tar-black tea, condensed milk and buttered naan.

He set it down brusquely and resumed his seat without acknowledging me.

No coffee. No soy milk. No internet. I know it was trivial to be disappointed at such things—but maybe this whole adventure would ultimately reveal that I was a trivial person.

JOURNALIST: How would you like to structure this? I can follow you around as you go about your mayoral duties, or we can talk like this—whatever is the best way to understand how things work.

MAYOR: I'll decide. Over the next three days, I'll provide the basics of Stoic ethical philosophy and answer your questions, within reason. You'll have time alone to process it, as I expect you'll need it.

There was no warmth in his tone. It felt less like an invitation and more like a dictated schedule.

MAYOR: Philosophy is something we practise daily here. Not as an edict pinned to a board, ignored by all, but as a way of living. You'll see the effects, or you won't; it makes no difference to me.

JOURNALIST: I'm interested in happiness. That's what I see this story being about.

I consulted a list of questions in my notebook.

Is the overall happiness higher here? Is quality of life good? What can you teach us that might make our society more successful? Do you eat special foods? Have an unusual diet? Eat many ultra-processed foods? What are your top tips for success?

MAYOR: 'Ultra-processed foods?' 'Top tips'? Is that what you think this is?

I could feel his condescension, though his tone stayed controlled.

JOURNALIST: My editor, Lou, told me this place was unique and special. That it could teach us something. He wanted a piece about the philosophy and the town—something like 'The Secrets of the Happiest Place on Earth'.

MAYOR: Secrets?

His green eyes blazing, he seemed to spit the word out. I held my nerve.

JOURNALIST: Secrets—like you guys in this faraway kingdom, away from the internet and all the decadence and decay of the modern world. What can you teach us? What I was thinking with this piece is something along the lines of 'A Sage's Guide to Happiness'—or some content like that. Accompanied perhaps by a six-part podcast about happiness hacks from the happiest mayor in the world. And if I can fix my phone here, we can film some shorts for Instagram reels or TikTok. Is there anyone here with high-quality camera equipment? We could film the interviews to go on YouTube and I could also get footage of the town, vox some townsfolk—

The Mayor leant back, his eyes narrowing as if I'd said something deeply offensive.

MAYOR: 'Secrets'? 'Hacks'? You're trivialising centuries of thought. Happiness is fleeting, a hollow pursuit. Contentment is longer-lasting, without the manic swings of dopamine chasing. But I doubt that will fit your headline.

I nodded but inside I felt crushed. Why was he being so unfriendly? I had come all this way and endured considerable hardship and danger to get here. I needed this story so I could land the next job. But it was dawning on me that my expectations were way off. I had assumed the Mayor would be a sweet old man who would be just busting to tell his story, to increase his clout and followers, who would be generous and cooperative with me in this project, who might even want fame for himself.

JOURNALIST: You agreed to be interviewed. I've come a long way . . .

MAYOR: I am now wondering if welcoming the media was a mistake. It did go against my initial judgement, inviting you here. And then you wrote that letter . . . the third letter . . .

JOURNALIST: That was from the heart.

MAYOR: Well, you got your access.

JOURNALIST: I think the world needs wisdom—and yes, happiness, more than ever. Sorry if that sounds corny to you.

MAYOR: Don't explain your philosophy; embody it.

JOURNALIST: Is it that you don't want to be anyone's guru? You don't go around proselytising or preaching your philosophy?

MAYOR: Definitely not. Your deeds and actions should speak for themselves. And you definitely shouldn't boast about being philosophical. Epictetus put it well when he said, 'If anyone starts talking about philosophy, stay quiet, because you might end up just vomiting out the stuff you've learned without digesting it. Sheep don't throw up grass to show a shepherd how much they ate . . . instead they digest it and use their food to produce wool and milk.'

Gross analogy but okay, they must have shepherds around here.

JOURNALIST: Okay—so, you learn it, absorb it, then act?

MAYOR: Yes.

The Mayor shut his eyes and silence settled over the conversation. A dragonfly buzzed from plant to plant in the sea of green in the Mayor's courtyard, its electric-blue wings catching the light. The tea was strong and bitter but the naan—still warm from the oven—made the bitterness more palatable.

JOURNALIST: How did you come to be here? And come to be the Mayor? You're not from here, are you? Your accent is . . . hard to place.

The Mayor looked uncomfortable and spoke haltingly.

MAYOR: No, I'm not from here. Like you, I'm originally from the rich world. But I've lived in what you, and other seekers, call Silver Springs for more than fifty years and I was elected Mayor three years ago. My term ends soon.

And how I came to be here? When I was young, I was a traveller, like your friend Lou, and maybe like you. I met a woman and followed her here. I didn't care about philosophy when I was young. I wasn't looking for a community. I wasn't looking for a peaceful life. I just cared about this girl and love.

So this was to be a love story? Interesting. But, if so, where was she?

JOURNALIST: So this girl you followed—what was her name?

MAYOR: Sandra. We met in Calcutta, over the border in India. She told me she'd grown up in a very unusual town beyond the

Davan province, and that town was run according to ancient philosophical principles.

JOURNALIST: Stoicism?

MAYOR: Yes.

JOURNALIST: What are the origins of Stoicism?

MAYOR: It's a philosophy that originated in Athens around 300 BCE, and flourished in Greece and Rome until the third century CE. It died out with the rise of Christianity. But in the years that it flourished, it guided individuals, communities and statesmen such as Roman emperor Marcus Aurelius. Back then Stoicism provided a unified account of the world, and incorporated physics, logic and ethics. It's primarily the ethics component that we still practise here today.

JOURNALIST: Do you like it?

MAYOR: Do I *like it?*

The Mayor's voice couldn't hide his disdain.

That's like asking a Christian if they *like* God.

I find the philosophy endlessly fascinating because it touches on all aspects of human nature and all aspects of life. Stoicism is a whole-of-life philosophy that provides a framework for everything that happens from birth to death. So you can never get sick of it as long as you're alive.

JOURNALIST: How exactly is Stoic philosophy used in the town?

MAYOR: Children learn it in school, just like they learn to speak English and Sanskrit; parents use it in parenting, teachers use it in teaching, and we use it in governing. When it works, the town hums along. We meet each week on Friday and are talking and teaching each other all the time. We have a room in town—you enter under the painted colonnade.

JOURNALIST: The Stoa? Lou mentioned it.

MAYOR: Yes. These meetings, this work, week in, week out, are what makes the philosophy stick. We are working hard, every day, to be peaceful—in ourselves and with each other—and we work hard to live up to the virtues of courage, justice, moderation and wisdom. All philosophy is meaningless without action. The theory and the praxis, together.

JOURNALIST: Praxis?

MAYOR: Practice, action, from the Ancient Greek. Turning theory into action. For me at least, all philosophy is essentially meaningless unless it translates into living deliberately. That includes thinking deliberately and acting deliberately. Initially when I agreed to this interview, my hope in sharing my knowledge was that people don't just read the article and think 'that's interesting' and put it to one side. Action is where it's at! Maybe the next step forward in humanity is not AI, but something that arises from a larger sense of connectedness and community, some sort of collective action, and enhanced feeling of solidarity. Although, of course, that is not something I have any control over.

JOURNALIST: How much do you know about AI?

The Mayor gave me another withering look.

MAYOR: Just because we are remote, doesn't mean we are stupid. We welcome the occasional traveller who brings us news of developments in the rich world, and many of our relatives in Davantown are on the Facebook.

JOURNALIST: So these travellers—are they pilgrims, like there were in the seventies?

MAYOR: We try to discourage pilgrims. Too many new people are difficult to manage, yes. The extra people . . . and their expectations.

The Mayor looked coldly at me, as if I was another of these annoying pilgrims. I felt something in me harden. I would not be his apostle or one of those lost and anxious pilgrims in search of a guru. I was here as a reporter, and I would be detached, even hostile, if he pushed me hard enough.

JOURNALIST: I'm reading Marcus Aurelius. What other writers do you recommend?

MAYOR: It's mostly the works of Roman Stoicism that have survived. What we are left with today are the works of the three main Roman Stoics: Seneca, Epictetus and Marcus Aurelius. Each of them is quite distinct and brings a unique viewpoint. Epictetus was born into slavery, was lamed by a cruel master, and later freed. He became a prominent teacher of Stoic philosophy. Seneca was born into wealth, and became influential as a playwright, tutor to Nero when he was a boy, and later a political adviser. He was ordered to kill himself by Nero. And Marcus was a Roman emperor and, at the time, the most powerful person in the world.

We also have works from Cicero, Heracles, Chrysippus and Musonius Rufus. Of the Greek Stoics, we have only fragments of their writing. It's a great shame; all the work of those brilliant Greeks that we've lost . . .

The Mayor looked genuinely pained at this.

JOURNALIST: And how do you use Stoic philosophy to govern Silver Springs?

MAYOR: It's used in an organic way. Stoic principles have been baked into policy. Each new Mayor has studied Stoicism and practises it in their own lives. It's assumed that, when making decisions, we consult the ancient philosophical principles of Stoicism. When we have disputes, or are trying new things, we apply Stoic principles. But we are constantly debating, in a friendly way, how the philosophy should be interpreted or if it's not relevant in particular situations. If it's not relevant, we don't consult it.

JOURNALIST: How do the debates stay friendly? How do the disputes not escalate?

MAYOR: Perhaps you should ask instead why, in your country, it is assumed that every disagreement will escalate. It's not normal to be in conflict all the time. You should be able to hear another point of view without feeling attacked or becoming enraged. There is something wrong with you, if you cannot do that.

JOURNALIST: Okay. But what about when you have disagreements about how to interpret some of the ancient Stoic teachings? How fundamentalist are you about those things? Are you strictly by-the-book?

MAYOR: Not at all. Seneca himself said, 'Let us be satisfied with what we have discovered and leave a little truth for our descendants to find out.' The philosophy was unfinished business. The Ancients anticipated that the world would change—and it did. And with that change, new truths would emerge—and they have. We are flexible with the philosophy, so we don't get trapped in something that doesn't suit the modern world anymore. I'm definitely not afraid of changing my mind if new information comes to light. Dogma is not encouraged.

But how much *had* things changed here? Although I was yet to explore, my interactions so far made me think this was not a modern community.

JOURNALIST: Okay, so you consult Stoic principles to make decisions. But is Silver Springs a democracy? How does it work?

MAYOR: Yes, it's a democracy. I'm not a monarch or a chief. We have mayoral elections every four years. Social cohesion is extremely important in Silver Springs. Maybe the most important thing. That, and community. They're the same thing really. The Stoa—and our friendships—are a framework to develop personal and communal resilience. We do this by discussing what we are going through and applying the philosophy to each other's situation, like a doctor might apply a remedy or write a prescription.

JOURNALIST: How do you define social cohesion?

MAYOR: The contract that exists between individuals in a society, and the contract that exists between individuals and, for want of a better word, the state, or in our case the Council. Our essential nature is to be part of a collective. What's good for the bees is good for the hive, said Marcus. So, in governing, we accept that in order to advance some protections and rights for citizens, other competing rights must be waived or altered. But underneath it all is the belief that we exist for one another, and that's the basis of how we operate both as individuals in the town, and as a community as a whole.

JOURNALIST: Sounds like you're trying to create a utopia.

MAYOR [*sternly*]: There's no such thing. This is not a town without problems. People have all sorts of issues here, just like everywhere else. People get divorced; people cheat on their spouses; people are awful to their children; children are awful to their parents; there are squabbles about money; there's alcoholism; there's addiction. We have a court system and a jail. We are all humans, and we have human problems: all the problems that you would experience in your cities in the rich world. But here in Silver Springs there are deliberate structures set up, formally and informally, to acknowledge the human struggles and suffering, and help people through them, therapeutically, using philosophy.

JOURNALIST: What are these structures?

MAYOR: What do we need to flourish as individuals and as a society? That's what I'm always asking. What do we need to flourish? We have the Stoa, and Stoicism is also practised privately and more informally. There are small groups around town who meet regularly using a combination of therapy, friendship, debate and ethical philosophical principles to support each other. We get very cold, very quickly, without community.

JOURNALIST: I wish we had more support where I'm from. I'm currently on a waiting list for an expensive therapist. So are many of us. And that's if you're lucky enough to have money to pay for therapy.

I remembered with a sudden pang that I would soon not be able to afford therapy when I was out of a job.

MAYOR: We need to commit to helping each other. I'm not saying therapy isn't important but you should be receiving support from your community. And also giving it.

He looked at me sharply with that.

MAYOR: Are you giving others support?

I bristled. I hated it when subjects turned the questions back on me. I answered lightly, and mostly untruthfully, 'Of course.'

I had to focus on myself. I had just survived a horrendous trauma. I was the one who needed support—not random others.

We took the cups and teapot to the sink and I tried to subtly peek around. Was there another person living here? Where was Sandra? But it was just our two cups in the sink. The rest of the house was still, quiet and dark. It was a simple structure made of stone, with slabs of worn slate for a floor. The roof was high with exposed beams, the kitchen and a large room were filled with books and a large, heavy table that could seat a dozen. In the gloom, I scanned for any photos scattered around the place. I couldn't have a story without a photo—and ideally it would be one of the Mayor and Sandra when they were young.

But before I got a chance to look around some more, the Mayor called from the door. 'Are you ready to learn the philosophy?'

THE CONTROL TEST—HOW TO WORRY LESS

SILVER SPRINGS, The Mayor's house, Thursday, 11.15 am— We sat on the verandah, another pot of tea brewing. The Mayor and I were seated across from each other, elbows on the table, an air of anticipation, like two opponents about to play a challenging game of chess. Deep breath—remember, don't be intimidated by this old guy.

JOURNALIST: Okay, Master—teach me your ways!

I pushed the dictaphone across the table and made sure it was recording. The Mayor looked at the machine with one raised eyebrow, as if deciding whether to swoop down and destroy it. His gaze switched to me with unnerving suddenness.

MAYOR: The first and most important lesson to learn is what you can and can't control. That needs to be your starting point for everything. Things can turn catastrophic for each of us, at any moment, always, all the time.

He was staring directly at me. As if every sentence was meant for me.

But how we handle what life throws at us, our attitude to setbacks, can result in us suffering less when a crisis strikes.

JOURNALIST: And how should we handle what life throws at us?

MAYOR: You should be relaxed, roll with it and realise there's not much you can control in life.

For someone telling me I should be relaxed, he didn't seem so relaxed himself.

JOURNALIST: Okay—unpack that?

MAYOR: So often we operate as if we are in control of life, instead of life happening in ways that we have no control over. But the Ancients, in their wisdom, said 'first things first': we need to get real about what we can and can't control in life.

JOURNALIST: And what can we control?

MAYOR: What do you think we can control?

Hmmm, it was evident, wasn't it—even though I had never given the matter much thought. We controlled what we wanted to control.

JOURNALIST: If you like being in control—like I do—you can control most things if you know what you want, have a list of goals, are relentless about achieving those goals, and keep trying—never give up. If you do that you will get what you want.

I'd read enough of my mother's self-help books to know what it took to get to the top—theoretically. Believe in yourself. Manifest. Get up at 5 am and make a list, then attack the list. Only problem is—reading these books hadn't changed much for my mother, who was still stuck managing a small team at a call centre and delivering UberEats at night, while I was weeks away from being broke and unemployed.

MAYOR: That sounds like you know exactly how the world works! Don't know why you've come all this way to talk to me then.

His sarcasm was jarring but I tried to keep my expression neutral.

Let's take a closer look at control. Can you control if you are successful? If you are well paid? If you become rich? If you are liked by everyone? If you get to old age without a serious illness? Can you control how others see you? Can you control how successful this interview will be? How successful the published story will be? Or even if it will get published?

And importantly, can you control if you meet the right person to marry? And if they want to marry you?

It was a bit presumptuous that he'd think I even aspired to get married. Had he seen the dating pool back home?

JOURNALIST: Err, no. Although many of those things I would *like* to happen!

MAYOR: Could you control being shot?

I felt a sudden shock at his words. My throat seized up. I didn't want to talk about that. Why did he go there so soon?

JOURNALIST [*shakily*]: No. It happened so fast.

MAYOR: There's a lot we can't control. A lot of really important things we can't control. Even when we think we have our hand on the wheel, even when we have strong desires, even if we are terrified of losing control: none of those emotions expands our area of control.

JOURNALIST: What can we control?

MAYOR: A Stoic believes our realm of control consists of our own actions and reactions, our character and how we treat others. The rest—including our bodies, the actions of others, our reputation and our fortunes both personal and financial—is out of our control.

This was different from the things in all the self-help books I'd read, which empowered readers to take control of their destinies.

JOURNALIST: That's not very many things that we can control.

MAYOR: Yes, only three. Actions, your character and how you treat others.

Pause. The Mayor laughed.

JOURNALIST: What are you laughing at?

MAYOR: Everyone who first hears about the control test has exactly the same reaction. And they have exactly the same look on their face! They initially react and say 'no, that can't be right'. You can see their brain whirring, trying to play catch-up. They get me to repeat it, and then they take it in, their mouth hangs open and they realise, yes, yes, it's correct, they don't control very much at all . . . And yet . . .

JOURNALIST: . . . And yet?

MAYOR: How you think about things, how you interpret them is within your control. And that's a very powerful tool. How you see the world, how you process into thoughts what you see and feel, leads to judgements, which dictate the experience you have in life: good or bad. And that is within our control: how we interpret what happens to us. Epictetus said, 'It's not what happens to you, but how you react to it that matters.'

JOURNALIST: I think what *happens* to you shapes your reality—not what you think. What happens matters.

MAYOR: It does. But you often, almost always, cannot completely control what happens to you. Whereas you are the only one in charge of your thoughts and your reactions. So why not focus on what you can control rather than flailing around trying to control something external and unstable?

JOURNALIST: What you're asking is actually quite difficult. I don't know if I can control my thoughts or my reactions. They come to me unbidden—I can't switch them off.

Although I wished I could. An hour alone with my thoughts and I was spiralling. Even before the shooting I was worried all the time; about money, the future, climate change, AI taking my job. And then there was the loneliness I often felt, and the loneliness I felt in others.

MAYOR: I agree that random thoughts come and go, apparently 65,000 of them a day! Most of them are junk, just appearances of consciousness that have no meaningful content. But you can steer the type of thoughts you have, which then feeds into your reactions. Using your rational mind, you have control over how you frame situations and the judgements you make. This then informs your responses. Your responses impact your mood. If you respond angrily, think about how you feel inside. You're all churned up, right? In turmoil? Poor decision making results from this frame of mind. You end up in a worse-off situation. If you respond calmly, you're more likely to feel calm, and make calm, rational decisions.

Lou was calm. That's what made him a good editor—no yelling when he was under pressure. But I tended to think calmness was a personality trait, not something you could develop.

JOURNALIST: Theoretically, yes. But how often does this happen in practice? People are emotional beings, and they have their biases and their patterns. And if something makes them angry, or excited—and they react as such—that can be difficult to change.

People don't change, my mother used to say, mostly when talking about my dad, and how unreliable and flaky he was.

MAYOR: But not impossible. The first step is being conscious of what you can and can't control. Think about the control test in relation to your journey here. You might be thinking that to get here is going to be easy because you were told that there was going to be a direct flight. But instead it took a week and involved many interruptions, diversions, digressions, great expense and danger. If you had assumed it would be easy to get here, you'd be upset by the journey. You'd be resisting reality—*what is.* And you'd be suffering unnecessarily.

Danger in Dav, danger on the roads, danger in the mountains. Warm close nights, breeze barely stirring the hammock, the drill of mosquitoes hovering nearby, the strange sounds—almost moans—of animals deeper in the jungle. Death seemed so close, it was walking with me. The black stick on the road was a snake. The wrecks of cars at the base of the cliff could have been my jeep.

The path could have been rigged with landmines. It struck me then, as it struck me that April afternoon in the newsroom, how thin the membrane is between life and death. And how weightless and terrible that realisation felt.

JOURNALIST: There was little I could control in the journey. I'm actually surprised I made it here in one piece.

MAYOR: Most modern people's moods can barely survive the upset of a plane being delayed for an hour, or a long queue at the airport. They suffer at the slightest inconvenience.

The Mayor seemed contemptuous of those he called 'modern people'.

JOURNALIST: We are taught to be very goals-orientated, where I am from. Do you think we can control outcomes?

MAYOR [*sighing*]: No. Of course not. I agree your society is very focused on outcomes. People look to the result, not the process. But the process is the point!

JOURNALIST: What is wrong with being focused on outcomes?

MAYOR: It can lead to a loss of tranquillity if you don't get the outcome you desire. Everything in your world, when it comes to love, in work, in investment, is trained on an outcome. People think they can control outcomes. That they can plot a path from desire to action to outcome. If you have your heart set on something, say a romantic relationship with someone you desire, or getting your dream job, or a scoop on a story—none of these things is fully within your control. The outcome is often out of your control. It's a recipe for unhappiness. And when the thing you want doesn't happen, you're upset or devastated. Your equilibrium is disturbed. But you shouldn't be upset! You never had control in the first place!

He paused meaningfully, as if willing me to take it in.

Accept that and you'll have peace. Call it peace. Call it happiness. But the misery ceases when you stop focusing on outcomes. When you are enjoying the process, letting it unfold, knowing you can't control the outcome, that's lovely. You're frowning . . . you don't agree?

This guy couldn't be serious. This was how capitalism and our society worked—we were motivated by results. We were rats on a wheel in a cage, laser-focused on the next piece of cheese. The outcome was the cheese. The wheel was life.

JOURNALIST: That theory robs people of agency; it devalues desire. Why be ambitious—why set out to do anything, if the result is not really in our control? If we ignore outcomes? If everyone lived like this, nothing would get done in our society. Ambitious and successful people set themselves a target in life and apply themselves with relentless drive, ambition and a fair amount of ruthlessness, until they get what they want. Society admires them. Rewards them. And we're encouraged to emulate them.

MAYOR: Stoicism doesn't say leave your ambition at the door. Far from it. Look at the Roman Stoics. Seneca was deeply involved in political life and was a self-made man who became extremely wealthy. Epictetus started life as a slave and became a teacher. And Marcus Aurelius was the most powerful man in the world. What the Stoics realised is that the reward is *doing* the thing. It's not the outcome. The effort *is* the reward.

JOURNALIST: I'm not sure I agree with that. I mean, that's what you hear when you get a participation award, but it's all made-up. Awards are important; recognition is important; status is important—these are all outcomes. They are how you get jobs, how you get status and how you get money.

Journalism awards night each year, the feeling of not winning again, nights of too much drinking to drown out the envy, avoiding the humble brags on social media the next day, wanting it really badly and pretending not to care. Awards mattered. This guy wasn't living in the real world if he didn't know that.

MAYOR: Are they important? I think they are all just by-products of some external definition of success. It's not a good idea to measure yourself against something you have no control over. Nothing is guaranteed; even though it may be great to get an award, it's not why you do something. Well, at least I hope it's not.

Think about your work. When you write a story, you don't know how it's going to be received. But instead of focusing on its reception, I bet you focus on the work, right? Like you are doing now? You focus on getting to the destination. You focus on the preparation and research before a big interview. You focus on getting there on time, and building a rapport with your subject.

You then focus on writing the article to the best of your ability. None of that is an outcome: *it's all process.* And all that effort? That is within your control.

JOURNALIST: Mostly—yes, it is.

MAYOR: And it's pleasurable, right?

JOURNALIST: It's why I do it.

MAYOR: It's probably in your nature to be a storyteller.

JOURNALIST: It definitely is.

MAYOR: Can I control the story you write?

JOURNALIST: No.

MAYOR: Can you control if I like the story you write about me?

JOURNALIST: No, I can't.

But I did have an idea of the kind of story he would like and the kind of story he wouldn't like. He would like one that made him look smart and humble. And he would hate one that made him look like an egotistical guru. But it was an angle I was free to take. I could (and I may—*it was tempting*) portray him as a bad or dangerous guru, if that is what he turned out to be.

MAYOR: But still, here you are: making the effort, doing the work, writing the story. Take the case of an archer, whose task it is to shoot an arrow straight at some target. Their ultimate aim is to do all they can in their power to shoot straight. Factors outside their control may intervene: a strong wind for example that throws the arrow off course. The same applies with your goals. Just focus on the process, doing your best.

You can do your best, always; you just can't necessarily control the outcome.

Lou aligned with the Mayor on this. Lou didn't look at the traffic on our website—ever. He said he couldn't control what people clicked on but he could control its quality. That a good story was a good story, no matter how many hits it got. In other words—the good story was the arrow, but other people reading it were the wind, conditions that were out of his control.

JOURNALIST: I guess that is right. But why the up-front emphasis on control? Is it because it's one of the single most basic human drives? The drive to control?

MAYOR: Yes. Think about all the things that humans want to control. We want to control how we live, in everything from what kind of job we have, to how many kids we have, money in the bank, status, our bodies. We think if we can control these things, we can protect ourselves, we are less at the mercy of the chaos of the world and we can suffer less.

JOURNALIST: I'm not sure if I believe in protection anymore. Can the government protect us? No, not really. Can we protect each other? Not if there are weapons or violence involved. It's everyone for themselves. Maybe we can only control how much we protect ourselves?

MAYOR: Or maybe we just accept that we are more defenceless than we'd like to be, and that's okay.

It's not okay.

The Mayor leant back and looked at me as if trying to assess what I was made of.

MAYOR: How are you with reality?

JOURNALIST: What do you mean?

MAYOR: I mean, do you live in reality? Or do you live in your head? Do you live in a dream that either makes reality more delicious and delightful? Or do you live in a dream that makes things more fraught and dangerous than they really are?

But reality *was* fraught and dangerous.

JOURNALIST: I think I live in reality—as it is. I'm dealing with reality in a very stark way right now.

Headaches all the time. Trouble sleeping. Throbbing hand. No phone in a foreign land. Always looking over my shoulder, never feeling quite safe. I worried about the future. I worried about money and not having or being 'enough'. I never had the luxury of going through life as if it was a beautiful dream, where desires easily become reality.

MAYOR: What about the darker version of reality? Seeing life in a negative way? Are you sure you are not looking through the glass darkly?

The truth was I didn't know anymore. Was I seeing life in a negative way—or was I seeing as it really was? A version of this disorientation was something I discussed frequently with Lou—something that had taken on increasing urgency at the newspaper. It was the rise of algorithms and misinformation, particularly on social media. People increasingly didn't know what was true and what was false and so an accurate picture of the world (was it heaven or hell?) was increasingly hard to see. With the merger swallowing *The Sentinel*, and so many jobs being lost, Lou was even more pessimistic about the future of information.

But what would the Mayor know of that? He spoke of archers and shepherds, relics from another age. Without technology he was living in a very simple reality—one where his world was small, and the truth was right in front of him.

MAYOR: One of the major problems with modern society is people aren't living in reality. They are living in their heads, in a version of what they'd like reality to be or what they fear reality to be. Both are bad. The control test is the first step to bringing us back to reality. We must look around, think critically, accept our current reality and work as best we can within that reality, within that system. Make a note of that: accept reality. Go on, write it down in that little notebook: 'Accept reality.' It really is crucial for reducing suffering.

I did as he said—and wrote *ACCEPT REALITY* in large letters in my notebook. The Mayor suddenly turned his attention to the tea, which was rapidly cooling in the fresh mountain air, and poured us another cup. It was strong. I grimaced as I swallowed and flicked to a page of questions in my notebook. I'd written *ACCEPT REALITY* so hard that it had marked at least five subsequent pages—creating literally a strong impression.

JOURNALIST: Why do we think we control more than we actually do? Is it to make us feel safe? Keep the vampire from the door—at least mentally?

MAYOR: If we think we're in control, we think we can control the outcomes. I get it. There can be nothing scarier than realising that we have no control over what happens to us. That the car has no driver. That's deep existential dread right there. That's deep anxiety right there. So, we create this fiction, the illusion that we have a lot more control than we actually do. To *not* have this illusion would tip a lot of people into a very frightening place. But squaring up to our lack of control is actually the key to liberation. The truth—*reality*—will set you free. And when you trust that you'll be okay, no matter what the outcome . . . well, that's a game changer. That's real freedom.

JOURNALIST: How is it a game changer?

MAYOR: Because you stop worrying and put your energy into what you can control. For example, you said your phone is broken.

Thanks for reminding me.

You're a long way from anyone who can repair it. Rather than worry about your broken phone, which you can't do anything about, you need to put your energy into establishing other means of communication. Or accepting that, until you leave the region, you will not be able to be contacted and you cannot film me, and that's okay. Accept your change in circumstances and move on.

My heart dropped when he said I couldn't film him. I wondered if anyone else in this town had a camera.

JOURNALIST: So essentially you're saying many of us in modern society—

MAYOR: Not many: *most people . . .*

JOURNALIST: —are operating under the illusion they have control?

MAYOR: Precisely. Illusion or delusion, take your pick. There's so little that we have complete control over, no wonder people develop a sort of mass delusion. You see it everywhere: helicopter parents, controlling spouses, psychopathic bosses, investors in financial instruments, growers of crops, and the people who do this thing . . . manifesting.

JOURNALIST: Oh yeah, I know that. It's a trend. If you think the thing will happen, it will actually happen.

MAYOR: Yes. That is totally delusional. I want a Mercedes-Benz sports car.

The Mayor closed his eyes.

I'm manifesting, I'm manifesting . . .

The Mayor opened his eyes.

Oh! It's not there!

The Mayor laughed. I didn't join him because I had actually used that technique in my own life, although it hadn't worked—yet. For a moment I thought about manifesting a camera or a phone.

The Stoic way is to presume you *won't* get the thing you desire, that your plans probably won't work out in an ideal way. Unless, of course, your plans are to develop an excellent character, the virtues that we spoke about before—courage, justice, moderation and wisdom. *That* you can control.

JOURNALIST: I've never heard of anyone desiring a great character. Most people want external things—power, money, fame, a hot body, a good job, lots of followers, a nice house, to be admired or envied by others, or an easy life.

MAYOR [*frowning*]: Good luck with that. All those things are unstable. I'm not judging those things as good or bad; people want what they want. But even if you do get one or some of these things, they only last for a short time. Who on earth has what you term 'a hot body' forever? No one! And don't say ninety-year-olds with plastic surgery. You can't buy 'hot'.

Dominic popped into my head and I suppressed a smile. Only yesterday on our journey, we stopped by a lake that appeared gold-plated across the surface in the afternoon sun, and although he didn't say much, we passed a companionable half-hour, laughing as we skimmed stones across the surface (well, all my stones sank to the bottom—while his glided across the water). When would I see him next?

Instead, you just need to work out what small areas are in your control, and go from there. And that is your character, your reactions and actions and how you treat others.

JOURNALIST: So this control test, how is it used? Is it something you refer to every day when you're making a decision?

MAYOR: It's hugely important. I run everything through it, and often refer to it multiple times a day. I use it when making an assessment about what I should and shouldn't worry about, and to determine where I can take action and best direct my energy.

JOURNALIST: Give me an example of how you use it.

MAYOR: I had control over whether or not to grant you a visa here.

He looked momentarily perturbed, as if he was regretting the invitation.

As Mayor, I can control the length of your stay. But I have no control over how you act when you get here, what sort of questions you will ask me and what sort of article you will write. So I'm aware of that when granting the visa. I accept my lack of control in the areas where you have control.

JOURNALIST: That seems to bother you a bit. That you don't have control over what I write. You said earlier that you were having second thoughts.

There was a pause, as if the Mayor were choosing his words carefully.

MAYOR: Control is something I'll probably spend the whole of my life grappling with. I'm human, not a sage. But I always return to Stoic philosophy. It never lets me down. It tells me where my control lies and reminds me of the reality of the situation. In reality, I have clarity over what is my domain and what is yours. Your domain is the story you write. My domain is my response to it. I accept that. And I am relaxed and I am at peace.

Are you relaxed? At peace? Really?

JOURNALIST: No matter the outcome?

MAYOR: Well, that's the whole point: not to care about the outcome.

JOURNALIST: Not to care about the outcome? Isn't the outcome the main thing?

MAYOR: No, because outcomes are mostly out of my control.

JOURNALIST: Who created the control test?

Someone brutal, I bet.

MAYOR: The test is very old and is common to most ancient philosophies. The one we use around here is found in the handbook of Roman Stoic Epictetus called the *Enchiridion*. Epictetus's handbook was published in about 125 CE. It still holds up today.

The Mayor reached for a slim book on the pile beside him and opened it near the start.

Epictetus said, 'Within our power are opinion, motivation, desire, aversion, and, in a word, whatever is of our own doing; not within our power are our body, our property, reputation, office, and, in a word, whatever is not of our own doing.' He knows from bitter experience the limits of control. He lived it.

JOURNALIST: So opinion—what we think. Motivation—why we do something. Desire—what or who we want. Aversion—what we don't want . . . These are all in our power?

MAYOR: Yes. And our body, money, what other people think of us—are not in our power. And this is the most liberating thing I can teach you.

JOURNALIST: Liberating how?

MAYOR: If all that's in our control is our actions and reactions, our character and how we treat others, we can stop expending energy on trying to control all the things outside this. It liberates us from unnecessary worry and anxiety, of putting energy into things we cannot change. Think of this situation: you hear that someone at work has been criticising you behind your back. Would this upset you?

JOURNALIST: Of course.

The newspaper was my home, my family, my community and my identity. I'd been at the paper for almost ten years. There were a lot of lifers—older people who thought they'd just be passing through but, to their surprise, found their forever home there. And, as the years went on, we were not only each other's colleagues, but also drinking buddies, shoulders to cry on, chosen family, best friends and—in the case of at least three couples who met at the paper—spouses.

What made it good? Probably Lou. He had an old newspaperman's instincts for a good story and would give you the time and space to pursue it. And at *The Sentinel*, he created this family. He couldn't afford to pay much but he paid what he could. Even just walking into the newsroom I felt a sense of home that I'd never felt anywhere else—not even growing up.

MAYOR: But you can't control what your colleagues think about you, and you can't control what they say. You can only control your response.

JOURNALIST: That's easy to say but if it were that simple, why is there an anxiety epidemic? Why are people so stressed about things outside their control?

MAYOR: Is that how it is now, where you're from?

Is that how it was? There's a whole pharmaceutical industry built on the back of worry. I took antidepressants, and after more than ten years I didn't even know if they were working anymore—I just couldn't tell. And, if I had a deadline, some dark-web Ritalin to keep me focused and off the internet where I just ended up losing hours. Drinks after work with the gang from the office to calm down after a stressful day. A martini. Some wine. Outside with Pete passing back and forth a cherry vape. Sometimes too many drinks, but it took the edge off and I actually found myself laughing and having fun and talking through our stories. And valium if I woke up at four from the drinking. Weed on weekends to unwind, as I binged something on Netflix. If I went out, cocaine at parties, music festivals, gigs. The best nights of my life, usually, at the time, followed by the most terrible anxiety that made me wish I was dead. But wasn't that everyone? It was almost everyone I knew. Just normal life.

JOURNALIST: For some people.

MAYOR: That's sad.

He didn't sound sad.

But you don't need to be stressed or agitated or unhappy. You just need to apply the control test. Stop worrying about things that aren't in your control. I wish I could wave a magic wand and get people to realise this.

JOURNALIST [*wryly*]: But, of course, you can't—because what others believe or how they act is not within your control.

MAYOR [*a small smile—finally*]: You're a quick learner. We try to change others, but in this we are doomed to failure. Parents try hard. Parents, politicians, lovers, colleagues, our bosses and family members, all of them trying hard to change others. But it's only a source of pain.

I thought of the long battles in my teenage years—Mum trying to control me, particularly in my goth phase, trying to stop me from going out 'dressed like that'. It never worked and it just made us angry with each other.

Other people's actions and their character are outside your control. We can, of course, try to persuade people but they have control over their own mind and actions. We cannot control them.

JOURNALIST: What about people who are jailed—surely that is society or the government, trying to control the actions of prisoners?

MAYOR: Yes, you can control someone's actions to an extent, when you take everything away from them. But you can't control how a prisoner reacts, what they think and their character.

JOURNALIST: True love is not trying to change the other person—or so I hear.

My mind strayed to Dominic again. What was he really like? Would I want to change him? Would he want to change me?

MAYOR: Yes, true love. But also garden-variety friendship can escape this burden, and that's why it's so delightful. You are you, and I am me, and we accept each other as we are. It's a foolish friend who tries to change their mate. Take friendship seriously. Nurture it. It's one of life's great delights. 'Nothing, however, delights the mind as much as a loving and loyal friendship,' said Seneca. Tell me, are you a parent?

JOURNALIST: No, I'm not. But my sister is. She's a new parent. And I'm a new aunt! The baby's name is Hannie.

I couldn't help beaming with pride. I had been there with Caroline when Hannie was born—was one of the first people to touch her, and, as soon as I did, I felt my heart explode. It was a new feeling, spontaneous and maybe the most authentic and true thing I'd ever felt. There was no ambiguity, no room for doubt, just pure big love. Suddenly I missed them so deeply it hurt. With a pang I remembered I had made them the wallpaper on my phone, and I no longer had the comfort of scrolling through photos of them.

MAYOR: It's common for parents to try to control kids, and to think they *can* control their kids. But it's never the case. You have a parent who really wants their kid to be a doctor or an engineer, who unconsciously or otherwise withholds love, approval or support until their child conforms to that aim.

JOURNALIST: I know many parents like that.

MAYOR: What about you? Did you feel controlled by your parents?

JOURNALIST: Ha, this is not about me.

My dad didn't try to control me because he wasn't there. My mum tried to control me but in retrospect. After I had acted, after I made decisions, after I had set a course—that's when the control would set in. Disapproval, silence, guilt, shame, anger, disappointment, withdrawal, smothering—she'd bring out her arsenal of things to try to get me to change course.

JOURNALIST: Did you feel controlled by your parents?

MAYOR: I was young a long time ago. But no, I don't think they tried to control me. They were of a very different generation. The opposite of helicopter parents. Possibly neglectful but in the best possible way.

JOURNALIST: What about Thida—did you try to control her?

MAYOR: Yes, I did. I'm not proud of it. I saw her as an extension of myself, so I was hard on her when she didn't conform to my ideal of what a child should be, what my *emissary* should be.

The breeze shifted and so did the mood. Both of us fell into our respective introspections. I didn't know what the Mayor was thinking about but there was a sadness in his eyes all of a sudden. He sighed.

MAYOR: We're sent mad by what we want, but do not have. It's the operating system that runs us. And it runs our life, if we let it.

The Mayor hesitated before speaking.

Sandra and I tried for many years to conceive more children, and it just never happened. Lots of miscarriages. We tried everything, including going to India for IVF. Thida was our only baby to term. We had to adjust to our lack of control in this area. Otherwise we would have been driven mad. Stoicism is about putting the brakes on all the things out of our control, that don't serve us, like the baby madness. It was a bad time, don't get me wrong, but we don't need to suffer as much as we do.

JOURNALIST: I'm sorry that happened to you. But if outcomes aren't the end goal, if drives towards external things are false gods to be overcome, what do you think will make us happy?

MAYOR: Living in accordance with nature. Desiring what you already have. Nature said one baby. What we already had. A beautiful, healthy girl. Thida. That doesn't mean that we shouldn't try for more children—but ultimately, after trying as hard as we could, we should accept our reality. The Ancients believed in fate: that everything is preordained, so don't fight against it, because what's happening to you or happening in the world is meant to happen. It's nature. Seneca said, 'Fate leads the willing and drags along the reluctant.'

The Mayor paused and looked at me kindly for the first time.

MAYOR: Fate is not always easy to bear; I know that from first-hand experience. As I'm sure you do too. But once you understand the control test, it will make more sense. You cannot change the past. You cannot control what has already happened. You can only control your reaction to it. I see you have brought a copy of *Meditations* with you. Good girl. What a book! Marcus says here—

He picked up my heavily annotated copy and flicked to a page.

'Whatever happens to you has been waiting to happen since the beginning of time. The twining strands of fate wove both of them together: your own existence and the things that happen to you.'

JOURNALIST: Do you believe that?

Instead of answering, the Mayor looked at me with his cold green eyes. It felt like the hawk had spotted its prey again.

MAYOR: Consider your life for a moment. Where were you born?

JOURNALIST: Um. In a small regional hospital. Or do you mean the city?

MAYOR: Doesn't matter. Think about it. How much of your life was dictated by where you were born? What about who your parents were? Would your life have been different if you were born to someone else?

What a stupid question.

JOURNALIST: Of course.

MAYOR: The truth is that the things that most affect our lives are not chosen by us. Who are parents are, where we are born, how intelligent we are. They are beyond our control. These incredibly important things, we have nothing to do with. They are set down. What is that but fate?

JOURNALIST: Fate is different. Fate means everything that is going to happen is . . . going to happen.

The Mayor laughed. It was a harsh laugh.

MAYOR: Yes. Everything that is going to happen will happen. And we can't do a thing to stop it, but I think 'determined' is the word you were looking for. Everything is determined. Is that what you were going to say?

JOURNALIST: Maybe.

MAYOR: A philosopher will ask, 'is life determined or is it free?' That's a false choice. The Ancients knew it was false. Fate is not something you choose to believe or disbelieve. Fate is something you realise.

I want you to think about your life, the one you have led.

I couldn't help myself. There was something in the air, something about being in Silver Springs, in front of this cold man, that drew me in. He said 'think about your life' and I was sucked back into it. I felt the slick vinyl seats of my mother's old car sticking to my bare legs in summer. I smelt the aroma of chips from a long-gone kiosk. I saw Paul's hand, smooth skin and fingers, and the spot where his hair parted on his forehead.

MAYOR: Well? What happened?

JOURNALIST: What do you mean? In my life?
MAYOR: Yes, what happened in your life?

Keep calm. He's using some kind of Jedi mind thing. He doesn't want an answer.

It's one thing after another, isn't it? Think about your life. Could anything have happened that did not happen?

I could have not been shot.

JOURNALIST: Yes. Many things.
MAYOR: How do you know?

JOURNALIST: It stands to reason. Something could have been different. One small thing could change everything.
MAYOR: That's what your intuition tells you, isn't it? Butterfly effect. And yet, we have only this one stream of events as evidence: the things that actually happened. The more you look at it, the more you realise that everything that happened had to happen, and everything that did not happen . . . well, it's just a fantasy. A control fantasy. Fate is unfashionable. I agree it doesn't suit the times. So call it what you want; the future is just like the past, a single stream of events that will happen come what may.

He waved *Meditations* at me and repeated the line.

'Whatever happens to you has been waiting to happen since the beginning of time.'

JOURNALIST: Why *not* resist the flow of events? Particularly if they are not to your liking? By resisting them, you are taking your destiny into your own hands. Taking charge! It's a less passive way to live.

MAYOR: Why not indeed! Resist, struggle, fight! Make your sandcastles. Rage against the world like a toddler. Or realise you can control very little and make life a little easier. Less friction. Less friction, less pain. The 'joyful yes' that your philosophers refer to.

We were silent for a long minute. Under the dappled light, and looking at the Mayor's shady garden, I felt like we had passed through a fever together.

Yet I remained resistant to the idea of fate. Where was the place for activism? For emotion? For bold and radical plays that might change the course of things? Instead the control test seemed to be suited to those living a small, quiet life. Those who had a low tolerance for disturbance. Maybe people like Thida or the Mayor, who had these slow, almost nineteenth-century lives, where they didn't have to worry about much except the things that were happening right in front of them, right now.

The Mayor's eyes lost their predatory glint. He looked at my hand.

MAYOR: Shall we have a break? Stretch our legs? You need to change that bandage. Your hand is bleeding.

He said it in his characteristically cold way, but receiving any caring attention from him was a relief. I nodded and was hit by a wave of exhaustion. I turned my hand and the bloodstain was as stark as a stigmata.

JOURNALIST: This is my writing hand. I worry about it—it's slow to heal.

MAYOR: So are many things.

The Mayor pointed down the hall to the bathroom, then went to make more tea. There were several doors lining the hall that were shut. I pushed one; it opened. A laundry. Across the hall—I pushed another door. A bedroom. Was it his? The bed was made with a simple indigo bedspread and one flat pillow. The walls were empty. It could have been a monk's room. Moving quickly and quietly, I went to the bedside table and opened it. I needed a photo of the Mayor, otherwise this entire trip was a bust.

Old notes. A folded booklet. A receipt. A comb. Bingo—a photo of a man and a woman wearing colourful batik kaftans. They were gazing at each other with a locked intensity. It was the Mayor! He was much younger. His hair was long and his lean face smiling and handsome. The photo was in colour but faded. (Could it be touched up with Photoshop?) Would he miss it, if I borrowed it until I could get it copied? Was it even him and Sandra?

I didn't hear the footsteps down the hall. But I almost jumped out of my skin when I heard a quiet tap on the door. Argh! I put the photo back and shut the drawer quickly.

'Are you in there?' asked the Mayor.

I walked out, face burning.

'I thought the bathroom was off the bedroom. Sorry—I got confused.'

If the Mayor registered a deliberate trespass, he didn't say. I had to remember to breathe as he directed me down the hall towards the bathroom.

I sat there on the toilet lid for at least five minutes, until my heart rate and breathing returned to normal. Then I rinsed my bandage and the wound. Looking into the mirror at my face still flushed with embarrassment, I cursed getting caught snooping. You can't come back from a loss of trust like that with a subject.

PREFERRED INDIFFERENTS—OR HOW TO WORK OUT WHAT MATTERS

SILVER SPRINGS, The Mayor's house, Thursday, 1 pm—When I returned from the bathroom, I hoped we might go into Silver Springs proper. I wanted to know if it matched Lou's recollections from the 1970s, make some notes, maybe interview a few locals—get their voices down on tape for the podcast. See if the Mayor was a dictator, madman or lunatic. He certainly didn't appear to be the kindly village elder, or so-called 'spiritual director' that I had imagined.

But the Mayor's house seemed far from town. Outside it was silent and hot except for the haunting, regular call of the koel in the canopy of treetops below the escarpment. The smell of the pines on the air reminded me of mountains I had visited back home, and I had a sudden yearning for people and civilisation.

I sat back on the verandah with the Mayor, the sun strong and hot on my back. We ate without speaking—water and naan—and then the Mayor turned to his dog. Teevee had been looking at us with silent longing since we sat down. Now he had his master's attention at last. He wanted a walk. We set off at a brisk pace towards the forest, below the escarpment and the low-hanging clouds.

We approached the trees that had been visible from the Mayor's verandah, a mass of dark green that resolved into ramrod straight pines and other unfamiliar evergreens with broad canopies. At close range their scent was even stronger. We walked into the forest and the Mayor spoke to me as he walked slightly ahead—turning to direct his voice towards the dictaphone in my hand.

MAYOR: As I do with all my students, I must warn you that over the next couple of days I will repeat things and come back to concepts. It's the best way, I have found, for things to sink in. Stoicism is actually quite intuitive and easy to understand but it's a practice where you return to the same concepts over and over again for your whole life. It's not set and forget. That's why we have weekly meetings at the Stoa: so things get repeated and repeated and repeated.

JOURNALIST: Understood. I guess it's like religion in that way where you have to go to church each week, to remind yourself.

MAYOR: You think this is like Christianity? You read the Bible, take scripture lessons, pray to God? People don't often think of the vast apparatus that goes into teaching religion. But that's how you get people to practise religion. You actually drum it into them! Week after week! And get 'em while they're young!

JOURNALIST: I take it you're not a religious person?

MAYOR: It's a shame that with religion there's so much dross served up with the gold, isn't it? And most of the time is spent on the dross. That's not how we do it here. We meet once a week . . . and we only deal in gold.

I could not take much more of this old guy's arrogance. Marcus Aurelius would have hated his guts.

But I recognise ritual is a useful tool, one many modern societies have forgotten how to use. It can bind communities together in powerful ways and can create meaning through sacraments and ceremonies.

JOURNALIST: Bind or restrict—depending on your point of view. What's your view?

MAYOR: You want me to start a culture war? Of course. You need a story. I'm not interested. Remember: don't try to control others. Don't invest yourself in changing others. I'm not saying 'religion is wrong' or 'religion is right'. I am concerned with my life and my beliefs, not yours or anyone else's.

I made a note to return to the topic of religion once I'd established more trust with the Mayor. It'd be a good, inflammatory topic to draw out some controversial quotes and make my piece a bit spicier.

MAYOR: After the control test, the second most important principle for Stoics is the principle of preferred indifferents. It also has the same natural logic to it as the control test.

JOURNALIST: Preferred indifferents? I've never heard of it. It's like you've just mashed two words together that contradict.

MAYOR: It makes perfect sense when you put it into action, like all of Stoicism. It means you might prefer something to be a certain way, but, because you can't control it, you should be indifferent to it. Your happiness should not be contingent on these things. Money, health, reputation and love all come under this principle.

JOURNALIST: That's a lot of very important stuff to be indifferent about. What's the Stoic position in relation to money? Be *indifferent?*

I felt an edge creeping into my voice.

MAYOR: You have a strong interest in money?

Of course. I never had enough.

JOURNALIST: Errr, yeah. It's on my mind. It's on everyone's mind. As I'm sure it is here. We're in the middle of a cost-of-living crisis in my country. Everything is getting more expensive. Groceries are the worst. A small bag with a few things in it costs around thirty dollars more than it did a few months ago. And my rent keeps going up. Plus I'm about to be out of a job. I'm staring down the barrel of gig economy work. So, yes—I have an interest in money.

I didn't want to go back to freelancing. No holidays. No sick pay. No protection. I didn't want to go back to waking at 4 am every night, worrying about money. Even just talking about it was making me anxious.

MAYOR: So a quick test for you. If you apply the control test, can you control how rich you are?

JOURNALIST: Yes and no. A lot about money isn't in my control, but I can control whether I work and how hard I work, and what I spend money on. But class matters. Sometimes money just flows to people down family lines, and the control test wouldn't apply to those people.

I knew inheritance wasn't in my future. I grew up working poor and remained working poor and yet was still surprised at how many of my colleagues and friends threw money around as if it wasn't important. Then I'd find out they got money from their parents or other rich relatives.

MAYOR: Class doesn't shield you from preferred indifferents! I've counselled many unhappy people who had assumed something would come to them in a will or legacy, and so didn't work hard themselves, or they overextended themselves financially, thinking an inheritance would come their way and pay for their lavish lifestyle or expensive mortgage. An inheritance is a gift and it is entirely up to another: that is, it is in another person's control if they leave you money.

JOURNALIST: Of course. But you can control money and get rich in other ways. You can work in high-paying jobs or try to work multiple jobs or make money through some sort of effort that you undertake. Effort is within your control.

MAYOR: You *can* make the effort, that *is* within your control. But the *reward* is not in your control.

JOURNALIST: I guess so. I work hard but I haven't had a pay rise in five years. But then again, I've chosen to work in a dying industry with rolling redundancies, vulnerable to the molestations of private equity and mergers.

I wondered what would happen to Lou and the others. Yes, they would keep their jobs—for now—but would they be sent to some sort of content farm where they pumped out articles to sit alongside AI slop?

MAYOR: It is within your control to leave and to try your hand in another, more lucrative industry.

But journalism was the only thing I loved. And the only thing I could do. Lou himself said in a rare moment of praise that I was a 'singular talent'.

JOURNALIST: Ha, maybe I'll retrain as a surgeon. I saw enough of them lately to know they're doing all right. Ski chalets and summer houses. Divorces to pay for, second—sometimes even third—families. But there are many structural barriers that stop people like me accessing careers like that.

MAYOR: But it's not insurmountable. Say you want the surgeon's wage. It becomes a top priority. You want that life, which quite frankly sounds a bit horrible and complicated, but each to their own. You might do all you can to retrain in medicine. But a lot of this process is only in your partial control. There are exams to sit, there are placements, and the question as to whether you actually have the skills to do the job. You can jump through all those hoops, and then something out of your control happens . . .

JOURNALIST: Like I developed a tremor . . .

Or I get shot at four in the afternoon in my workplace by a stranger.

MAYOR: Exactly. Or, in the many years it takes you to learn how to be a surgeon, there are huge advances in AI and the profession becomes obsolete. That's just one example but you can apply it to so many ambitions that people have for getting rich.

JOURNALIST: So getting rich is an external thing that you only have partial control over?

MAYOR: Yes. You may prefer being rich to being poor—that's only natural—but you should be indifferent to making money because it is out of your control.

JOURNALIST: So *prefer it* by all means, but be indifferent?

MAYOR: Precisely. For a Stoic, wealth is preferable rather than neutral because you can do good things with wealth: give it away to worthy causes, build a company that employs people, support a family. If wealth comes as a by-product of the virtues, of living a Stoic life, in harmony with Stoic principles, you shouldn't reject it. But the key word here is *harmony*. You can also accumulate a lot of stress trying to create and maintain wealth, and this can ruin your equilibrium or, as the Stoics call it, 'ataraxia', your joy. So be indifferent to money because the acquisition of wealth is not something in your total control. Otherwise everyone would be rich, right?

I was beginning to wonder if Stoicism was a capitalist conspiracy, designed to make people accept their shitty lot in life and not make a fuss.

JOURNALIST: More of us need to be rich. Right now there's a vast amount of inequality with a small number of people owning the majority of wealth. The middle class is disappearing. The poor are getting squeezed so hard that life has become about survival. That's stressful in itself.

I had been walking next to the Mayor, but now he stopped. We were on a path, still in the woods. The koel called somewhere deep inside the trees, and the air smelt clean, almost laundered. The Mayor, though old, was taller than me. He turned and looked down into my face.

MAYOR: I have lived here for fifty years, you know.

JOURNALIST: Yes, you said.

MAYOR: When you're old, you tend to see things negatively. Because you have lived a long time, you remember how things were, and when you compare them to how things are . . . well, it doesn't look so good. The world of the past seems so much better, even to those of us who think, who remember. So we go on, always comparing what is to what was. Judging. Seeing decline everywhere. This is the arrogance of the old. We forget nothing except the most important thing: that this age of decline is someone else's golden age of youth, full of promise.

You say life is hard. The rich are richer, the poor working harder than ever. Maybe you are correct. That is where you are from. Things are not the same everywhere. You are like an old man, arrogant and lost in thought, harking back to a better time. You don't even have the excuse of having lived a long time! You are young, and believe what you are told. You are told life is hard, that people are anxious, that everything is rotten everywhere. But that's not the case. Be in reality! Not everything is a dystopia. Here, things are different. We work to make it different. Here no one is poor. Here we have enough to eat, enough wood to heat our homes in winter. But no one is obscenely rich either. I prefer it here, with things more evenly distributed and so here I am. I do not sit around complaining about life.

I felt something in myself further harden towards the Mayor and his message. What did he know about life in my world? Why was he gaslighting me about income inequality? But I kept my cool.

JOURNALIST: Prefer it—but remain indifferent to it?

MAYOR: Yes. Exactly.

JOURNALIST: What about other stuff? Holidays? Cars? Better clothes? Don't you want them?

The Mayor looked at me for a moment more. I could see the sunlight on his eyes, the green changed to flat yellow-brown, the fine mesh of lines on the skin of his face etched deep now. He smiled, turned and began walking again. I raced to keep up.

MAYOR: Where's my new car? Where's my holiday? You know how remote this place is. If you can manage to get a car up here, you are not swapping to a new model car every couple of years. That's if you are lucky enough to have a car at all. They come up here in parts, you know? And they have to be re-assembled! It's a helluva job. And if you do have a car, you lend it to your neighbour when they need it.

JOURNALIST: What about travel? Holidays?

MAYOR: 'To keep your mind within bounds, you must first stop your body from running away.' Travel for the sake of it is a sign of a restless and disquieted mind, of someone wanting to run away from themselves.

JOURNALIST: And don't you want more money?

MAYOR: No. I have enough to live, and that's plenty. But let's bring down the questions of money from a societal level to a personal level, where your control lies. You can't control the whole of society and a society-wide distribution of wealth, but you can control your own attitude to money. Even if you succeed in getting a high-paying job or having successful investments, people with money lose money all the time. They might make it as a surgeon or whatever: an investor, a famous writer but then make a bad investment, or get swindled, or get divorced and find their assets are cut in half.

And it's not always a catastrophic loss: what is money for, after all, but to be used? It is in the nature of money to flow, to move from one person to another, to change. Like life.

We stopped climbing, me panting a little—and the Mayor paused at a stone bench, with a view high across several valleys. The valleys were drenched in light and unfolded in dramatic, almost cinematic peaks. We sat and he took a ball from his pocket, which he threw at the delighted Teevee.

The mistake is to think of it as *your* money. That will only cause you suffering, and you will suffer twice: once when you actually lose or use the money, and twice when you think about what you have lost and are filled with bitterness, anxiety or regret. The second suffering is entirely up to you: it's your choice.

JOURNALIST: Wow. I think it would be natural to be upset if you've lost all your money. There are real-world consequences if you can't afford rent and food. Your actual survival is threatened. Explain to me how I can avoid suffering if I am homeless and hungry? How is that not upsetting?

I felt my pulse race, the quickening of anger. What a heartless old man!

MAYOR: Just stop for a minute. What are you doing right now? Are you letting your thoughts upset you? Are you choosing to be aggrieved?

JOURNALIST: It just doesn't sound that compassionate. You're saying, 'okay, you lost your house and you can't afford food—too bad, be indifferent'?

MAYOR: The Stoics aren't compassionate people. Compassion wasn't one of their virtues.

JOURNALIST: What do you mean? Isn't compassion one of the emotions we should be trying to cultivate?

MAYOR: Buddhists have more emphasis on compassion. They explain it as wishing others to be free from suffering. But do you have control over whether others suffer? How others feel? How other people react to their circumstances? You've just learnt the control test: apply it!

I looked sideways. The Mayor almost looked happy as he schooled me.

JOURNALIST: No. I don't have control over other people's emotions.

MAYOR: So what place does compassion have? You are wanting something that you have no control over, which ironically can lead to more suffering if you don't get it.

I rolled my eyes.

JOURNALIST: I guess if you existed in a world of pure logic, you might think that way. But most people feel as well as think.

MAYOR: I'm not anti feelings. I'm pro dealing with feelings rationally. There's a lot of suffering in your society. You told me so yourself. People drugging and drinking themselves so life doesn't feel so bad, self-administering anaesthetics to stop themselves from feeling. That's more crazy than anything I'm proposing. What I'm proposing is a way of reducing or eliminating suffering by thinking differently, by coming to terms with reality. Living in it and even loving it! Marcus said, 'To be mad at anything that happens is to remove yourself from the world as it is.'

Loving it? Was he for real? My life *did* feel bad—particularly after the shooting. But even before it had been an anxious grind, with a sense of foreboding and uncertainty about the future. Taking the edge off by numbing yourself—well, who wouldn't? This hillbilly hypocrite was judging me! The Mayor was pointing at my notebook.

MAYOR: Look what you wrote there.

I flicked it open, confused. Then, appearing first as an impression in blank pages and then written in capital letters: *ACCEPT REALITY.*

MAYOR: Get back there. It sounds very obvious but not everyone who desires money gets money. In that gap between what you have and what you want, there can be an awful lot of suffering. Even when you get all the money you desire, enough to buy a mansion ten thousand times over, it doesn't solve things deep down. You will always want more. You will always be vulnerable to loss. And anyway, you're going to die. Each of us is headed for extinction; our lives, with all their momentum, accomplishments and energy, will all at once just cease. Whoosh! Over! So do you desire to live this short, sweet life in a constant state of dissatisfaction and wanting?

I felt almost assaulted by the Mayor's severe and challenging questions, his talk of death. I needed a self-help guru who was more like Oprah less like Hannibal Lecter if I wanted to make a pitch for a Netflix show, if I wanted to make Silver Springs palatable for viewers.

Then from the distance, away from the valley, an alarm sounded, rupturing the silence.

MAYOR [*sighing*]: Fire call. We're trying to be a good society, but that doesn't make us immune from natural disasters.

JOURNALIST: What's a fire call?

MAYOR: Hear those sirens? The town's firefighters have to scramble to tackle a blaze in the forest. They are volunteers, spread across the town. They hear the call, gather near the Stoa then head out on one of the trucks. The militia owned them before they were upgraded, and we repurposed them as fire trucks.

Clouds passed across the sky and smoke came from the forest in big gusts.

MAYOR: It's been happening a lot lately but not to worry: the trucks are good; we are quick and can contain it.

The Mayor held Teevee close, calming him until the sirens stopped, then continued his train of thought.

A lot of very wealthy people have visited us here. Wealthy people, famous people, some of the most powerful people from your country have been pilgrims. To get to Silver Springs is a status symbol, albeit a secretive one in the communities of the ultra-rich. These pilgrims have all those external things, all the money they could not even spend in several lifetimes, but what's striking is that they are not content. Not one iota! So much money but it never seems to be enough. They are still not happy. They come and visit me and say 'Mayor, Mayor, what can I do, I'm so unhappy!' Want what you've got, I say. Nothing more. And I say that to you now.

If only it were that simple.

'Treat what you don't have as non-existent. Look at what you have, the things you value most, and think of how much you'd crave them if you didn't have them. But be careful. Don't feel such satisfaction that you start to overvalue them—that it would upset you to lose them.'

JOURNALIST: Marcus?

MAYOR: Marcus, yes. We suffer when we become preoccupied with what we don't have.

JOURNALIST: Lifestyle creep. Relevant. How does Stoicism reduce suffering?

The sirens started again, making me uneasy, and smoke flew our way in great clouds, as if from a giant vape.

MAYOR: By bringing you into reality. The idea of being indifferent to money or riches is about recognising that riches come and go. You don't have to suffer if you are prepared, and if you judge your situation as not being harmful.

JOURNALIST: Talk me through it. How do you not just see your situation as harmful? Say I was scammed—do you have those here? Every second person I know seems to be getting scammed right now, losing a tonne of money.

MAYOR: Yes, I know what being scammed is! Scamming and being scammed are as old as time. There have always been scammers; their methods just change depending on technology. For the Ancients it would have been a fake gold thread in a bolt of cloth at the market, or an exotic spice that was actually sand.

These days it's not a fucking bolt of cloth. How are they meant to be indifferent? I thought of Lois Bond—a 73-year-old I had interviewed who had transferred her entire life savings to what she thought was a representative of her bank, who had warned her of a computer virus, but instead was a scammer's account. She was now homeless and living in her car. I spent three days visiting her with soggy cardboard containers of hot food, pulling out a camp chair in the grey light of the winter's day, eating and talking together, interviewing her for a series on scam victims.

JOURNALIST: Now it's people's entire life savings! I've interviewed elderly people who are homeless because they were scammed out of every cent in their bank accounts.

MAYOR: Think of the suffering in this case. There is the first suffering—being robbed and losing the roof over your head. That's happened. That can't be changed. The second suffering is *within* their control. It is the suffering of regret. Of anger. Of bitterness. It's spending the last of your days here on Earth furious with rage at your scammers. That rage you *can help*. That *you can* control.

JOURNALIST: I don't think I would react in any other way except to be livid with rage. And upset with the discomfort and danger of the situation I now found myself in—not having a roof over my head, not having enough food, not feeling safe or secure. None of these things is something one should be indifferent to.

MAYOR: Then prepare for it! Ready yourself before it happens! Look at what the Ancient Greek and Roman Stoics did, what their practices were. So much of it was designed to minimise suffering if they lost their money. This includes practising starvation, in case they could no longer afford food. They would go a few days a month without food, to prepare in case they lost all their money.

Seneca wrote, 'Set aside a certain number of days, during which you shall be content with the scantiest and cheapest fare, with coarse and rough dress, saying to yourself the while—"is this the condition that I feared?" It is precisely in times of immunity from care that the soul should toughen itself beforehand for occasions of greater stress and it is while Fortune is kind that it should fortify itself against her violence.'

JOURNALIST: So toughen yourself before disaster strikes?

MAYOR: Yes. This has several benefits. You're not as afraid of disaster because you have experienced it, given yourself a taste. Your body knows what to expect, so you become less stressed on a mental and physiological level. And you realise the thing you feared most is not as bad as your thoughts about it.

The Mayor looked at me almost beseechingly.

MAYOR: It's what you should be doing now, in preparation for soon losing your job. Just as Seneca suggested, you are lucky in some ways: you know the loss is coming. 'Let us become intimate with poverty so that Fortune may not catch us off our guard.'

JOURNALIST: I grew up poor—I don't need to cosplay being poor like Seneca did. Wasn't he the richest man in the world at the time? Today's equivalent would be Elon Musk giving everyone the same advice.

MAYOR: I don't know who that is. But look, if you've grown up poor, then you have a better idea than most about how you need to develop resilience to cope with financial insecurity. Do you put money away? Have any savings?

JOURNALIST: No.

MAYOR: What was the last thing you bought before you embarked on this trip?

I cringed. I knew the Mayor wouldn't understand or approve.

JOURNALIST: Don't laugh, but I have a subscription to a luxury handbag rental service. I just got a new rental Louis Vuitton the day of . . . the day before my last day in the office. It's dumb, I know. But actually sometimes I do like to cosplay—just like Seneca. But I like to play being rich.

To my surprise, the Mayor smiled. That made two smiles and a laugh in one day. Progress.

MAYOR: You need to cancel that service. It's unnecessary. Prepare for poverty! Eat simply. Vegetables, lentils, rice. Tap water. Why carry a Louis Vuitton when you can use a canvas bag? Why use a bag when you have hands with which to carry things?

What I didn't say, what was really stressing me out, was that at this moment the Louis Vuitton handbag was sitting in a plastic bag at the bottom of the wardrobe in my studio. It was covered in blood, and totally fucked. It had been with me in the office that day. I couldn't cover the $17,500 to buy it and I couldn't return it covered in the bodily fluids of my dead colleagues.

JOURNALIST: These treats—the rented handbags, UberEats, the cocktails and cherry vapes—they actually make me feel great. They have a mental health benefit. I'm getting a dopamine hit.

The Mayor pointed to my notebook again.

MAYOR: Reality. Look it in the face. Don't fool yourself.

I thought about how much easier it was to have no money when everyone else had no money. When I was just out of school, I waitressed and lived with roommates in a dodgy part of town. We'd pool our tips at the end of the week and buy a heap of cheap sausages, hamburgers and beer and have a big dinner on Friday night—everyone invited, everyone fed, people pulling out guitars and singing, no need to dress up, no need to go out, just doubled over with laughter all night, talking shit. I couldn't wait to leave that dead-end job and the falling-down house with one bathroom for six of us. But the strange thing is, looking back, it was the best time of my life.

JOURNALIST: Why not enjoy the good times while they're here? Why go hungry just to prepare?

MAYOR: Stoics *do* enjoy the fine things in life; they're just not attached to them. They drink the good wine if it's available. But they prepare for when it's not. The Ancients knew that, as well as the fine things in life, we also get our share of discomfort, deprivation and hardship. Misfortune is inevitable for everyone, at some point. I mean—do you know anyone who *hasn't* suffered? Anyone who's lived forever?

Plenty of people in the rich world are trying—freaky CEOs and tech titans who injected the plasma of teens, anyone who posted about 'protocols'.

JOURNALIST: There were kids at school who seemed to get everything—all their parents' love, good holidays, nice siblings. They were rich, and popular at school.

MAYOR: And what about after school? How did their lives turn out?

JOURNALIST: Probably just as nice and privileged as how they started out. The worst thing that happens to them is they say something stupid and get cancelled for like five minutes . . .

MAYOR: No one escapes suffering. Everyone gets sick, everyone dies.

Speaking of [*he pointed at my bandaged head and hand*] health is also another preferred indifferent.

We do our best here with our tiny hospital. But really sick people have to go to Davantown, or just suffer. Can you imagine someone going to Davantown to *get well*? So we are all trying to be as healthy as we can. We prepare for the foreseeable. We don't live in la-la land, where we pretend we have specialist cardiac surgeons around the clock.

JOURNALIST: So you prepare for the foreseeable? How do you do it? What are your protocols?

MAYOR: I fast for one week a month—just water. And once a week, I sleep on the floor. Your body, all our bodies, are fragile. Bodies get sick, stop working. This is natural. Accept it. Certain illnesses are curable; others are terminal. You still have control over your responses—your character, your courage and wisdom—even if your illness is not within your control.

The Mayor turned away at that point, and for the first time I realised he was not only talking to me, but also reminding *himself*. How old was he exactly? How many years did he have left? Was he already sick?

JOURNALIST: That's a hard lesson. People who are told their illness is terminal often want to fight on. As they should! Life is precious!

MAYOR: Ha! Yes, so precious it's worth letting go. Living with self-deception, this belief that you can control what is going to happen to you, is a betrayal of life. Most people live with this lie right to the end. It's better to let go. This is what happens in nature and it's what happens to us. Getting sick is natural. Dying is natural. It will happen to you. Seneca said we are dying every day—and he was right about that.

I knew more about dying than he did. I had looked death so closely in the face that I could feel its hot breath on my cheek.

JOURNALIST: Hang on, I'm supposed to be indifferent about the state of my health, but prefer to be healthy? Isn't that just like an envious person who pretends they don't secretly covet what another person has? Isn't this just putting it on—ultimately, just another, bigger self-deception? But I *do* care about my health because I love living! I love it, and I don't want to die! I don't want to suffer!

The Mayor gave me a surprised sidelong glance. I was surprised too and could feel my cheeks redden. I thought I was jaded and cynical but there I was blurting out to a stranger that I loved life. I didn't remember ever telling anyone that before. I didn't even remember *feeling* that before.

MAYOR: Whatever happens to you, happens. Calamity is a great teacher. As you now know, if you didn't before, what happens to your body is only partially under your control. I understand there's an industry in your world, the wellness industry. It's selling you the lie of control.

JOURNALIST: There was a sportswriter on the paper—Joe. He was a vegan, cycled everywhere—and he died in the shooting. Two kids! I still can't believe it! He had done everything right. His wife visited me in the hospital. I have a memory of her coming in to see me and being so angry. She was saying over and over again, 'Why him? It's not fair. It's not fair!'

That day at work I was hungover. I'd been out with another reporter—Vin—the night before and we'd had too much to drink. I'd stumbled into work the next morning. But Joe—he would have been to bed early, so he could get up early and help his wife get their kids ready for school. Then he would have gone to the gym before work and packed a healthy lunch. When I thought of what happened to him, I felt sick with guilt. While I had recovered and was on the road, reporting, Joe was dead and Pete was dead.

MAYOR: The idea of fairness is completely irrelevant. You might say nothing is fair. Equally, nothing is unfair. Why did your sportswriter get shot? Why did you get shot? Why *not*?

Accept what has happened, move on and you will recover from setbacks quicker. Release yourself! Health as a preferred indifferent doesn't mean that you should trash your health. Of course you should look after your body. The Stoic virtue of moderation, which we'll get to later, extends to things that affect the body, such as food and drink. But when you get sick, accept it. Sickness is a form of change, and the one iron rule of the universe is that everything changes. Accept it, and suffer less.

I looked down at my hand, which had started to throb again with pain.

JOURNALIST: I worry that my hand won't get better, that it will get infected, that I won't be able to use it.

MAYOR: Do you have another hand?

JOURNALIST: Yes.

MAYOR: Well, you can use that one.

JOURNALIST: And what if something happens to that hand?

The Mayor shrugged, unconcerned.

MAYOR: Does having no hands prevent you from being a good person?

JOURNALIST: No.

MAYOR: Well, be indifferent.

This guy was asking too much. I would definitely not be indifferent if I had no hands. For a start—how would I drink wine? Or text?

JOURNALIST: Even if they are not sick, people still resist decline. Loads of people I know are getting injectables and fillers, or just taking a tonne of supplements and doing ice baths so they can stay younger looking and healthier for longer. Why do they have to accept it?

I was thinking about getting some Botox myself, even though I wouldn't call myself vain. I had a line between my eyebrows. I was in my early thirties, looking old, the worries of the world on my shoulders and between my eyes.

MAYOR: You need to accept change because it is the way of nature. Maintain your tranquillity, your ataraxia. Realise that just as nature changes with the seasons, so it is with people: we are part of nature and subject to the same laws.

At that moment, an old song I had heard in the hospital came clearly to mind, with its ringing guitars and harmonies: 'To everything there is a season.'

No one stays young forever. Bodies age. Problems are inevitable, even if it's just stiff joints.

JOURNALIST: You're not afraid of getting older?

He looked at me in disbelief.

MAYOR: Look at me! I'm already there. And I'm not afraid. Why would I be? Every human and animal on Earth experiences what I'm going through.

JOURNALIST: You're not a health freak?

MAYOR: A freak? No. I do what is in my control. Stretching. The gym. Walks with Teevee. My diet is pretty simple, lots of fruit and vegetables, very little meat. Just whatever is available from the farms around here. Even with healthy living, some days it's hard to get out of bed. There are aches, particularly in my knees. But I know that life is short, and my aching body reminds me of this. The aches spur me on to get up and make the most of the day. They also prepare me in both subtle and unsubtle ways that I'm going to conk out and one day conk out for good! People who want to never feel any of the pains of ageing or see any of the ravages of time, it's a sort of death denial. They're shocked when the breakdown actually happens. They're suffering twice. Be in reality!

In the distance the smoke still plumed but not as strong and as dark. An acrid, charred scent hung in the air. The koel's call returned and for some reason this made me feel relieved.

The Mayor, out of nowhere, started chuckling. Was he mocking me again?

JOURNALIST: What?

MAYOR: I'm thinking of someone I know who learnt about health as a preferred indifferent the hard way.

JOURNALIST: Was it me?

MAYOR: Ha, no. But it could be you. There was a man in Silver Springs who was very proud of his body. Now, *he* was a freak! He spent a lot of time working out; in fact, he built the jungle gym right near the Black Lake. He was an early proponent of what you call 'cold water therapy'. He'd be working out in these tiny shorts then he'd jump in the freezing water and then back to the jungle gym. He was amazing, inspirational even, except for one thing.

JOURNALIST: He was annoying?

MAYOR: Yes, in a way he was. A real peacock. But that's not the important thing. He was extremely fit but there was no moderation there. Moderation is for all things, including the things that we think are good for us. Place too much importance on the body, too much stock in its strength and physical appearance, and you'll die a thousand deaths when something goes wrong. Actually, it doesn't have to go wrong; you just need to age and that is enough to destabilise people who place all their emphasis on external appearance.

JOURNALIST: What happened to Mr Cold Plunge?

MAYOR: He got bitten by a mosquito!

JOURNALIST: What?

MAYOR: The tiniest little creature was able to teach him quite a big lesson.

JOURNALIST: Was it dengue?

MAYOR: How did you know? He was in a lot of pain. High fever. Drenched in sweat when I went to see him on the third day of the fever. I spoke to the doc. It didn't look good. He had to be transported down the mountain to Davantown.

Dav. I shuddered involuntarily.

MAYOR: Have you ever had it?

JOURNALIST: Dengue? No. But there's always time.

MAYOR: Sandra and I both had it, though thankfully not at the same time. You really do think you're going to die. They don't call it broken bone fever for nothing. On the fourth day, the worst day, it feels as if your whole body is being crushed in a vice, while simultaneously being cooked from the inside. You'll beg for death! I was begging for death. My Stoic training deserted me on day four.

JOURNALIST: Really?

MAYOR: Yes. It was hilarious in retrospect but not at the time. I can still remember Sandra laughing at me as I begged for something milder to afflict me, like a double amputation without anaesthetic. She thought I was a lousy Stoic, not up for the challenge. She said, 'You can talk the talk, but you've got to walk the walk!' I said, 'Honey, how can I walk the walk when I can't even get out of bed?' It was like those early days back in India, when she first met me at my weakest.

I thought of the photo I found of him and Sandra. Was that taken soon after they had met? They were looking at each other with such intensity and love that the photo took on a mesmerising quality. I had to work out how to get my hands on it.

What's the point of me telling you this story about the cold plunge guy? Well, he recovered but he walked through hell first. It was a reminder of how fragile our bodies are. Even if we do all we can to keep them strong, a tiny mosquito with a tiny bite that we can hardly feel can cause us the most immense amount of pain and discomfort, even death.

JOURNALIST: And it can happen to anyone—even if you are fit and strong.

MAYOR: And if it can happen to anyone, it can happen to you or me. Although you need to use your rational mind and good information to see what the statistical likelihood is. You need to deal in facts, not fears. That is the key to reducing anxiety.

Ultimately the Stoic ideal is acceptance of whatever happens to your body. You realise health is an indifferent, and you appreciate and nurture a healthy body while you have it. But when things go wrong, like being the victim of a violent crime or when the normal signs of ageing appear, you realise that many things are beyond your control. Embrace acceptance and focus on how you respond to these circumstances. You can control how you respond, so why not use the adversity to respond with virtue? To be courageous in the face of reality?

JOURNALIST: And having a sick body doesn't get in the way of developing virtue?

MAYOR: On the contrary: the virtues are often developed during times of illness and misfortune.

JOURNALIST: What about when a young person or a person in the prime of their life becomes ill or injured? That seems to defy nature. It's callous.

MAYOR: Defy nature? I don't think so. Nature is lovely and violent. How many chicks in their nests are killed by a hawk? No living thing, neither animal nor human, is promised anything. Know things for what they are. We are born, we have a short time here and we die. 'The first rule is to keep an untroubled spirit. The second is to look things in the face and know them for what they are.' That's Marcus again. Those destined for a short life, like your friend Joe, live just as well as all of us. Sometimes better.

JOURNALIST: That sounds cold.

I was beginning to disassociate. I didn't want to dwell too much on the dead. I did what the hospital social worker had told me to do: focus on the real things in the world that I could see, smell, hear, touch. The mist that came off a distant mountain, the smoke from the fire, the clean pine scent of the forest, the sound of the highland koel, and all the different bird calls from the forest, Teevee's silky coat, warm and alive under my hand.

MAYOR: It's not cold; it's realistic. All these things are preferred indifferents, including life itself. Yes, I would prefer to be alive, but I need to be indifferent because ultimately when I die is out of my control. In the natural course of things, none of us knows when we are going to die, and if that death will be long and protracted or short and sudden.

JOURNALIST: I think a slow death is better—so you can better prepare. I was not prepared when I was shot.

When my colleagues started screaming it was so weird, like being in a different dimension. Amid the carnage, I almost started laughing. Maybe I did laugh?

MAYOR: Yes. But that's not something we have a say in. We must prepare for the end, long before we see an ending loom. Because we never know how much time we've been allotted. Often when people get a diagnosis that gives them, for example, a year to live, they say it focuses the mind wonderfully. Everything becomes more beautiful; even water tastes good, sweeter . . .

Like the river rum, that special rum, made with the silty river water that made me feel so good and later dream so vividly.

When you know you are dying, *really know*, you will no longer binge on mindless television when you could be watching the sunset, or being with people you truly love. Those who know life is finite and could end at any time, not of their choosing, stop squandering time. When everything is imperilled, everything becomes both urgent and precious. Seneca put it like this: 'You live as if you were destined to live forever, no thought of your frailty ever enters your head, of how much time has already gone by, you take no heed. You squander time as if you drew from a full and abundant supply, though all the while that day which you bestow on some person or thing is perhaps your last.'

I didn't want to think about death, particularly out here, surrounded by such dramatic beauty, such warm golden light.

JOURNALIST: What about place? Is that an indifferent? Is Stoicism neutral to what the external world is like? And so you don't need to be in a beautiful place like this in order to practise Stoicism?

MAYOR: Yes. In fact, Stoicism might actually suit a harsh, ugly or inhospitable place because of its focus on inner peace and inner contentment. Place, location is an indifferent. Stoic training aims to make it possible for us to salvage some form of a good life under adversity, and to be able to handle sudden, massive changes in our circumstances. In short, to live anywhere. Even, in your words, a total 'shithole' like Davantown.

Silver Springs was stunning, even if the Mayor lived in a fairly basic house. Butterflies and birds flew around us and, despite the smoke in the distance, there was a sylvan lushness to the landscape, a sense of being in a hidden fairytale kingdom, inaccessible and remote, where the taint of modern life couldn't touch us. Looking at the Mayor on the bench—his face a bit softer now, less forbidding—I thought of what a strong photograph this would make. Him on the bench in the sun, Teevee by his side, surveying his idyllic Stoic kingdom. Maybe there was a photographer in Silver Springs who could re-create the scene and shoot a portrait? I saw my page one now. Lou always said there was no story without pictures—and I realised with some alarm that, without an image of the Mayor, I would struggle to get anything published.

JOURNALIST: Why not live in Dav then? It sounds as if you have been training to live in harsher circumstances. Why are you living in such a remote and pretty place, where everything is so lovely and easy on the eye?

Except you can't get a car up here, other than in a thousand different pieces, or an internet signal or—judging by what Thida was wearing—modern clothing.

MAYOR: For decades I've been training to live somewhere grim. And I like being tested. Where I live is a preferred indifferent. I prefer to live here but ultimately I need to be indifferent to my home here, as one day I may be forced to move. Climate change could have an impact and make Silver Springs uninhabitable. Wildfires could destroy it. Or we could all succumb to the next pandemic. The junta could make an incursion up here. Maybe the peace we have with neighbouring villages could dissolve with a new political regime. After all, many of them think we are pagans.

I recalled with a shudder the recent history of the region: fake news on Facebook about villagers in a neighbouring area forming a rebel militia. A mob descended on the village and massacred several dozen people. If it could happen there, it could happen here. Even utopias are fragile.

The Mayor smiled again. Three times! And I felt a sudden surge of concern for the old man.

JOURNALIST: You must be careful! Fake news travels fast these days. There have been terrible crimes committed against whole peoples because of mobs, because of lies on social media.

MAYOR: New technology but old hate. There's a long history of philosophers being exiled or killed, which would make all of Silver Springs—a whole town of philosophers!—a target. The Stoics in Ancient Rome were expelled by Emperor Domitian. Epictetus himself was expelled. It's throughout history. Look at Pol Pot in Cambodia. Anyone who was an intellectual, among many other groups, was killed as being threatening to the regime. Safety can never be taken for granted, no matter what time in history you're living in.

JOURNALIST: You sense a threat to your community? An invasion perhaps?

Although I was worried for the Mayor, this could be a bigger story than even Lou imagined. I needed to start documenting the town, taking photos, before anyone—or a random mob—ran through it with torches and machine guns.

MAYOR: Why not? What is built can also be destroyed. But what is more likely to happen is much less dramatic. I'll just get too old and feeble to live independently, and that's when I'll leave Silver Springs. I keep all this in mind. It could happen any day now. And if I need to relocate to Davantown or somewhere else, I would do so and be okay with that because I have prepared. The Ancients had experience with exile and wrote extensively about how to bear it, even thrive. So, I am curious to see how I go when it's a permanent state.

JOURNALIST: Not dreading it?

MAYOR: No. I'm looking forward to it. We call this a Stoic challenge. We want to be tested. We want to see if all that reading, journalling and thinking pays off and translates into action. Into grace under fire. It's no good reading the preferred indifferents unless you can put the theory into practice when you lose something like your health, your reputation or your money. Or maybe all three, all at once!

The Mayor sounded almost excited at the prospect. I hadn't been prepared for the shooting, and now I was suffering—but I wondered how *could* I prepare for it? Get someone to fire bullets at me while I sat filing a story at my desk? Walk through the kill floor of an abattoir, so I could get used to being covered with blood, bone and brains?

The Mayor stood up. We were on the move again—a brisk walk across the hills. Teevee trotted joyfully ahead. The unfamiliar sky was huge and blue around us and the air was now sweet and cool, no trace of the fire, the temperature dropping.

JOURNALIST: So you have trained for exile—tell me what that looked like for you?

MAYOR: Sandra got sick. I took her to Davantown, then beyond, for treatment. It was a form of exile. But then so is life without her.

JOURNALIST: What happened?

MAYOR: She died.

JOURNALIST: I'm sorry.

MAYOR: That's okay. I'd been preparing for it.

JOURNALIST: Where did you go for treatment?

MAYOR: To your country. A better health system. I had some money left to me from my family, so we used that to make the trip and to get treatment. But it was like taking a sick person to a sick place and expecting them to get well. It felt like an exile. Stoicism helped us accept this time, even enjoy some aspects of it.

In the distance, the hills were a vivid, deep purple. We turned a corner and there was a heath of purple wildflowers that smelt like clean grass and sweet like jasmine.

Exile is what the mind makes of it. That's what I've come to believe. In ancient times some philosophers were exiled to places that we'd consider quite pleasant today, holiday islands now, but others were exiled to very harsh and inhospitable islands. Seneca was exiled to Corsica; Musonius Rufus exiled to the arid, desolate island of Gyaros in the Aegean Sea. Knowing they could do nothing about the exile, that they must serve their time, they accepted the set of dire circumstances and made the most of it. Some of them even came to see their hardship as benefiting them. They had time to think and write, away from the social life and temptations of Rome.

JOURNALIST: I guess it's just how you frame the situation.

MAYOR: Exactly. You're learning! If you welcome these dire circumstances, if you see them as something that could help you become a better person, it transforms the whole experience.

JOURNALIST: I wonder if I could have done that in hospital?

I was there for so long and it felt like an exile. I felt like I was dying. It was terrifying.

MAYOR: In pain it would be hard to use reason and get clarity, particularly if you were given lots of opioids and other pain relievers. But I wonder if the point of *your exile*, your time away from your ordinary life in hospital, would have been to allow yourself to be the vessel of love and care from others? To be able to truly receive the patient tending, prayer, medicine, love from those who treated you and visited you?

That you were in exile, for sure, but you were not alone? For someone like you, who seems fiercely independent, that would have been a difficult exile. But to yield to the love and care of others is such a rich experience. A Stoic experience. And from that courage and wisdom are born.

I nodded noncommittally, but had to remember to breathe. I didn't like to think of my hospital stay and the precarious and nightmarish aspects of it; the way the drugs made my eyes roll back in my head as they came on, and the endless blood extractions, the drawing of the needle and looking for a vein (the black hand that scared me at first sight was my own, bruised from the cannula). At night, the mechanical beep of the machines, the slanted light coming in through a half-open door, and the songs on the radio at the nurses' station were of bad times coming—a Doors triple play before the news: 'Riders on the Storm', 'Crystal Ship', 'The End'—filling me with deep dread. I changed the topic.

JOURNALIST: What would Musonius Rufus think of modern times, when everything is orientated towards making life easier, more frictionless? You had labour-saving devices like washing machines, cars and planes, then twenty or thirty years ago the internet, so maps and personal navigation systems, Facetime, Uber. Tech that turns on the lights for you when you get home, plays your favourite playlist, adjusts the heating. Now AI, doing a lot of our researching, writing, creating and thinking for us.

MAYOR: I would ask—for what end? You free up time with all of these things, sure. But what are you doing with this extra time?

JOURNALIST: I don't know—binge-watching Netflix, ordering someone to come over on a bike with a bowl of ramen?

MAYOR: That's all passive stuff. Being entertained to death. People in the rich world becoming simultaneously exhausted and overstimulated. They are hungry but too tired to cook. Yet too wired to sleep. I'm all for less housework and less drudgery but the time that we save, we need to use properly. Otherwise, what's the point?

JOURNALIST: What's a good use of time?

MAYOR: What we are doing now. Walking in nature, breathing the fresh air, the sun on our faces, feeling the slight static in the air before the storm rolls in. The finer feelings of being alive and part of the natural world. And talk! Talk like this. Reflecting on life. Asking questions. Getting to know each other. Arguing! Creating experiences! Sharing experiences! It's wonderful, don't you think?

I nodded but was yet to be won over. Stoicism seemed, to my ears, hard and unyielding, demanding a discipline I didn't possess.

JOURNALIST: Okay, place is a preferred indifferent, so is comfort and health. And you mentioned earlier that reputation was a preferred indifferent?

MAYOR: Yes. Once again, your reputation is out of your control and having others think badly of you, for whatever reason, doesn't prevent you from acting with virtue. The Ancients put this to the test, just like they put voluntary starvation or fasting to the test.

They wore ridiculous or unfashionable clothing, to test their ability to cope with the disdain or ridicule of others. Zeno, the founder of Stoicism, used to beg people for money, even though he had plenty. Cleanthes, another Stoic philosopher, worked as a manual labourer for so long, some in Athens thought it might be a front for something illegal. Seneca experimented with vegetarianism at a time when it was deeply transgressive in Rome. Cato, a Roman senator, used to walk around bareheaded and barefoot, wearing shabby clothing. And Marcus Aurelius, the Roman emperor, wore a poor man's cloak and slept on a hard bed.

When Stoics learnt that ridicule didn't hurt as much as imagined, and didn't affect their characters, they were freed from caring so much about their reputations. One less thing to worry about!

JOURNALIST: They didn't care because they couldn't control their reputation?

MAYOR: Reputation falls outside the control test. When they experienced the public ridicule, they asked: is that the worst that can happen? Someone just laughs at me? Well, that's not so bad and, anyway, it says more about *their* character than it does about mine. There is so much freedom in that. Think about the freedom of not caring. Not caring what other people think of you. Not caring if you were unpopular. If you had a good character, and you knew you were doing the best you possibly could in relation to your character, it didn't matter what your reputation was.

JOURNALIST: Wild that they practised being uncool!

MAYOR: Yes. And they found that it didn't truly diminish them; this knowledge released them from the burden of conformity. Conformity is still a scourge today.

JOURNALIST [*sighing*]: The amount of pain I caused myself when I was young, trying to fit in.

MAYOR: People spend their whole lives conforming, trying unconsciously or consciously to meet the expectations of others. Maybe it's having a beautiful house, or money, or in relationships. It's definitely in work. The stress people experience when they think they're in trouble with the boss, when they haven't measured up: it wreaks havoc with your physiology, releases stress hormones. It's the modern equivalent of being chased by a tiger.

JOURNALIST: I'm hoping I care less as I get older. I still care what Lou thinks, but the list is dwindling.

MAYOR: Try to get it to dwindle to one. Just you! You can't control another person's thoughts or words, so it's far better to be indifferent about what others say about you.

JOURNALIST: What have you done that invited ridicule? The fashion here—maybe you don't have the latest trends—so that's not an issue I imagine.

MAYOR: I've done plenty that's invited ridicule.

He didn't elaborate. What was humiliation for me? Anything connected to social media. The pile-ons—sure. But being ignored was worse: if I posted something that got no likes. Parading my avatar through the internet with posts that were cringe and got no acknowledgement or interaction—that was worse than wearing dingy clothing. (Come to think of it, wasn't I wearing dingy clothing now?)

MAYOR: The practice of all these discomforts is freeing. And that freedom can be felt on several levels. On one level, it's freedom from worry about the future because you know you had been preparing or training for an adverse event over many years. And it's also freedom from fear. You don't live meekly or anxiously, anticipating some dreadful event in the future that would affect you in an unknown way. You know how it would affect you, because you've been practising for it. And for a modern Stoic, it's freedom from materialism, from the empty promises of advertising. You have experienced going without, not buying, not having. When you realise you'll be fine, it's a very powerful lesson.

JOURNALIST: But if you live inside the capitalist system, like I do—how can you be truly free of materialism?

Just as I was thinking the Mayor had loosened up and we were speaking easily, almost as friends, he turned on me.

MAYOR: What are you talking about? Have you not been listening? Abandon these grand ideas you have about systems and historical movements. Capitalism, materialism. You speak like the fools I left behind half a century ago. Ask yourself: what do you have control over? Yourself, what you think! There's no magic answer beyond that! There's nothing I can tell you, no moment of revelation, that will set you free. Live according to nature.

The Mayor raised his voice further. I took a step back from him, eyebrows raised. He continued his rant.

Free of materialism? You are part of the world, and you will be a materialist insofar as you need materials to survive. What I am saying . . . please, just listen to me . . . is that you can do this a little better. You can be more intelligent, more wise, more virtuous. Less stupid. When it comes to reputation, you can know, in your heart, that what others say about you is beyond your control. And things beyond your control should not concern you.

I felt powerless and angry—like I once did when I was a child, and didn't have the tools to defend my position.

JOURNALIST: What about defamation actions then? They're a very consequential attempt to control your reputation. Reputation is taken seriously by society. There's a whole, lucrative substratum of the legal industry that exists because of defamation laws.

MAYOR: What's your point exactly?

JOURNALIST: Well, clearly reputations are important, or there wouldn't be a whole industry based around them.

We arrived back at the house. I noticed the Mayor hadn't locked the door before going out.

MAYOR: People *think* reputation is important. They also make the mistake of thinking they can control their reputation through court actions like defamation, as you mentioned. But control is an illusion. It's in the hands of a judge and jury, or a judge alone. I would advise anyone taking out a defamation action to prepare themselves immediately for loss and humiliation.

A better way is to be indifferent to your reputation. You will be more tranquil. And richer! Usually the only winners in defamation cases are the lawyers. Become a defamation lawyer, not a surgeon! They'll always be in work as long as people think they control what is said about them. As long as people's egos are writing the cheques.

JOURNALIST: But if someone is spreading lies about me, and it is causing me harm—saying bad things about me—I need to be able to correct the record and repair my reputation. Reputation is incredibly important. I spent years building mine up. I'm not from a rich family. I don't have money. I couldn't afford to do unpaid internships and so I worked really hard to get in from the ground up and build my reputation. My reputation is my inheritance. It's my bank balance. It's my contact book. At the end of the day, it's all I'm going to be left with when I leave *The Sentinel*.

MAYOR: Wake up! Your reputation exists in the minds of other people. And it's not one singular, static thing. Every person you interact with will have a different view of you, and that view will keep changing. Because *you* are not a static singular thing. How crazy to think you can control that! To think that you can control a shifting image in the minds of every person you know. You may as well try to control the wind.

After pulling me off Paul that day back at my friend's house—yes, it was teen pregnancy that my mum railed against but it was also something else. Reputation. What would people think of me? What would people think of her if they knew her daughter was having sex with the neighbour's older cousin? Then the generational cycle would begin again—teen pregnancy, single mother, struggle and poverty. A good reputation was a way out of this but a bad reputation could be a trap that kept you down and impoverished.

MAYOR: You would have seen people who, in an attempt to protect their reputation, end up destroying it. Right?

JOURNALIST: Yes. I've seen it backfire. People's dirty laundry being aired in court when they have brought an action to protect their reputation.

MAYOR: Reputation . . . who cares! I'll be back shortly.

He abruptly disappeared down the hall, leaving me to play with Teevee.

The light was dim, but ten minutes later, from the gloom, there appeared a tall woman, walking towards me. Who was she? A housekeeper? A friend? Teevee ran to her and I gasped. It was the Mayor—dressed in women's clothing and an oversized sunhat, with a slash of hot pink lipstick on his mouth!

JOURNALIST: What the actual fuck?

The Mayor sat across from me, looked at the dictaphone and smiled broadly. He had lipstick on his teeth. He was the worst-looking drag queen I'd ever seen.

MAYOR: Where was I? Ah the irony of defamation actions. One of the four Stoic virtues, which we'll discuss further, is justice, so, if there is injustice to the slur, then it should be pursued and rectified but also the person defamed needs to be aware that the results of any action they bring is out of their control. They need to be relaxed about the outcome.

My mouth hung open, like a fairground clown. The Mayor exhaled and his shoulders dropped. Suddenly we both started laughing—and just when I stopped, I looked at the Mayor with his badly applied lipstick and too tight dress, and I started laughing again. He looked ridiculous lecturing me about defamation while dressed like that. And he knew it too.

JOURNALIST: This is what you wear when you want to drive home the point about reputation?

MAYOR: Yes. Just like Cato wore ridiculous clothing and was laughed at in the street and Marcus wore a rough cloak, I wear this to prove that it makes no difference to my character.

JOURNALIST: You have outdone Cato and Marcus!

MAYOR: I say to people, this is no big deal. This dress is just a piece of cloth, cut differently from pants. Lipstick is just wax, fat, dyes and oil. It doesn't change or damage my character wearing this. I am still the same person. I am still a man, and my masculinity is not dependent on external things like clothes.

JOURNALIST: If you say so!

MAYOR: I know so!

JOURNALIST: Do you dress like this around town?

MAYOR: Sometimes, if I feel that it's relevant. If it's a lesson that needs to be learnt.

JOURNALIST: A lesson for the people of Silver Springs?

MAYOR: No, a lesson for me. What others think of me is a preferred indifferent. Every time I get too puffed up or prideful, I need to remember that reputation, being a big man around town, that's a dangerous idea to have. It stops me from being humble, and it makes me reliant on the esteem of others and social status. Both of which could disappear tomorrow.

I had to hand it to him—it took courage to walk around looking so strange.

There's this old story, from the very dawn of Stoicism. When Zeno, the founder of Stoicism, became Crates's pupil—Crates was a Cynic—he was too modest to properly live the Cynic philosophy.

Crates, to cure this defect in him, gave him a potful of lentil soup to carry through Athens; and when he saw that Zeno was ashamed and tried to keep it out of sight, Crates broke the pot with his staff. As Zeno began to run off in embarrassment with the lentil soup flowing down his legs, Crates chided, 'Why run away, my little Phoenician? Nothing terrible has befallen you.'

It was just soup. And this is just a piece of clothing. No harm has come to me. And no harm came to Zeno.

ATARAXIA—OR HOW TO BE RELAXED

SILVER SPRINGS, The Mayor's house, Thursday, 2 pm—After washing his face and changing back into his plain cotton button-down shirt and a blue longyi, the Mayor said he was going to demonstrate how to cook a simple, cheap and healthy vegetarian meal. 'To help you prepare for your new, more insecure life.'

From his pantry he gathered ingredients for what he called lahpet thoke, a tea leaf salad mixed with crunchy peanuts, sesame seeds, fried garlic and lime. He told me it cost only a couple of dollars a serve and would fill me up until dinner.

I stood at his elbow as he sautéed the garlic and toasted the sesame seeds. He waved away my offers of assistance.

I asked him about ataraxia. I was curious as to why Stoicism—the word that has such austere overtones—had such an emphasis on being relaxed.

JOURNALIST: Not caring what other people think of you, not minding being scammed out of all your money, not worrying about looking weird or foolish, not stressed about ageing and ill health—even death—you keep coming back to this concept of ataraxia. Why is it so important to be relaxed?

MAYOR: If you are relaxed, untroubled, steady, then you are less likely to be rocked by the events of life, such as losing your job, being injured or getting a divorce. And you're less likely to be an arsehole to other people. It's that simple. We've talked about world peace but where do you think that starts? It starts with being peaceful in yourself, no matter what happens.

JOURNALIST: Easy to say—hard to achieve. What's the origin of the word?

MAYOR: The Ancients had a concept called 'ataraxia', meaning equilibrium. In Ancient Greek philosophy, ataraxia is generally translated as equanimity, or tranquillity. An ongoing freedom from distress and worry. It's being even, relaxed, unperturbed. It's a very important state to be in if you want to remain unaffected by external events. This is not a Stoic thing. In the ancient world almost all schools had a word for the concept of internal stillness. Ataraxia is a state that you should be working to cultivate. Think of it like a duck paddling hard with its feet underwater, while remaining calm and unruffled up there on the surface.

JOURNALIST: A drug company should invent a tranquilliser and call it Ataraxia.

The Mayor indulged my humour.

MAYOR: I'm surprised that hasn't happened yet.

JOURNALIST: We could go into business together—a joint venture! Make some money! I hear there are some labs just over the border . . .

The Mayor raised his eyebrows and laughed.

While I would say it's a great aim to be relaxed, it's normal to have changes in moods, to suddenly feel uneasy or unhappy. Isn't that part of life?

I was a child of someone whose moods would mercurially change, seemingly from one moment to the next, without outside stimuli. As a result I was a watchful child, forever ready to fight or flee in case I was at the receiving end of my mother's temper. Sometimes I wondered if I had inherited this too, along with her blue eyes.

MAYOR: But you *can* control your moods. Your reactions and your responses are within your control. As soon as you feel like you're starting to get upset, be conscious of the change of mood and return to the place of calm. Most people don't need a drug to get them there, and to keep them there. When force of circumstance upsets your equanimity, lose no time in recovering your self-control, and don't remain out of tune longer than you can help. Habitual recurrence to the harmony will increase your mastery of it. Just try time and time again to get to harmony.

JOURNALIST: Before you get angry?

MAYOR: Yes, definitely before the anger or bad mood erupts. Once it's unbottled, you can't put it back in. With this habitual return, with ataraxia—continual calmness, contentment and peace—it's actually easy to not get angry, or to not get provoked, because you are not emotionally primed to. You are so far from being triggered because you are just resting in that calm state of emotional homeostasis. It becomes your natural place. You have made it that way through habitual recurrence. You return there again and again and again until it becomes second nature.

The Mayor diced a capsicum and took out some plates. The smell of the toasted garlic and sesame was making me hungry. This was the first home-cooked meal I'd had since before the shooting and I enjoyed being cooked for, sitting on a high bench and watching a meal unfold from separate elements. The Mayor moved around the kitchen, selecting bowls and water glasses, cutting a lemon for the water, pushing a pile of papers and books down to the other end of the table, and served lunch.

JOURNALIST: Are you an angry person? Prone to mood swings? This looks amazing by the way!

MAYOR: Not anymore. I was. Parenting revealed my anger and lack of patience. It was a real lesson in self-control, to learn how to parent better. I'll often use fake anger though.

JOURNALIST: What's that?

MAYOR: It's pretending to be angry at someone to make a point. You don't get out of ataraxia within yourself but you act a certain way to impart something strongly. It can be used to great effect with students or young children.

JOURNALIST: And journalists?

The Mayor shrugged and grinned.

MAYOR: You're not the only one who has professional tricks. Anger is a whole other topic for tomorrow, when we talk about the passions: anger, desire, arousal and so forth. Things that arise from the body. But today I want to focus on contentment, which can occur when you make it a priority. As I said earlier, happiness has its opposite. If you are always seeking happiness—and happiness that depends on outside factors—then you're risking suffering. Because you can't control those outside forces. Contentment, which you might also call ataraxia, a calm, equanimous state, is less vulnerable to highs and lows. The aim is to get into emotional homeostasis where you can better access your reason and negotiate life in a calm manner. In a state of ataraxia, you won't become agitated and liable to make poor decisions or lash out at others and make their lives miserable. We all know someone like that, don't we? They take out their unhappiness on others because they can't control their own moods. They smear their bad mood around, tainting the atmosphere around them. No one wants to be around those people.

JOURNALIST: That's the worst—walking on eggshells around moody people. But what about the upside of strong moods? I love the exhilaration and huge rush of excitement when something good happens. Falling in love, or getting a page one, or being nominated for a prize. I don't want to give up that feeling for a more chill, stable state, for the homeostasis. If I really thought about it deeply, I'd say I live for that feeling of exhilaration.

Dominic came uninvited into my mind again. And with that thought, I remembered all the highs: me and Pete running through a parking lot, chasing Ferdi Zolo, a dodgy developer, and finally cornering him at his car, him cowering and Pete getting the perfect page one shot. Me and Lou at dawn, meeting at the newsagent when the trucks came in with the first editions and there it was—my story on cover-ups in the local council that would eventually bring down the deputy mayor. Me and my sister, when we were young, blagging our way backstage to meet the Ledjets and partying with them all night. Lou calling me to tell me I got the job at *The Sentinel* and, after putting the phone down, dancing around the kitchen with my mum. Big highs. I loved them all.

MAYOR: Once you experience true contentment, ataraxia as your normal state, you won't want to go back, not for all the quick highs in the world.

JOURNALIST: I can't imagine that.

MAYOR: That's because your culture actively works against your maintaining that state. Think of any big city and all the things that stimulate and distract you. And that's not even taking into account people's phones. These ultra-powerful entertainment machines put you in a state of hyper-arousal that fractures your attention span, prevents you from going truly inward, but also makes you unable to look away.

I was missing my phone badly, even if all these things were true.

What about all the things each day that you see on your phone, whether by design or accident, that agitate you, rile you up, make you angry, make you envious, make you smile, make you afraid? You're cycling through this never-ending entertainment. It will never be over—

JOURNALIST: —and so you have to keep watching.

MAYOR: Think about all the time, that amount of time, sheer time in hours and minutes per day, months a year, years a decade you are on your phone. It's going to be working on you, changing you. It's not some passive entertainment that you all depend on, but it is something active and it's changing the way all humans operate. As a society, we need ataraxia more than ever to compensate for the constant state of arousal and agitation we find ourselves in.

JOURNALIST: It's been more than a week now since my phone was working. So theoretically I should be adjusted but I keep reaching for it, and I really miss it. It's like I'm missing an arm—truly! I'm bereft. Do you feel like you're missing out?

MAYOR: We never had portable phones, so it's hard to answer that. But I've noticed how it changes cities—and changes people! When I have a couple of years without travelling and go into big cities now, I see how they have completely changed.

JOURNALIST: Like how?

MAYOR: For a start everything just looks different. The people are different. When Sandra and I went for her treatment and the plane landed, I won't forget it: the first thing people did was they all got out their phones and turned them on. The eagerness! As if to be separated only for a short time was too much! And the relief to be told by the captain that you could turn on your phone. It was palpable. Then taking the train that day—a normal commuter train—and looking down the carriage, every head was down, eyes fixed on their phones. I thought, uh-oh, something is happening here. There's a different type of presence, a different type of attention. It's all directed to that small box.

JOURNALIST: It must have seemed like zombies had invaded.

MAYOR: It *was* strange. But I also noticed on that trip that it has become a more volatile world. Maybe the two are related. You see more public anger. A generation ago, it would have been unthinkable to raise your voice at a stranger in public, let alone someone working in a shop.

So you have to be more deliberate, more conscious and more aware of how these external forces rile you up. And you have to combat them with a seriously stable, fierce inner calm.

I smiled. A *fierce* inner calm?

JOURNALIST: Just my luck to be born into this shitty time.

MAYOR: C'mon, we've been through this. It may feel bad, but is it really any different from other times in history? Think of the Ancients. They had to invent the concept of ataraxia because there was so much suffering, so much to struggle with. They needed a coping mechanism, otherwise it would have been unbearable.

'What need is there to weep over parts of life? The whole of it calls for tears,' wrote Seneca, two thousand years ago.

Wars, famines, plagues, a life of slavery for many, or, if you were an aristocrat, plots and schemes to get you murdered should you get in the way. Women died in childbirth, along with their babies: there was no modern medicine. Look at the Roman Stoics: Seneca, ordered to suicide by his former protégé. He had a child who died young, in his mother's arms. Marcus, he lost seven of his thirteen children, and lost his own father when he was three. And Epictetus: born into slavery and lamed by a cruel master. When was this mysterious Eden free from suffering that you are nostalgic for? It never existed. Life is a struggle, no matter what the age.

JOURNALIST: It feels worse now.

He looked at me derisively.

MAYOR: How do you *know* it feels worse? Were you there? You're caught up in the concerns of your time and think them the worst there ever was. Worse than the invasions of the Mongol hordes that killed maybe up to sixty million people? The Thirty Years' War, the great plagues, the Irish potato famine, the horrors of the world wars? History repeats itself in large cycles. That's why we should learn from the past. All that we experience has been experienced before. 'Look back over the past, with its changing empires that rose and fell, and you can foresee the future too.'

And you know what?

JOURNALIST: What?

MAYOR: We have always needed people who, through it all, throughout history, demonstrate steadfast inner calm and relaxation, who can bring the temperature down a bit, who act with virtue and rationality. After all, you can always choose how you react.

That's why I agreed to this interview in the first place. We need a shift in collective consciousness, away from anger and towards peace. We need more people to bring the temperature down, and this philosophy can help them do that.

There are techniques that can help you focus on getting to ataraxia. Marcus talked of the inner citadel. Even in battle, even with a tumultuous external world, you should be able to retreat inwards.

JOURNALIST: To your citadel . . . what's that?

MAYOR: Your tower, the part of you that can't be touched, assaulted, warped or upset by the world outside.

JOURNALIST: You're talking about disassociating? Numbing yourself?

MAYOR: No, quite the opposite. You are fully present. Acutely, exquisitely conscious. But you refrain from being reactive in certain situations. You detach your emotions from what's going on. You observe and stay calm. It really is a great skill to have.

Marcus had a version of it called the 'view from above', where in times of distress or worry, he would imagine himself looking down on the world from a distance. It gives a better perspective on our problems, to zoom out.

JOURNALIST: I've heard about astronauts—how seeing Earth from space can radically change them.

MAYOR: Yes, a profound cognitive shift can take place. Astronauts talk of seeing the Earth anew, and developing a heightened sense of connection to other people and the Earth as a whole.

JOURNALIST: How do you get there without having to go to space? To ataraxia? To the citadel?

MAYOR: It's work you need to do. Just be conscious that you can retreat at any time: from a hot situation, from an angry reaction, from a fight. And once you get there you need to keep working at making ataraxia part of your make-up, like going to the gym. Remember: 'habitual recurrence'. Every day. Building up the muscle. Ataraxia doesn't just descend down on you like a magic cloud. You work at being calm, at not reacting. And you do it over and over and over again.

The Mayor scooped another serve of lahpet thoke onto my plate and took some more warm naan from the oven. I was hungrier than I'd been in weeks—like part of my body was waking up after being so sluggish following the shooting.

With ataraxia, with calmness, contentment and peace, I meditate twice a day but of course this is just my own practice, not something Stoic. I learnt in India, from the best. This helps me keep a calm mind. And at other times, I visualise an inner citadel. It could look like a spaceship, where you are enclosed. Or a fort. Or a place where you feel particularly safe. Your bedroom or your home? When I'm in a difficult council meeting or there's a dispute that I find myself being emotionally drawn into, I just go there, to the citadel, until the storm that threatened to agitate me passes. I say to myself 'don't react', and so I don't. Or I say 'return to harmony', and I go back. Regular meditation makes it easier to keep reverting to being calm.

JOURNALIST: I tried meditating on an app but then I got bored after like five minutes.

MAYOR: You have the attention span of a goldfish. Boredom is the whole point. You get to boredom, where we so seldom go now, and you stay with that boredom. Get beyond it and you find peace.

I thought of the sweaty, feral days and nights in Dav, the journey across the river, the ascent into the mountains and jungle. Boredom, discomfort and terror all smashed together. Could peaceful Silver Springs, this destination, be the proverbial ataraxia—the state made manifest, at the end of a long struggle?

MAYOR: But achieving ataraxia isn't just about meditation. It's deeper than that. It's a mindset. The other crucial condition for tranquillity is accepting the flow of life, that nature is change and life is change and that there is only suffering in resisting what is. Said Marcus, 'Accept the things to which fate binds you and love the people with whom fate brings you together—but do so with all your heart.'

JOURNALIST: That's actually kinda romantic, that line.

MAYOR: But there's also tough love in there. People getting hurt and upset because they didn't get their way, the world didn't conform to their internal desires? That was never going to happen! Wake up! Accept the things and people in your life!

I was now used to the Mayor's sudden sharp, urgent and hectoring tone, so I just smiled and nodded. In my head I was trying to think of a nickname for him that I could use in the piece. Uncle Hector? The Stern Stoic?

MAYOR: People in your country talk about freedom and how important it is. And I agree. I love freedom too. But the only sort of freedom truly in your control is how you feel, and how you think. Do you feel free? Are you free to think critically?

I had thought about this. Sometimes I didn't know. I sometimes wondered if I'd just accepted some orthodoxy or another without really questioning it. But to start questioning everything was to invite instability, disorientation and chaos. Sometimes in moments of crisis, the only stability I felt was my political identity and my beliefs.

The Mayor didn't wait for the answer.

Where does ataraxia fit in with this? In order to have a truly free life, free not just in the mind but lighthearted in the spirit, you need to be able to roll with it, to be able to cope with anything that comes your way. This includes other people's beliefs and positions. It includes their weird personalities and their foibles. That's true freedom. If you just roll with it, not only will you find life easier to bear, but people will also want to spend time with you. No one wants to spend time with an anxious, stressed-out person. Because that attitude catches. No one wants to spend time with a person who doesn't accept them or wants them to change. Just keep a sense of humour about things. We were given one for a reason.

JOURNALIST: Not everyone is funny.

MAYOR: Yes, but everyone can have a lighthearted approach to life, if they choose to. Don't take yourself so seriously! The Stoics loved to laugh at things. Life is funny. You see people get perturbed or embarrassed about small things all the time. Waving back at someone when they are actually waving at someone else? That's funny! Laugh at yourself! Toilet paper on your shoe? Laugh. Slipped on a grape and fell on your backside? Hilarious. Walking around all day with a piece of mango in your hair—that's kinda funny.

By now I was laughing at the Mayor, who had turned himself into Mr Bean—demonstrating the mango in the hair, slipping on a grape, the paper on his shoe—to great comic effect. When he loosened up, the Mayor was actually very funny, like stand-up comedian-level funny.

Let's explore shall we, while the sun is still shining? I want to take you down to a very special place. I've always wanted to make my own wine, and the climate here is well suited to pinot. The grapes are looking healthy—and soon, we'll be able to harvest.

CHARACTER—HOW TO BE A GOOD PERSON

SILVER SPRINGS, The Mayor's vineyard, Thursday, 3 pm— The vineyard was further afield, so we climbed on the Mayor's small motorbike (less powerful than Dominic's—almost a moped) and headed off in the afternoon sunshine down a lane towards the outer reaches of his property. I'd never been to a vineyard before—and found the rows of vines heavy with grapes to be very Instagrammable, if only my phone had been working. We walked between the rows, the Mayor stopping from time to time to assess the firmness of the grapes—or to make a note of a particular bug or parasite on the vines. I followed, holding my dictaphone out—hoping to catch his words despite the very noisy cicadas that surrounded us. Their sound picked up force as the afternoon lengthened, like a choir reaching a crescendo.

MAYOR: So, we've talked about the control test, preferred indifferents, ataraxia, comparisons, judgements and reactions. The other crucial element in Stoicism's ethical philosophy is character. Remember your character is one of the three things within your control.

JOURNALIST: You know, now that you mention it—wouldn't you say your character is something *not* actually in your control? After all, kids are born extroverted or shy, gentle or boisterous. Did they choose that?

MAYOR: Character is not to be confused with personality. Your personality is specific to you—it's something innate—whereas having a good character is something that anyone can develop and control. As long as you have reason, you have the ability to monitor, assess and develop your character.

JOURNALIST: You rarely hear people talk about character these days. And it seems like the worse someone's character is, the more likely we are to reward them with fame or riches or a powerful office.

MAYOR: And the Stoic would say, 'So what?' A wise person is indifferent to power, fame and riches, both their own and those of others. *Particularly* those of others. You know that it's your industry that is most to blame here, don't you? You give the most attention to people with the worst characters. It's almost like you're incentivising people to have a poor character, with the amount of attention you pay to scandal, extreme behaviour and crimes.

JOURNALIST: What do you think I'm doing here? I'm trying to counter all that with a story that focuses on a community that is swimming against that toxic tide.

MAYOR: Well, you've come to the right place. Character is very important here, because we know it's one of the few things that is within our control. There were four virtues that the Stoics isolated as being incredibly important in terms of leading a good life and developing a good character. I mentioned these earlier. These virtues are courage, wisdom, temperance and justice. Values that have existed since ancient times are still relevant in our modern age. That's the great thing about the virtues. Regardless of your religion, cultural background or gender, you'll find wisdom, courage, moderation and justice are truly valuable.

The virtues sounded okay, but a question kept turning in my mind—how did the control test accommodate social good? It was good to see justice named as a virtue but how did it all play out in real life? There seemed to be tension between trying to change the world and improve people's lives and recognising the limits of control.

JOURNALIST: How do you define these so-called virtues?

MAYOR: Wisdom is knowledge that has been refined through experience. One way I gain wisdom, apart from just existing and getting older, is by the study and application of philosophy. Through contemplating the day I've just had, and contemplating my actions and the actions of others, I'm gaining in wisdom all the time. But I'm unwise if I act rashly, without thinking or from a lazy, careless or bad habit. Self-reflection and the ability to change both one's mind and one's behaviour is key.

JOURNALIST: And justice?

MAYOR: Marcus said justice was 'the source of all the other virtues'. And it includes acting for the common good of all.

And moderation is similar to self-control. It involves not going overboard. Too much alcohol, for example, can lead to loss of self-control, sickness in the form of a hangover, and possibly addiction down the line. Just take it easy. Don't have too much of anything. You don't want to compromise your tranquillity. Temperance is what you should be shooting for: nothing excessive, nothing deficient.

JOURNALIST: Says the man who owns a vineyard.

The Mayor smiled.

MAYOR: Touché, Goldfish.

Goldfish? So he had a nickname for me, before I got to call him Uncle Hector? Quick.

Yes, I need to exercise restraint when it comes to getting high on my own supply. 'No man is free who is not master of himself.'

JOURNALIST: And there was a fourth virtue?

MAYOR: Yes. Rounding it out is courage. It's facing fears, whether they be fear of being disliked or unpopular, fear of being harmed, fear of being rejected, fear of sickness, fear of death. As a Stoic, you are going to need courage to stand up for justice. And you are going to need courage to do what is right, particularly when you're alone or your actions make you unpopular.

Courage was straightforward. I had always needed it for my work; I needed it for my recovery; and I needed it for this journey. I summoned it more easily than I once had but only because of practice and necessity.

JOURNALIST: Virtue is such an old-fashioned word.

MAYOR: Bring it back, I say!

JOURNALIST: Wisdom, temperance, courage, justice . . . Why those four things? And not some other good qualities?

MAYOR: Well, for a start these four things are all within your control to develop. Everyone can develop courage; it's not just something you are born with. Same with wisdom. And we can learn to recognise justice. You know the concept of 'natural justice' used in most common law systems is descended from the Stoic notions of justice? It follows nature. What feels right, or natural, is the way justice should bend.

JOURNALIST: What's an example of natural justice?

MAYOR: It's found in a lot of legal systems. Fairness to all sides. If you are charged with a crime, it's natural justice that you be told exactly what you are charged with, and you be given the opportunity to defend yourself. In the workplace, say, employment law, firing someone without telling them why they are being fired is a denial of natural justice. Natural justice would be giving someone a performance review or a warning, and giving that employee time to correct their performance or behaviour. That's natural justice. A fair go, a fair hearing, a right to be heard, to know what the crime is, if you are being charged. It's the opposite of a show trial or what regimes have done down the ages and continue to do: lock up their enemies without charge, imprison them without trial, deny them access to legal representation.

JOURNALIST: How is it within our control to develop the virtues?

MAYOR: Often it is a matter of just being conscious of what the virtues are and practising them. Epictetus used the example of the banquet in an analogy of the benefits of moderation: 'Remember that you must behave as at a banquet. Is anything brought round to you? Put out your hand, and take a moderate share. Does it pass you? Do not stop it. Is it not come yet? Do not yearn in desire towards it, but wait till it reaches you.'

JOURNALIST: So don't be greedy?

MAYOR: In Silver Springs we take only what we need. We don't overfish, over hunt, clear too much land or grow large quantities of crops that we cannot use. We do not hoard. In food, drink and life, exercise temperance. The virtues, being a good person, having a good character, were of huge importance for the Stoics. It's better to die than corrupt your character. And die they did, rather than do something that was outside the good. Some died horrible, violent, vile, bloody, wretched deaths in an effort to preserve the sanctity of their good character.

JOURNALIST: That sounds a bit extreme. Give me an example.

MAYOR: Cato killed himself because he didn't want to live under Julius Caesar. He felt he would not be free under his rule. He stabbed himself but didn't die straight away. He ended up injured and falling on an abacus, getting stitched up, then pulling the stitches out, before dying.

JOURNALIST: An abacus?

MAYOR: Yes! And, in more recent times, Major James Stockdale, who followed the teachings of Epictetus and was a prisoner of war in Vietnam, also tried to kill himself rather than give up any American military secrets when being tortured by the Viet Cong. But it doesn't have to be as dramatic as all that. For the normal person, through keeping a diary, meditation and contemplation, we're able to keep an account of our character: where things are going well and where they are deficient. This is why reputation or another's assessment of your character is really not that relevant. Only you know the secrets of your own heart, and the state of your own soul.

JOURNALIST: I think people's character can be shaped by trauma. It's not fair to put all the responsibility on individuals to shape their character. Sometimes, particularly in childhood, the shaping is done for them.

MAYOR: Again, Goldfish, we come to the Stoic point of view. It's always personal, always inward, always concerning what *you* should be doing. It's not about the right and wrong of what *others* are doing. Take responsibility for yourself above all other matters. Awful things happen to people all the time: as adults, as kids. It leaves a mark for sure, but *you* always have the option to control *your* own character, to develop virtue. That's your choice, and your background doesn't hamper that choice. No matter what, you can always strive for those virtues we talked about: courage, justice, wisdom and temperance. That's in your control. You always try to choose to do the right thing. Always.

Blossoms fell from the cherry trees, I thought of confetti and weddings, we were still walking side by side, the air was still, with the faintest hint of tension and the smell of steel in the skies—like you get before a storm. The Mayor took me into a shed by the side of a field, where the wine was made. He cleared tools from the workbench and pulled over two chairs, and got two glasses and a bottle from a high shelf.

You know . . . don't blame a shitty upbringing for your shitty behaviour.

Whoa. That was a line I could use if I was writing a Bad Guru piece. It could get him cancelled.

JOURNALIST: That sentiment flies in the face of credible research in the role trauma plays on people's lives and their character.

MAYOR: If I were an eye-roller, I'd be rolling my eyes now. To say that a person can't be courageous or wise because they've had a rough upbringing, wouldn't you say that's insulting to those people? It presumes they are too unwilling, or stupid or incapable to work on their own character, to become good people. Goldfish, don't look so pious all of a sudden.

JOURNALIST: But trauma can limit growth. All the experts say—

MAYOR: All the experts on social media? Trauma can also extend growth. It can be a catalyst for growth. And the chronic stuff, not just a bad experience, but a lifetime of poverty, ill health, no opportunity—you'd think that would breed people with terrible characters. But no, it doesn't. Some of the most brilliant, kind, exemplary people whom I have met throughout my life and in my travels have experienced the most hardships. They've experienced hardships, but they are *not their hardship*. They transcend their experiences. There is such strength and beauty in that. Such real triumph. When I travel over the mountains to some of the poorest places in the world, that's where I receive the most generous hospitality. They will spend what little money they have to buy you meat, a delicacy over in the next province. They have endured all manner of suffering, seen their children die because medicine was not available in their village, seen tuberculosis race through their communities. Their children have been enlisted in the army and died in battle. How do these people deal with their trauma? Their chronic, lifelong, never-ceasing trauma? They keep going! They just keep going. With grace and goodwill. They must. And they do! 'You may break your heart, but men will still go on as before,' wrote Marcus. And it's true: they do!

I remembered my rough-and-ready travel companions on the way here, ready to share with me their food and water. Half a banana, a cup of noodles, a pot of tea. It was a contrast with all the rich people I knew who had easy childhoods and were wealthy as adults—and how stingy and mean they could be, totting up the restaurant bill at the end of the night to avoid subsidising an extra entree, who complained about the slightest trivial disturbance: slow service in a restaurant, a blueberry shortage, a burnt coffee.

MAYOR: You must see there is a choice. You might not be able to choose the circumstances of your life but you can choose your reaction. You might not be able to change the character of other people, but you can change your own—for the better.

JOURNALIST: Okay, thinking about it, I agree that character can often flourish despite hard experiences.

MAYOR [*scoffing*]: Despite? How about *because of* those hard circumstances? There is almost no other way. These things like courage and wisdom you can't just conjure from air. They must be earned, they come from experience, age, time, hardship—often. They are excavated from harsh soil. And so Stoics desire these hard experiences. A nightmare for anyone's Stoic practice would be to have a soft and comfortable life, where everything is done for you and you are idle and unchallenged.

JOURNALIST: We could have a reality TV show and call it the *Stoic Challenge*. Get people—maybe celebrities—to fast or to sleep on the ground or eat stale bread . . .

MAYOR: Are you always so flippant? Take yourself seriously, even if you don't take me seriously. Think about it: your whole journey here was a Stoic challenge. All of it!

Fucked up on rum, in the hotel in Dav, falling into bed then hours later waking in a sweat. Being followed at dusk by the moustached creep from the bar. The bad dream was over. The bad dream had just begun. I didn't want to feel anything because everything hurt too much, and so I'd disassociate.

JOURNALIST: And for the average person?

MAYOR: You might have a really difficult boss or difficult colleague who's going to test your ataraxia, your wisdom and your temperament. You have to rein in any feelings of anger before they surface. I saw you doing it at lunch, and I was impressed. It was a hard conversation, I could see it in your face, but you didn't become reactive.

The storm broke and rain started lashing the side of the tin shed.

JOURNALIST: This is good, a storm could put out the last of the fire!

MAYOR: While a lightning strike could start a whole new one.

Just on cue, from the shed door we could see lightning illuminate the dark afternoon sky in dramatic forks.

JOURNALIST [*wincing*]: I can be reactive. And I definitely encounter people every day who annoy me.

MAYOR: Tell me about that.

JOURNALIST: I don't want to speak ill of her but I had real problems with Julie from work. She was constantly on my back, waiting for me to fuck up some fact, some story. Then she'd send a message around to the whole newsroom, saying that she'd spotted an error in my copy. It used to drive me crazy. She'd cc the whole office!

MAYOR: Are you sure you don't want to talk ill of her? Because you're being pretty enthusiastic about sticking the boot into poor Julie. Look at your role: could you have foreseen the error that you had made in the copy?

JOURNALIST: Sometimes I was sloppy—it was my fault. Other times, I had no way of knowing or I was filing on deadline and just ran out of time to check stuff.

Like I was that day.

MAYOR: Only worry about what you can control—and that is your own work performance. Strive to be better. Not because Julie is on your back but because it is within your power to improve, and you want to be as good as you can be.

JOURNALIST: That is true. But Julie had the power—or I gave her the power—to totally ruin my day. Sometimes my week. I'd stew over those emails. I can still recall every passive aggressive word, even now. I wonder if it's only possible to be totally peaceful if you seal yourself off, far away from annoying people. But even then, you have to be peaceful with yourself—which I think can be the hardest kind of peace.

MAYOR: I agree. And you will come to feel at peace with yourself in due course. You're right: that can be one of the most difficult things to attain. After all, most of us have a voice in our heads that doesn't shut up, that drives us crazy and nags us every waking hour with wants, needs, criticism, anger, most of it directed to ourselves. But when it comes to being peaceful with others, Marcus wrote this in his nightly diary, and it still holds true today. I'm going to read you the whole quote, because there is so much gold buried in this one paragraph. Do you mind?

The Mayor sipped his wine slowly, gestured towards my backpack, pulled out my copy of *Meditations* and flipped to an already marked-up passage.

'When you wake up in the morning, tell yourself: the people I deal with today will be meddling, ungrateful, arrogant, dishonest, jealous and surly. They are like this because they can't tell good from evil. But I have seen the beauty of good, and the ugliness of evil, and have recognised that the wrongdoer has a nature related to my own—not of the same blood and birth, but the same mind, and possessing a share of the divine. And so none of them can hurt me. No one can implicate me in ugliness. Nor can I feel angry at my relative, or hate him. We were born to work together like feet, hands and eyes, like the two rows of teeth, upper and lower.

To obstruct each other is unnatural. To feel anger at someone, to turn your back on him: these are unnatural.'

JOURNALIST: Great quote! If it wasn't so long, I'd get it tattooed somewhere.

MAYOR [*sighing*]: I think Marcus would be horrified at that. Nothing should be fixed! Everything is change . . . regardless, let me break that entry down for you. What Marcus is saying, quite rightly, is you cannot change other people. You can accept that other people are annoying or horrible. But at the same time, you must accept they are human, just like you are, and will contain good along with the bad. But more than that, they are your brothers and sisters. To be angry at someone, to hate someone, that is unnatural. 'We were born to work together.' Or as Seneca says, 'We are bad men living amongst bad men and only one thing will calm us—and that is we must agree to go easy on one another.'

JOURNALIST: Huh? *We are bad men living amongst bad men and only one thing will calm us—and that is we must agree to go easy on one another* . . . I like that. It still holds true today. When you accept other people, are you less likely to be rocked by them when they try to hurt you? Or do something petty?

MAYOR: Precisely. You don't want to be thrown off balance by the actions of other people. With say, this woman Julie, the first time she sent around an email about you, possibly seeking to undermine you, well that is information *about her*. How she operates. Receive that information neutrally, without emotion, and accept that she is showing you herself. When someone shows you themselves, take note. It's important information. It's reality. And it can help you navigate them in the future.

The Mayor gestured to my notebook, where earlier that morning I had written *ACCEPT REALITY* in big letters.

And when she does it again and again, don't be surprised. Just accept this is her, this is reality; you cannot control her. And do not lose your calm. You are prepared for Julie then.

I felt a sudden pang when I realised the person we were talking about was dead. Julie was dead, killed at her desk. Even though she had been the bane of my existence at certain times, she also cared deeply about the newsroom, and the accuracy of the stories. I remembered the light on above her desk, seeing it from the street, long after everyone had left—checking pages, checking facts, valuing accuracy. Why did I waste so much energy stewing on her, when I could have put down my weapons and tried to understand her a bit more? Only one thing will calm us—if we agree to go easy on one another. I finished the wine in a gulp. The rain settled into a soft beat on the tin roof.

JOURNALIST: In relation to character, you say it's our nature to be good. I'm not so sure. I don't know if I'm a good person.

MAYOR: What was the last good thing you did for someone? And don't say writing a story that helped someone, or some cause. What did you do independent of your job that was purely altruistic?

My old friend Jasmine. The last good thing I did was for Jasmine. I didn't have much money, but she had even less than me. I hadn't seen her for a while—had reached out a few times, but she was ghosting. Then one day, I got a message out of the blue, asking me to meet her for lunch. She had a favour—she hated to ask it, but she had an issue, just a small issue with cash flow. And she was good for it. Just in a month or two.

JOURNALIST: I lent some money to a friend.

MAYOR: Did that feel good?

JOURNALIST: I don't know. It felt complicated.

It was quite a large sum. I was shocked at how much she wanted. 'I can't cover all that,' I said. 'Why do you need so much?'

Behind on rent—months behind, behind on credit card payments. Her last boyfriend took out a card in her name and then disappeared, taking the card and leaving her with the debt. Sexually transmitted debt, she joked, before saying, 'It's been a nightmare.' 'I can lend you 5K,' I said. 'That's all I've got.' She hesitated and then said, 'Thanks, babe. Pay you back, I promise.'

MAYOR: When you gave her the money—was it a loan?

JOURNALIST: Yes, but I didn't get it back.

It wasn't so much the money that hurt. Although that did hurt. It's that, after she got the money, she stopped speaking to me. I could still see her on Instagram, and to my irritation, she was partying up a storm. I'd leave her messages saying I needed the money back, and she kept saying 'yeah babe, you'll have it soon, just scraping it together' (well, stop going out!). Later she blocked my number, but I could still see her stories. I stopped asking because it made me feel sad. It's just guilt, my sister said. You haven't done anything wrong. But it felt bad to end like that.

MAYOR: Getting it back would be out of your control—and that could affect your tranquillity. Make every bit of money you give someone a gift. Not a loan. Whether they give it back to you is out of your control. It could ruin your tranquillity worrying about getting the money back, so just give it.

JOURNALIST: That's what it ended up being, I suppose.

MAYOR: You look sad.

I felt sad. I wondered if I had contributed to the friendship ending, but I was too prideful and wounded to make contact, to extend an olive branch.

JOURNALIST: I'm okay, just tired.

When we stepped outside, the mist was coming in off the hills and the easy, drifting smell of woodsmoke from a nearby farm filled the air. I wondered for the first time what it would be like to stay. The Mayor put his hand on my arm, which felt warm and reassuring.

He apologised for rambling and said he hoped I was getting the material I needed. I hesitated.

JOURNALIST: Do you have any photos I could use in the piece?

MAYOR: What of?

JOURNALIST [*speaking quickly*]: You and Sandra? Maybe a recent one, and one of when you were young.

MAYOR: That can be arranged. I'd be happy to help you. Now if it's okay, we might break so I can rest. At my age, going into the night is only made possible by a siesta.

STOIC TRADITIONS AND THE EVIL OF SOCIAL COMPARISONS

SILVER SPRINGS, The Old Bar, Thursday, 6 pm—Back at the inn, I had fallen asleep on an armchair in the library, a book spread on my lap, hands spread across the book. I woke to Thida shaking my shoulders, looking concerned.

'I wondered, do I just let you sleep? You look so exhausted. But then Dad was adamant that I wake you before dusk. He wants to meet for dinner in the square.'

Hours had passed! My limbs felt heavy, like I'd been drugged. I tried to steady myself, but had to grip the mantelpiece. The room was too warm and I could hear soft rain outside. Uncertain of what time it was, I knew one thing—I'd like to go to bed right now. Fatigue had hit me like a brick. How easy would it be to sleep these three days away and miss my chance at a story?

Thida guided me to my room, where she said there was a pitcher of water, so I could splash my face. Septimus, Thida's son, had been deputised to take me into town.

Whereas Thida was taciturn and shy, Septimus wouldn't shut up. He confided that he found English a bit too easy, because he spoke it sometimes at home and with his grandad. He was eight, he told me—and at school he's learning 'everything' but 'my favourite is the biology of butterflies'.

For such a small boy, Septimus moved quickly. He took my hand—he dragged me and prodded me, pointing out the houses of his friends that we passed. I tried to take in my surroundings but a fog had rolled in. A light mist fell and threw a veil over everything.

We appeared to be on a ridge-line path—the flagstones were worn smooth. On one side was a brook, the other side the walled jungle gardens of brick, stone, mud and cement houses. The houses looked solid—tall and square with large and long shuttered windows and painted in faded yellow, brown and orange.

There was a carved sign to the Yellow Flower Cafe—and the path barely widened before either side of me were tables, empty in the rain, with hanging blossoms in orange, bright pink and purple. I saw, once the fog shifted, that the houses had concealed the topography—we were walking along a cliff with a deep green jungle below. Mountains rose above us—marbled white with snow at the peaks and streaked with green, brown and white streams of melting snow. It was beautiful.

Shortly we arrived in what looked to be the centre of town—a square. Around the square there was a clocktower, a flower seller, a fruit and vegetable stand, some chairs and tables including a cluster of tables where people were playing chess.

This was the first time I had seen Silver Springs in the day—and I was impressed. While not particularly prosperous looking by Western standards, it seemed planned and orderly, with substantial buildings, mature trees and established paths, in stark contrast to the impoverished, ramshackle Davantown.

When the Mayor arrived (and I was ashamed to admit that I was relieved he didn't turn up in a dress—which shows I have work to do on preferred indifferents!), we sat angled towards the chess players in the pale afternoon light. He gave Septimus some coins to buy a sticky white rice cake from a street cart, then sent him home.

People passed by, greeting the Mayor with hugs and handshakes and when they were introduced to me they bowed slightly and said they were honoured that a visiting journalist would be interested enough in them to come all this way.

MAYOR: Look at you! You're a celebrity! Tell me, did you rest?

JOURNALIST: Yes. I picked up a book from Thida's shelf—Seneca's plays. I had barely opened it when I fell asleep! That never usually happens to me. *Thyestes* . . .

MAYOR: Oh—that's a good one to start with. No one has written a gorier story of revenge. When you look at his philosophical writings, compared with his plays—*Thyestes* really is a dispatch from his shadow side.

JOURNALIST: Seneca seems complex.

MAYOR: And debate rages—well, at least here—about his hypocrisy. Can you really be preaching virtue if you are implicated in murder? If you work for a crazy despot like Nero? If you are one of the wealthiest people in the world?

JOURNALIST: No, you can't.

MAYOR: You need to think about these things with more nuance. Use your rational mind. You can agree with some of Seneca's teachings, and reject other points. And you can read Seneca without endorsing his biography. If you demand moral purity from every teacher, from every writer and philosopher, you will remain ignorant.

The Mayor sighed, like he thought I was ignorant. He wasn't very good at hiding his feelings.

We've covered a lot of ground already: the control test, preferred indifferents, judgements, virtues and ataraxia. All the things of the mind. Tomorrow, we cover Stoicism as it relates to the body. Do you have any questions so far?

JOURNALIST: I have a lot of questions!

MAYOR: I guess that's your job.

JOURNALIST: But first, tell me about this town. It's so mysterious—not even in the old Lonely Planet!

MAYOR [*drily*]: I'm sure there are lots of towns in the world that you've never heard of, which aren't in the Lonely Planet.

JOURNALIST: But towns that are run according to a philosophy?

MAYOR: It's not a big deal. Many places in the world are run according to a religion, many communities are religious. So why not a philosophy?

JOURNALIST: Fair. What's the history here? Before this philosophy you were just like any other town?

MAYOR: Early stone tools and flints have been found in my vineyard when we were planting, indicating that there were people here in the Stone Age. But, as with many places around here, there was not much in the way of outside influences. The town's remoteness—those enormous mountains, the difficulty in getting here, the unpredictable weather, and wild animals—meant that for a millennia it didn't have any outside influences. I mean any. How unusual is that? Before the British, the occasional Dutch or Portuguese missionary made it over the pass—and was so emaciated and desperate that they lacked the energy or belief in God by then to try to proselytise. Over the years, buccaneers and businessmen, hearing rumours of rich seams of gold and diamonds, also tried to come. But once again they were largely defeated by geography and the tribes that lie to the north. Eventually basic roads were built. Burma got a railway. Nothing quite reached us, only what could come up the goat track that starts at the monastery. But by then, rumours had spread far about this beautiful place, green lakes encircling the town, deep, cool forests, the freshest air, cleanest water, most enlightened citizens. Word of this paradise reached the British. They colonised India, of course, and Burma, but our kingdom was spared. Silver Springs didn't participate in any of the three Anglo-Burmese wars. Our isolation saved us. But when the British found the track, and got donkeys—they put a toe in our waters. But we kept everything on our terms. Towards the end of British rule in Burma, Silver Springs became popular with administrators escaping the heat. For a time it was a hill station. Some of the architecture is colonial; you'll see when we go for a walk later. Then the Raj fell, the British pulled out in '48 and we were left with their fine china, stores of tea, some farming equipment, officers' holiday quarters and a good library of English-language books to go alongside our existing collection of Sanskrit, Ancient Greek and Latin.

JOURNALIST: I heard rumours of Nazis hiding out here after the British left. And the CIA before the Vietnam War.

MAYOR: The Nazis? No. Just a wild rumour, among many wild rumours about this place. The CIA, yes. They were all over the north from the time the British pulled out, supporting the Nationalist Chinese movement. But it did not concern us. Anyone here long enough will see power rise and fall. Nothing lasts. Everything is change. That's why I prefer philosophy to politics.

JOURNALIST: Safer?

MAYOR: Not necessarily. Philosophy can be way more radical than politics. But a decent philosophy lasts a lot longer than an ideology.

JOURNALIST: What about Jack Kerouac? Someone told me he came to Silver Springs in the early sixties and stayed for a while and got right into stargazing.

MAYOR: After the war, hippies and beats came. Allen Ginsberg arrived via northern India, or so the rumour goes but there's no record of Kerouac ever visiting. Others tried to come. Take Americans for example. They were not explicitly banned from visiting Myanmar last century but there were many periods of turmoil that made getting here, and being safe, difficult. If you were visiting northern India, you could access Silver Springs but again, with great difficulty. You had to climb that peak to the west—and you need to be a mountaineer to do that.

JOURNALIST: A light plane?

MAYOR: The old military helicopters couldn't go high enough to get up there. Too risky for light planes, too. Plus you need clearance.

There's a road from China, an ancient trading route, but now it's controlled by the cartels.

If you could get here from India, great, but we have strict visa rules. Come to visit, if you get permission. You just can't stay.

JOURNALIST: Why is that?

MAYOR: We have to protect what we have. Materialism and greed kill communities like ours. Too many seekers looking for answers, and a place to start over, swamp communities like ours. Disease has wiped out other comparable small and isolated communities, but we've never had a pox. We never even had Covid.

JOURNALIST: That's incredible. I thought it spread everywhere.

MAYOR: Not here. And in keeping it out we referred to Stoic maxims. Cicero, who was actually a Sceptic but sympathetic to

Stoicism, said, '*Salus populi suprema lex esto*', which translates as 'The safety of the people should be the supreme law'.

When there are two competing interests that cross my desk, for example, the need for free trade versus letting in travellers who may be carrying the most recent plague—in this case, Covid—we consult that maxim and say 'yes, the safety of the people should be the supreme law'. So we make rules to protect their health, which may involve sacrificing some other important things, such as trade or freedom of movement. You can't have everything.

JOURNALIST: What about bringing in food and goods if the borders are shut?

MAYOR: Remember, we're largely self-sufficient. We grow our own food, farm our own animals, share the few resources we have. Cars—we have ten in the village; two fire trucks; most people have motorbikes; people ride horses, donkeys, bicycles. We're good at fixing stuff that is broken. Septimus, for example, could take apart a motorbike and put it back together. He can raise livestock, plant fruit trees, tend to the crops here. He's knowledgeable about the animals in the region and the seasons.

JOURNALIST: But can he make a meme?

MAYOR: What?

JOURNALIST: Don't worry. It's a joke. What about medical stuff? What if someone is sick?

MAYOR: We have two nurses here and a doctor. Essential medicines are shipped to Davantown and come up via donkey. We have medical and urgent supply runs to Davantown a couple of times a year. But you don't want to get seriously ill here. There are people who have lived here for many generations and they are good with plant medicine. There are sacred plants, deities within nature. And there are very talented midwives. Old knowledge is intact here. Not all of it. But a lot of it. We also like progress. I mean, c'mon, look at pharmaceuticals. It's incredible and in short supply here. If a new virus swept through, we'd be in trouble. If you have a complicated illness, it's Davantown or you travel to a more developed country, or elsewhere if you have relatives abroad and try your luck there.

JOURNALIST: What about schools? Septimus seems very bright.

MAYOR [*beaming*]: He's taken to philosophy like a young Plato! We teach philosophy in school. It's not that different to other towns. There's all the usual stuff in a town this size. We're not wanting for anything: food vendors, sweet and savoury, a restaurant, library, a roadhouse, a tea house, a schoolhouse, the town square and the Stoa.

People who travel bring us books. They're highly prized here. Septimus has devoured everything, including the so-called adult books. He has a hungry mind and I suspect he will leave for further education. People leave if they want when they finish secondary school and move to Davantown or the West. We hope they come back. Many do, often bringing a spouse or new partner with them. And that is how we continue.

JOURNALIST: And tourists?

MAYOR: Before Covid, the occasional wanderer and traveller came through, like Lou said. They have always been treated with hospitality and grace. We love visitors. Just like the Benedictines, who lived by the motto 'the stranger would be welcomed as Christ himself'. One of those strangers was me. Another is you.

You can visit, but you just have to leave . . .

Another of those visitors—a couple of millennia ago—a trader and explorer who came from Athens, brought the gift of philosophy.

JOURNALIST: Who was that original traveller?

MAYOR: Xoko—a philosophy student and stargazer. The local legend has it that he arrived from the far eastern edge of the Roman Empire in 100 CE. He heard about the region from traders in the Parthian Empire in the Near East, who travelled by sea then horses, to trade spices and precious stones. These traders had been through and talked about the beauty of the landscape, the pure mountain streams, the clear skies and the extraordinary sight of so many stars and the occasional aurora. They thought the aurora was a visitation from the gods and twice a year, at summer and winter solstice, they would have a festival celebrating the night skies that went from dusk to dawn.

Legend has it that Xoko visited and loved it so much, he stayed and married into the local community. Other stargazers and traders followed. Xoko was an adherent of Stoic philosophy and had learnt under the tutor Arrian, who, of course, was a student of Epictetus. Although he was an outsider, Xoko became venerated for his wisdom, and gradually his philosophy won over the entire village. It has stayed with us ever since.

JOURNALIST: And now?

MAYOR: We have the Stoa. It keeps the tradition alive. And we adapt the philosophy to modern times.

The Mayor's face lit up when he saw a couple walking arm in arm across the square. He exclaimed, 'My best friends!'

An elderly couple, walking with a middle-aged man, came to our table and embraced the Mayor.

MAYOR: Nay Chi and Bo. Schoolfriends of Sandra, and my friends of fifty years. And their son, Ian.

He seemed proud of this, to have friends of fifty years standing. Immediately in their presence he looked a generation younger, animated from inside.

He spoke to them in a language I did not understand, and they looked at me, smiled, and bid their farewells.

JOURNALIST: Were you just talking to them about me?

MAYOR: Only to say you are a charming young woman who is interested in philosophy.

JOURNALIST: They were pointing at my head. Did they want to know what happened to me?

MAYOR: They were concerned, yes. But I told them you were okay.

An elderly waiter came out to take our order. He bowed deeply as he greeted the Mayor and nodded at me shyly. The speciality of the house was the local rum. I ordered mine with a wedge of lime.

JOURNALIST: So, would you describe yourself as a Stoic? Is it part of your identity?

MAYOR: My identity? I would hope not to have a fixed identity. I'm always evolving and changing. But right now, yes, I am a Stoic, an imperfect one with a collectivist bent. I love community. It's our best medicine against loneliness and alienation. All the philosophy in the world is useless if you don't have anyone or anything to love. But community doesn't just appear. It's like marriage. It needs to be worked at. You need to have ways for people to disagree and debate things without it turning feral. You need to be able to compromise. You need to be able to share. You need to be prepared to help out: with the children, with the old people, with the farmers who need an extra hand for harvest.

JOURNALIST: Where I am from, we've really let go of community. People love to be home alone, work from home, socialise on their screens at home. Everything is there. Why go outside?

MAYOR: And other people?

JOURNALIST: They are your competition for resources.

MAYOR: I'm sure it's not as hellish as all that. You just need to connect. Only connect, wrote E.M. Forster! That's the natural human way. Up here, we are consciously aware that there is an art to living well, and we try to apply it every day. Connection is natural but you also have to be deliberate about things, otherwise you get swept away, pulled this way and that by things designed to capture our attention. And those things may not always be good for us. Who in the rich world do young people look to, as a guide on how to live well?

JOURNALIST: I wish it were philosophers—but in reality, it's probably celebrities or influencers on social media.

The Mayor reached into his pocket and pulled out a woollen scarf.

MAYOR: Let me know if you get cold; we can go inside.

I nodded but I liked being out here, watching the last bit of sun hit the faded paint of the buildings and turning them briefly into vibrant glowing orange, as birds dipped then soared over the square. Three old men and a young girl were bent over chess boards. In the tableau, there was something timeless. Lights were coming on in the buildings around the square and groups of people greeted each other at doorways.

MAYOR: There's an evening class up there, the painters. They do still life; this week it's a ceramic bowl. And another over there, the philosophy and theology group. This year they're studying the Veda.

JOURNALIST: Are they a breakaway group from the Stoa?

MAYOR [*laughing*]: No, it's all complementary. Knowledge of all religions is encouraged.

JOURNALIST: Sorry to harp on it, but I really think this town would take off if you had social media. It's so pretty right over there, in this light—it would be great on Instagram.

The groups of people coming and going, the snatches of conversation and laughter reaching us, the lengthening shadows mingling with bright post-storm light—everything about Silver Springs seemed warm and agreeable.

MAYOR: We *don't want* the town to take off. Kids like Septimus, and the older ones, they grow up knowing about all the other places in the world. And I'm sure they'll get out there one day when they're old enough. But they're also fully immersed in the world, in nature, and their own lives, and the place they are living in. They're not sitting there with a screen looking at someone else's town, someone else's life, and feeling bad about their own. This is not a wealthy place. People don't have a lot of stuff. To get a second-hand book from a visitor is exciting. To get a Bic pen is like Christmas. Why open up a portal where you can compare yourself to the richest people in the world, while simultaneously being marketed to? Why open the gate to comparisons?

JOURNALIST [*sighing*]: That scans.

MAYOR: I'm not saying comparisons don't happen here. Of course they happen here. But on social media, you're comparing yourself to the whole world—to the richest people in the world. Here you might compare yourself to a neighbour. That's it. But for those in your society, with the internet, it's very hard to get out of the mental habit of looking around and measuring yourself against how other people are doing, what they have, how their lives look. And you will often do it so frequently and so consistently that these comparisons happen below the surface of your awareness.

So you don't know why you're constantly miserable; you just feel bad. It's always there. Here we don't even have outdoor advertising. I think to add social media would be a sort of assault.

JOURNALIST: What do the Ancients say about comparisons? How would they even know about it?

MAYOR: Comparisons are as old as human history. In today's society they are just amplified, and turbocharged by social media and capitalism. But what would they say? It goes back to that old adage 'comparison is the thief of joy'. If you want a life of joy, you need to stop comparing yourself to others.

JOURNALIST: Easier said than done. Although I guess I'm not doing it here, because I don't have my phone.

I longed for my phone, fifty times a day at least.

MAYOR: But it's worth trying to stop comparing; it's worth the fight. When you free yourself from comparisons you start feeling gratitude for what you have and feeling happy with where you are at in life. You don't waste any energy wishing things were different. In contrast, comparisons fuel the hedonic treadmill, where as soon as we get one thing, we crave the next thing.

JOURNALIST: Mo money mo problems, as the song goes. I wonder if comparisons are why I feel pretty terrible about my life, most of the time?

MAYOR: And yet you are saying 'bring social media here' . . .

JOURNALIST: It's because I'm an addict.

MAYOR: It seems social media is just distracting you and a good chunk of your society from sadness, from depression—or at least dissatisfaction—but you've rolled over so easily and just let this product take all your time, without any question or much resistance. And as a result, you've prevented yourself from having true agency over your situation.

Ooofff.

JOURNALIST: I blame microplastics. I reckon they are doing something with our brain chemistry.

MAYOR: Your eyes tell me you're sad.

JOURNALIST [*sighing*]: Why do you think much of modern society is sad?

MAYOR: Big question. You know comparisons are a huge part of it, but there's also something else I wonder about. I think about your economic system, and the lack of language around spiritual matters, the absence of ritual, of community. And I think that's somehow connected to people's mental health.

JOURNALIST: What rituals do you have here, if you don't have religion?

MAYOR: Oh so many, probably too many. People love a festival and they love a party! There are rituals that have existed in this town for thousands of years: things around harvest and solstice. Pagan things, traditions that existed before the philosophy came along, which the town has kept going. It almost doesn't matter what the festival is. What matters is that there is something marked, and that people come together. Rituals slow down time: they create a container; they give it space. A world without rituals becomes a blur. Think about Christmas or any feast day—

JOURNALIST: Christmas is stressful.

MAYOR: It can be. But it can also be a pocket of time for you to pause, to return to something: family, a place, a book, a memory, yourself. Currently, what you have in your society isn't feeding people in the right way. In fact, it's having the opposite effect; people are starved of something even though they live in overabundance. Like a man dying of thirst at an overflowing aqueduct.

JOURNALIST: And so we numb ourselves to stop the sadness?

MAYOR: What is the high number of opioid overdoses or antidepressant use but a symptom of this? No judgement from me. No one wants to feel pain, physical or psychic. But it doesn't have to be like that. There is joy and meaning to be found in life all around you, even the painful bits. You just have to develop a framework for accessing that joy and minimising that suffering. You have to resist the comparisons and what society is trying to sell you, not just in terms of material goods, but values.

JOURNALIST: Like a desire for fame? Lots of people I went to school with aspired to be influencers. You know—live like them, look like them, buy certain products that they're promoting.

The Mayor looked horrified.

JOURNALIST: Who's to say that the Stoics weren't the influencers of their day?

MAYOR: There were lots of competing philosophy schools in Athens in the ancient world, and yes, I suppose the schools, by virtue of teaching, were trying to influence their students but the product was knowledge. It was virtue. They were moral teachers, not selling skincare. They also didn't care about fame. Fame was not their motivation.

JOURNALIST: What did the Ancients say about fame?

MAYOR: That it's an indifferent. You cannot control it, so you should not want it. Becoming famous depends on other people's reactions to your talents or skills, which is out of your control.

You should also consider the worth of fame. Use your rational mind to properly examine it. People who are famous often complain of not being able to have any privacy or having a bunch of false friends, who are just using them. And even if fame is pleasant, it doesn't last. 'Consider the lives led once by others, long ago, the lives to be led by others after you, the lives led even now, in foreign lands. How many people don't even know your name? How many will soon have forgotten it? How many offer you praise now, and tomorrow, perhaps, contempt. That to be remembered is worthless. Like fame. Like everything.'

JOURNALIST: I think being famous—for a story, for a show, for a podcast—would open doors. It would lead to more opportunity and more money. And that means more security.

MAYOR: But pursuing fame, which is unstable, will disrupt your tranquillity. You may get to one level of fame but there will always be someone more famous than you, so you will not be happy until you climb higher. This is bad news for those trying to maintain ataraxia.

Social media tells you to desire fame but it's a very wobbly framework to base your life on. A sturdier frame is Stoicism, and you're learning that framework now, with me. And there is time, you're young.

JOURNALIST: Youngish.

MAYOR: You are young. You are still a child in your culture! I mean here, it is very different being in your thirties, but for you, you still have time to work things out.

Talk about a backhanded compliment.

Plus, already there are great things in your life. A mother and sister who love you to death. You have the freedom to travel and meet interesting people; you have a job you love.

JOURNALIST: Had . . .

MAYOR: Okay, but you'll get another job. You have a great friend in Lou; you are curious, brave, smart and kind—the world is your oyster. You might feel poor compared with the richest one per cent in the world, but you are probably richer than ninety per cent of the planet. And you have the sort of luxurious life that can only be dreamt of by people in the ancient world, particularly as a woman.

JOURNALIST: But women still don't get paid the same as men, and they do more housework!

MAYOR: Life for women in ancient societies was unimaginably worse than in the twenty-first century. In Greece, women could not own property. They were under the guardianship of a male relative—even their sons!—for their whole lives. No public office; no voting, of course. Rarely appeared in public. Like Saudi Arabia now, but more restricted. In Ancient Greece you had no political rights of any kind, and your lives were run by men.

Interestingly the Stoics advocated, at least theoretically, for women's equality.

My ears pricked up.

JOURNALIST: How?

MAYOR: Musonius Rufus, a Roman Stoic, said that anyone who possessed a rational mind was capable of virtue. And that included women. He thought women should be taught philosophy and that philosophy, specifically Stoic philosophy, was the most useful thing a person could learn. Stoics more broadly thought that sexual inequality was contrary to the laws of nature. And they were right! They were following the Cynics—an adjacent philosophical school—in this regard. Cynics argued for men and women to have the same clothing and receive the same education. They thought gender demarcation was just a fake, nonsense, societal thing, and should be challenged.

JOURNALIST: Wow. Okay—I'm coming round to Stoicism.

MAYOR: Even so, that is a theoretical position they held. You would not have wanted to be a woman in ancient times. Look at your life now! The richest man in Rome wouldn't have had the lavish existence that you have. Think about it. When you wake up in the morning, you step out of a warm and comfortable bed, in a room that is perfectly temperature controlled for the climate. You step into the shower; hot water gushes out. And you have soap to clean yourself. You wear clothes cleaned by a machine. You get into your car and it takes you across town in twenty minutes, a distance that the Ancients might have taken a day to cross. And most importantly, on the way you stop at your favourite cafe and for a few dollars you get a hot, delicious coffee and something tasty and warm to eat. You didn't have to go out and kill your breakfast or wait in fear and dread for a famine to pass so you could eat breakfast. And you say you feel terrible about your life? Compared with others? What others? Not the ninety per cent of the world who are poorer than you.

JOURNALIST: But I'm not comparing myself with them. I'm comparing myself with the one per cent, and they are in our faces more than ever before thanks to social media. You know one of the issues with the friend I lent money to, the one we talked about?

The Mayor nodded.

After I lent her the money, I was seeing her all over Instagram with great hair, new clothes, at a beach resort. That shit costs money. What am I going to gram? The school covered in asbestos? The chemicals in the town water that I'm investigating? Abattoir conditions? The second-hand coat I wear? The holidays I never took?

MAYOR: Stop feeling sorry for yourself!

The Mayor was muttering under his breath—it sounded as if he was saying 'you have so far to go . . .'

What matters is your experience in the real world. In real life. Does the coat keep you warm? Does the work make you feel proud? Yes. Yes!

JOURNALIST [*begrudgingly*]: Yes—it does. It does.

I flagged down the waiter and ordered another rum. It was delicious. The Mayor stuck to water. The sun disappeared behind the buildings. Groups of people, carrying jackets and bags, left the courthouse—long shadows thrown on the stone square. A sudden cold gust. I shivered. What would it be like to live here? To work in these buildings, to join the life drawing class, or study the Veda, to cross the square at dusk—linger by the chess games, stop for a drink on the way home? Have a friend for fifty years?

Then suddenly I saw Dominic. He was with a group of guys kicking a soccer ball as they crossed the square. They were laughing and jostling each other for the ball. Two of them walked with their arms over each other's shoulders, the way you don't see much with men anymore. Dominic was in animated discussion, walking backwards before the ball suddenly came our way. He turned and saw me watching him. I tried and failed to look serious. I had a dumb grin on my face; I could feel it. A jolt of nervousness passed through me—a funny, almost unfamiliar feeling. The Mayor was watching me watch him. Dominic waved and smiled. The first genuine one I'd seen. I waved but he didn't come over. The pain that the Mayor was talking about hit me. And just like clockwork, I longed for distraction from this feeling. Come over here. Why won't you talk to me?

Another rum was set down. *Best rum in the world is made from the river water. The silt comes down from the rainforest—'sweet water' they call it—and once you taste the rum, you can never get enough.* Sweet like river water. Sweet like Dominic. The Mayor broke the silence.

MAYOR: Dinner? We have a booking.

HOW TO BE MODERATE, JUDGEMENTS, THE VIRTUES

SILVER SPRINGS, Adi's restaurant, Thursday, 7 pm—Walking to the restaurant, I realised, probably too late, that I was on my way to getting drunk. Everything was blurry and slurry, and not at all frightening or unpleasant. Twenty-four hours ago Silver Springs was just a name, an abstract idea, not even a place on the internet. Now I knew Dominic, had met Bo and Nay Chi, Thida and Septimus. I was an honorary citizen of the town, strolling around the square with my new best friend, the Mayor, like I'd been here forever.

The light was low in the sky, giving it a blue velvet sheen, and, with the rain gone, clouds cleared—a spray of stars appeared above us. I felt incredibly relaxed, at peace even. It was an expansive, good feeling—the first time I had really felt my guard go down since before the shooting.

A flock of doves, heading to roost, filled the sky. We walked off the square, along a dark, unpaved path, and the Mayor offered me his arm, which I took. I wondered if he could tell if I was drunk? But in those moments, something between us also relaxed after the wariness and hostility that had characterised our interactions at the start of the day.

From an open window, music drifted down. 'Beethoven,' the Mayor murmured and I wondered how they managed to get a piano up the mountains. I could imagine Dominic and the other young men, ropes attached to their waists, donkeys and a cart—climbing up the mountain with a piano on their backs. We paused by the window, as the 'Moonlight Sonata' poured out. Everything felt slowed down and liquid almost. Listening to the music, I had a sudden impulse to release a sob. I pushed the feeling down and we walked on. It was now very dark—and, looking up, the stars seemed more vivid, closer and brighter than they did back home. No light pollution to cover their brilliance.

I asked the Mayor to tell me more about how he came upon this place, and it really was a tale from a different time. He had travelled through Iran and Afghanistan in the late sixties, through rugged mountains and meadows filled with flowers, but what stuck with him most were the incredible villagers. Hardy mountain people, who never turned away a stranger, because that would be turning away God.

Then India.

MAYOR: I thought I knew it all. The answers were to be found in the East—in the old temples and the ashrams. I had my own guru in India. I learnt meditation from the maharishi who taught The Beatles. That was something else.

And I saw him there, in my mind's eye—'Dear Prudence' and yellow blossoms, small cups of chai, and pretty girls, sitting cross-legged on the ground.

When I was young, I was an idealist. I was interested in knowledge, self-improvement, fixing society, all that stuff. My parents were socialists of the old school—trade unionists and teachers. We read a lot in our house. They saw the path to improving society lay in politics, in the labour movement. I was attracted to more individual forms of betterment. The monastic life. Meditating for months on end. Being silent. A vegan. I was hardcore all right; I burned my ass off meditating, solving the problems of the world from my cushion.

JOURNALIST: Ha ha—I know the type . . .

MAYOR: The type is evergreen. A motorbike accident in India put a stop to my soul-searching. It was quite a bad one. That poultry truck killed my ego more than any guru. In the hospital, I was reduced. I was nothing but functions. Pissing. Shitting. Trying to escape pain but being stuck, literally in my own shit. There was no escape from myself and from my own foulness.

JOURNALIST: That sounds awful.

MAYOR: It was. Poorest hospital, in a poor country. Cast made badly from that old plaster of Paris, that weighed a tonne and itched in heat that seemed to come straight from hell's furnace.

The discomfort was epic. I wanted to hack off my own leg. There seemed to be nothing to do but die there. But I just couldn't die quickly enough. That's when I met her.

JOURNALIST: Sandra?

MAYOR: Yes. She was volunteering at the hospital. An angel. I wouldn't have traded the vision of first seeing her for all the opiates in Afghanistan.

JOURNALIST: And she brought you here to Silver Springs?

MAYOR: She brought me here. Fifty years ago now.

JOURNALIST: Not homesick at all?

MAYOR: No. When I first arrived I thought I had died and gone to heaven. They were days and nights of ecstasy in nature. The freshest air and the purest water on Earth. A hike down a mountain on a hot day, and you'd land at a deserted lake and swim in the clearest green water with fish darting between your legs. It was Eden. Total. But this place, Silver Springs, is not only beautiful and wild, it's got something additional. It's an ongoing project. A never-ending conversation. An experiment in community. Don't say 'utopia', because it's not that. It's more real than that. It's not just a theory. You see, the experiment had been going on so long that it didn't feel like a risk anymore; it didn't feel like an experiment even: it just felt like Silver Springs.

JOURNALIST: The experiment being the philosophy?

MAYOR: Yes, the experiment being the philosophy. The binding being the rituals. And the values, the values that we strive to hold in common. People can leave, and do. But those who stay—most of us want the same thing.

JOURNALIST: And what's that?

MAYOR: We want to live peacefully. We want to minimise the effects of suffering. We want leisure. We want community. We want loving relationships. We want connection to each other, nature and the cosmos. And we want beauty.

We arrived at the restaurant, a large, plain room. I recognised some of the people I had seen crossing the square (but no Dominic). Friends celebrating a birthday. An elderly couple, another table of teens playing cards. They all knew the Mayor, and he stopped by each table like an old Don, kissing babies and promising favours to fix this pothole or that leaky roof in the community hall.

The restaurant itself was a step up from the roadhouse on the terraces—simple but solid, rustic tables and chairs, pretty faded tablecloths with small vases of flowers a low roof made from wooden beams.

The owner greeted the Mayor with a hug and then to my surprise hugged me.

Once seated under the lamplight, the Mayor discreetly stuck his leg out. Rolling up his pants, he showed me the scar tissue there, decades after the motorbike accident. Puckered and pulled—it was like the flesh had been burnt off or melted.

JOURNALIST: Wow. It still looks raw. That must have hurt.

The Mayor grimaced.

There were no menus in the restaurant, explained the Mayor, instead the chef, Adi, would bring out the dishes of the day.

JOURNALIST: Are you having wine?

Now that I had two rums, plus the Mayor's wine, I had a taste for alcohol and wanted to keep going, to maintain the buzz. I was drunk—yes, but not too drunk.

MAYOR: Not for me. I drink in moderation, but not regularly. Never more than two drinks.

JOURNALIST: Is that a Stoic thing? Or a Mayor thing?

MAYOR: Alcohol is an indifferent. Seneca wrote: 'Eat merely to relieve your hunger; drink merely to quench your thirst; dress merely to keep out the cold; house yourself merely as a protection against personal discomfort.' He's saying, indulge yourself as much as your actual needs are, as opposed to your wants. They are two different things.

JOURNALIST: Sometimes my need is overwhelming.

MAYOR: If you were in ataraxia, Goldfish, your need would be zero. You'd be at peace and not need something to relax you or make you sociable.

He tapped my glass.

MAYOR: Does Goldfish want another drink because of her unconscious assumption that if one was good, two must be better, and so on?

Because I hate to say it . . .

JOURNALIST: No—you love to say it, I bet.

MAYOR: This assumption that two must be better is clearly not correct, and yet it remains as a foundation to many of our thoughts and actions.

The Mayor sighed.

What you drink is none of my business. I'm not the fun police, and neither were the Stoics. Of course they drank wine, like so many of us. But, as you will remember, what the Stoics sought to do with their philosophy was not to needlessly suffer. They wanted to safeguard their rational thinking. Avoiding a very predictable hangover may be called Stoic but it would also be called commonsense.

The Mayor warned me that all the food came at once. And so it did—a parade of plates and colour, and the table quickly became crowded. Snacks of rice pancakes filled with vegetables, fried tofu served with spicy dipping sauces, then a sour soup—made with tomatoes, herbs and pork. Turmeric-flavoured rice with flaked fish, boiled green vegetables and a flat noodle dish served in tomato broth. And while the wine was dry and cold—and went down well—my mood was turning, from the joyful, almost romantic feeling I had had listening to Beethoven to something darker. My hand, injured a week ago now in Dav, was still throbbing with pain, a continual reminder that something terrible had happened to me.

The Mayor had referred lightly in one of his letters to 'the tragic business of being alive'. But when would the pain lift?

JOURNALIST: So . . . I feel like you're sidestepping the question of the suffering of others. Especially the role we need to play when it comes to social justice.

MAYOR: Sidestepping? That is one thing the Stoic doesn't do. Is this a journalistic trick: you just ask the same question many different ways until you get the answer you want?

It *was* a journalistic trick but I didn't admit it.

You seem to want a philosophy that is an answer to every question, a remedy for every ill. What about *x*? What about *y*? You want *the answer*. That's not Stoicism. A Stoic looks to their own state, their own self, what is in their control. And in that, they work hard. They make a positive difference in the world. They do this realistically, seeing the world as it is, not as they want it to be. Goldfish, *remember*: this is not a philosophy to beat others over the head with. It's about you. Do the right thing.

JOURNALIST: How do I know what the right thing is?

MAYOR: Be guided by reason and the virtues. Act, and if you don't get the outcome you want, deal with it calmly.

JOURNALIST: There are real problems in the world, problems that lead to our mass extinction, not to mention the suffering and extinction of the natural world—plants and animals—and your main aim in life is to keep calm?

MAYOR: Should I meet anger with anger? Anxiety with yet more worry? Without calm, without rational thinking, we won't come to any solutions about the problems we face in this world, which are complex and difficult problems. Take climate change. Someone who's angry all the time is unlikely to be able to build the sort of consensus we need to establish with manufacturing, government, mining and communities to come to some of the solutions to reduce emissions.

JOURNALIST: And how's that working out—that consensus? It's not happening, because people aren't energised enough. They're too busy looking for inner peace and not dealing with the urgent problems that lie outside them.

I took another swig of wine, trying to slow my breathing and calm myself by thinking of the river with pink lotuses, emerald-green lakes, the ferns in the Mayor's garden, the purple heath, the almond trees in bloom growing on the sides of the hills.

MAYOR: We have a responsibility to know reality and then act from that place of reality. The real grunt work of improving society involves a much more grounded approach than angrily denouncing everything, calling for revolution, and then becoming disgusted when not everyone agrees with you.

JOURNALIST: All the great changes in the world—all the revolutions are because people have refused to accept reality. They are fighting reality! Not accepting it!

The Mayor served me some fish, murmuring that I must try it, and continued in his even, neutral tone.

MAYOR: Marcus wrote 'we are made for each other'. And the Stoics believe that we are designed to be part of a community that all works for the common good. When we strive for the common good, which we should always do, we understand that we live in a society where not everyone will agree with us, where we could be mistaken and where much of what we seek is outside our control. To allow the *outcome* of this process to dictate our emotions is to condemn ourselves to frustration, anxiety, and anger. It's inevitable. Don't allow your tranquillity to depend on external matters.

I wondered if it were possible that the Mayor didn't know that climate change or the threat of nuclear war was a *thing*. Maybe cut off from the world, no one here knew about current woes in the rest of the world?

JOURNALIST: I am certainly not feeling tranquil about climate change. Look, it's here! And don't say you don't have it in Silver Springs. On the way up here, the weather was strange—the rain that stops and starts, the streams down the mountains of the unseasonal melting snow. Where I am from, climate change is well and truly kicking in and already making life shittier. Wetter winters are flooding farms, cancelling music festivals, transport and sport, overflowing sewerage systems and making groceries more expensive. Places that have never flooded are deluged. Places that have never seen drought are parched. Wildfires are burning in cities. People are collapsing in their thousands on pilgrimages to Mecca. Farm workers in India and Mexico are dropping dead from the heat. Tranquillity? Let me tell you—I do not feel tranquil.

The alcohol and climate change talk were aggravating me. The gentle teasing that we were enjoying earlier had evaporated. It was unprofessional but I realised it felt good to express myself. So much of interviewing people was a passive exercise. You were not meant to assert yourself—but I felt energised being off the leash finally, letting this quasi-monarch, high up on his throne, have it.

With your philosophy, it's not fit for purpose anymore! You're trying to have a bet both ways. Trying hard and acting collectively to reduce the harms facing the world and others but being detached about the outcome. That feels completely mad.

I couldn't eat anymore. I wondered if I'd be ill. I had some more wine though, as there was still some left in the bottle.

MAYOR: We have a natural responsibility to act in the best interests of the whole, not just individually. This accords with your earlier example about advancing the cause of women or protecting the natural world. Just as we want to minimise suffering for ourselves, we also want others to suffer as little as possible. The virtue of justice is very important in Stoic philosophy.

The Mayor was definitely dodging my questions. He was as wily as an old politician. Which, as a mayor, is exactly what he was.

JOURNALIST: You talk about Epictetus and slavery as if it's in the past, but there are still fifty million people enslaved—mostly women in forced marriages, and children. It's not over!

MAYOR: Is that supposed to be a rebuttal? What if I gave you this simple answer: it's not a perfect world.

JOURNALIST: That's your comeback? It's not a perfect world—yeah sure. But from what I understand, Epictetus—who was a slave—accepted his slavery. Are you saying these fifty million just need to bite it?

If all you can control is your character, actions and reaction and how you treat others—then how are you supposed to effect change on a larger scale? An example might be—advocating for climate justice or women's rights. The activism of those who came before us gave us the rights that we enjoy today. Imagine if they had been Stoics—nothing would have been achieved.

MAYOR: You don't want to hear me, do you? Perhaps you are too attached to your own anger and fear. It's difficult to have conversations with people who have no commitment to change. I have said that Stoicism is not about the world out there. It is about the world in here.

The Mayor extended one wiry arm and pointed at my chest. To my surprise, I saw his hand was shaking.

I didn't like being pointed at—it felt like an aggressive move.

JOURNALIST: Why not be back in the city doing this? Silver Springs is very removed, a society that only a privileged few can join. It's like you saw societal collapse, the rise of authoritarianism, and you all tried to get out. And you are kind of doing it—you got out! But what about the rest of us? We are still in there and—

My voice cracked with the injustice of it all.

—only a lucky few thousand get to experience this way of life.

MAYOR: This town wasn't just magicked up. It wasn't just conjured out of air. The people who live here have worked hard to live in a more thoughtful way. Although human nature is the same the world over, if you work at it, you can improve yourself and make a better reality. That is true anywhere, even in places that are authoritarian. Think about what you could do to create this community back home.

JOURNALIST: But I'm going back to no job. To my community destroyed by an act of violence.

MAYOR: You must find a new community—and if you can't find one, you must start one. Take what we have done here, and copy it. Put the word out in your area: 'Let's meet each week and talk about how we can help each other suffer less.'

Could I really start something like that? Something flared in me. Maybe I could? But my negativity bias kicked in, and I thought how difficult it would be to change my corner of the world, with all the nihilism and depression I saw all around me.

JOURNALIST: It's easier to go in the direction of virtue if the currents you are swimming in are all carrying you a certain way.

MAYOR: Maybe that's what I want from the article you will publish—a sense for other places in the world that you *can* make a change in your own community. You don't have to separate yourself off from the world to make things better. Our geography makes us separate, and remote, but this philosophy is designed to be used anywhere and everywhere. The more difficult the conditions, the better!

JOURNALIST: With such a remote location, can you really say you are teaching Stoicism from experience? I just don't buy it. Your community is too sheltered from some of the worst aspects of modern life. Being indifferent to the body? Being indifferent to money and reputation? Being okay with not being in control? All this talk of being relaxed? This is all theory to you guys up here—but for me, I've actually been through some heavy shit lately. I've seen some things, man, you would not believe. And I've listened to everything you say—and I got to say, I'm calling bullshit.

Was I slurring my words? They were not coming out as fluently as I hoped. The Mayor's eyebrows raised slightly but he remained silent.

I was shot. In my workplace. I saw my colleagues die. Your theories minimise that trauma. This is making me feel worse, coming here. I shouldn't have come here.

Instead of firing back and arguing with me, the Mayor looked as sad as I felt. Adi was in the shadows, listening, waiting to clear the plates.

MAYOR [*speaking softly*]: I'm so sorry. Remember Marcus's words. 'Humans have come into being for each other, so either teach them or learn to bear them.' And that goes for me too: please, go easy on an old man who leads a quiet life, in a remote village. I am learning from you too.

The Mayor excused himself from the table, while all the energy of indignation left me like air from a deflating balloon. Why did I go so hard? Why was I taking things out on him?

The Mayor hadn't quite done a runner. He'd paid for the meal but when it was clear he wasn't coming back, that he'd gone home without me, I felt angry and bereft. Adi offered to get me back to the inn but I wanted to revel in the hurt of being abandoned. Leaving the restaurant, I wandered drunkenly around the closed, prim, boring town with no wi-fi, kicking a bin off its brackets and watching it roll noisily down the square, then kicking it again. That'll teach them. Think they know all the answers!

But it was dark and quiet and soon I felt lonely and remorseful. The bin rolled back and forth in the winds, making aluminium music. Why was I so awful to the Mayor? I suddenly became mortified. What if word of my behaviour got back to Lou?

I hadn't been raised to be a brat but here I was having fights in restaurants with my host. With the town's Mayor! I knew almost nothing of him. What private pain might he be experiencing? I wasn't the first or only person in the world to suffer. Yet I had made it all about me—and in doing so, had broken the most important rule of journalism. *It's not about you.* Tears started to fall and I let them.

I could have sat in the square all night, the mild evening air carrying the charred smell of fire from the nearby forest, the full moon washing the square with a column of silver light, the tears feeling good, in the way that feeling sorry for yourself can feel good. But I heard footsteps approaching and I saw a figure crossing the square. A man. I shivered. Could he see me? In the moonlight I caught a glimpse and gasped—tall, handlebar moustache, his right hand held behind his back, in the other the tip of a glowing cigarette. It looked like him! The scary man from Davan! I rubbed my eyes, stood quickly and stepped into the shadows, but when I looked again, he was gone. A hint of cigarette smoke remained in the air and I felt afraid.

Then I heard the waft of music coming from a side street.

It sounded like . . . The Strokes. Someone was having a party.

The house lights all around me were off—it was an early-to-bed kind of town—but, after turning in circles a few more times, I found a laneway where a small light burnt bright and there was a kid on the door dressed in one of the nineties rave smiley T-shirts. Music could be heard faintly from within. He looked me up and down, before opening the door.

The Mayor had mentioned it was a town that liked a party but had not mentioned this, and I was happily surprised—Silver Springs had a club!

I descended the stairs and found a dark cavernous space, filled with music and people dancing. In the dark, it was hard to make out any faces, and so I joined the mosh pit and danced hard to the music of my youth—the Strokes, LCD Soundsystem, the Yeah Yeah Yeahs, The Vines.

I was drunk but also overcome by a physical sensation of nostalgia that made my knees buckle. It also felt good, like I was actually back there.

A random teen passed me a cup of something foamy. It tasted of cough syrup with lemonade, and after two large cups of this almost medicinal-tasting drink, I felt the borders of my body fade as I was absorbed into the mass of bodies. No separation, no ego, unified in a pure mass of sound. I wanted to leave tonight's sadness behind. I wanted to change my state of consciousness. I needed more of whatever that drink was.

One song tripped into the next and became heavier—more primal—like a more guttural and exciting style of EDM. For a brief, vibrant time I felt I had abandoned my body and my mind. I was no longer thinking, processing, viewing myself from outside myself and, simultaneously and horribly, trapped in the cage of my never-ceasing internal dialogue, and my pain-racked body. I reached forward and my hand ran down someone's sweat-soaked limb or torso, or something. I threw my head back and let the bass thrum from my back through my organs and out my stomach—like it was a real thing with force, a poltergeist hand that moved through me.

The dance floor filled even further, pushing our bodies closer together. Who were these people? Where did they all come from? I no longer felt self-conscious about the wound on my head and the bandages on my hand, about being a stranger in a small town, a foreigner that only spoke English. We were all breathing as one—and that's when I noticed Dominic, hair wet with sweat, shirt off, shining eyes on mine. I elbowed my way to him and, with an audacity that I had never felt before, I breached the space between us and—with his head in my hands—started kissing him. In the ecstasy of vanishing boundaries, I suddenly came roaring back to a different sort of life, broke through the container of numbness (how long had I been numb? forever it felt like) and felt the full body force of pure desire.

THE BODY

MODERATION, JOURNALLING, THE PASSIONS, DESIRE, HEALTH AND AGEING

SILVER SPRINGS, The Mayor's house, Friday, 8 am—I turned down Thida's offer of an escort to the second day of interviews with the Mayor. I was too hungover for small talk and so, slowly and silently, made my way, passing an old man walking a dog who smiled and said 'Hello', and Septimus and a friend heading across the fields, schoolbags over their shoulders.

The air was very still and quiet except for a couple of hawks that flew overhead. In the silence I could hear their wings cut the sky.

Hit by a wave of nausea, I paused by the farm gate. Last night felt like a dream—sensuous, heavy, full of whispered things, hot rooms, a thrumming bass that felt material, made of flesh and muscle, and later, Dominic walking me home, holding my hand.

Who was it that said love disordered the senses—apart from every poet? Plato said 'love is a serious mental disease', and after all the talk about rationality yesterday, it was easy to see why. I felt scrambled and strange.

But then there was what happened before. Dinner with the Mayor.

In the clarifying sun and stiff breeze, I gulped air, trying to quash the nausea and shame. Arriving at the Mayor's house, I lowered myself into the chair gingerly and shuffled closer to the fire. I was feeling very fragile, my stomach lurching, a splitting headache. It was a Defcon 1–level hangover. Then there was the Mayor. He seemed awkward too. I couldn't quite make eye contact, not before a mug of the strong tea with sweet condensed milk.

JOURNALIST [*shamefacedly*]: I guess I should begin by apologising for last night. I played back a bit of the tape this morning and wanted to die. It's not just that I hate the sound of my own voice, but I really lost my shit. I'm so embarrassed.

MAYOR: I don't care. I'm happy to test my beliefs. Although the alcohol meant it wasn't a fair fight. It's always amusing to see someone who isn't used to drinking lose their inhibitions.

Was he serious?

JOURNALIST: You have no idea. I wish I could say it's unusual for me to drink too much—but truth be known, I'm one of those people who, once they start drinking, find it hard to stop. I just love the feeling—at least at the start. Not cool to say in these health-conscious times, but there you go.

MAYOR: I understand. After all, I have a vineyard. I like wine. And although I can't drink as much as I once did, I can remember finding it hard to resist finishing a glass or two more on a warm day, particularly after harvest. I'd roll home in the twilight, with a smile on my face, my dinner gone cold.

JOURNALIST: Would Sandra be mad?

MAYOR [*a bit wistfully*]: Sometimes.

JOURNALIST: I get it. I also like the loose, slightly hazy feeling of a few drinks. Not being fully in control. It feels good, you know. I don't feel so anxious. I stop overthinking things and just go with the flow. But, after every hangover, I'm like—never again. I feel embarrassed a lot of the time, the next day.

MAYOR: The embarrassment you can control, but obviously not the physical effects. A hangover just has to pass in its own time.

JOURNALIST: What's the Stoic approach to drinking?

MAYOR: We went over this last night! The Stoic approach would be moderation, which is one of the four virtues. Roman Stoic Musonius Rufus was of the belief that self-control came via mastery of your intake of food and drink. In your situation, after a night drinking, you can't control what you've said or done, because it's already in the past. The past is over. It's gone. Embarrassment about the past, or 'shame' if you want to use that word, is useless. The only real use you have for embarrassment is if you *remember* the emotion. *That* is the key: remember the feeling of embarrassment, shame or guilt, feeling ill, saying something stupid, whatever it is you've done, and use that to correct your character and the virtues, into the future.

JOURNALIST: So use the hangover as a learning experience?

MAYOR: Yes. And use *this* hangover as a learning experience. Start this practice right now; for example, you have such a short time here in Silver Springs, so why waste one of your three precious days feeling sick? You can't change getting sick—last night has already happened—but it's a reminder not to do the same thing tonight, and waste tomorrow as well.

Sorry, I should have offered you some water. And I'll make some tea and breakfast.

I downed the water in two gulps.

JOURNALIST: How do you remember the hangover and the emotions that come with it? All the big nights tend to roll into one.

MAYOR: You make a note each day in your journal. That's what the Ancients did. What they wrote was *not* about what *others* did to them, it's about what *they* did to others, or *they* did to themselves. That is where true control lies. In yourself, in monitoring your actions and then changing your own actions.

The thought of journalling when I got up in the morning with a hangover seemed to be sufficient punishment for the hangover.

JOURNALIST: So journalling was like giving themselves a report card every day? Or a report on the wild night before, or what you can remember of it? I'd usually go through my photo roll to remember what happened the night before. That, and my banking app.

MAYOR: Seneca used to write at night, reviewing the day and how he responded to challenges, measuring improvements or slippages in his own character. He said, 'I examine my entire day and go back over what I've done and said, hiding nothing from myself, passing nothing by.' Then he would go to bed, finding that 'the sleep which follows this self-examination' was particularly sweet.

Marcus wrote in his journal in the morning and, of course, the *Meditations* is the result of that. He was following the instructions of Epictetus, who would tell his students that philosophy was something they should 'write down day by day,' that this writing was how they 'should exercise themselves'. It was a spiritual exercise, and how they kept track of their progress.

JOURNALIST: Do you keep a journal?

MAYOR: Yes. I've kept a journal for more than fifty years. It's the only way to chart my inner journey. We're unreliable narrators of our own progress, particularly how we progress on interior matters like development of character. We can't really properly see ourselves.

JOURNALIST: I agree—we are our own blind spot.

The Mayor selected some eggs from a bowl, cracked them and whisked them lightly.

MAYOR: Watch yourself like a mother watches the growth of her baby. Chart the growth and the challenges in your journal. If you pay attention, you'll be shocked by how different you were from only six months ago. We are changing, and I hope, evolving, all the time.

JOURNALIST: Do you see growth as progressing with age? So the older we get, the wiser we get?

MAYOR: No. Some of the most stupid people I know have been around for a long time. Sometimes they get worse as they get older; their character deteriorates rather than strengthens. They get more selfish; their ego gets stronger; they dig in their heels; they are less likely to see their own faults or want to see their faults. And the entitlement!

You must chart a different course. The higher road is always available to you, and don't underestimate keeping a diary as a way of getting there. I see it as not an optional extra but an essential part of Stoic practice. Stoicism is practised through thought and action, but the action is directed by self-reflection. The self-reflection gives you the map of where you need to go. And the self-reflection takes place when you write in your diary. Come and have a look in here.

I stood up, a bit wobbly, and we walked down a corridor into a small, light-filled room. All around the walls were shelves filled with notebooks of various sizes and signs of age, some held together with rubber bands. By the window there was a small desk with a solitary lamp and a half-drunk cup of tea on a saucer.

JOURNALIST: This looks like thousands of notebooks.

MAYOR: It is! All my journals since I arrived here more than fifty years ago. Sometimes I'll just open one at random, like this . . . 1994.

He flicked through it—got lost in a page—then remembered where he was and looked up.

MAYOR: This one here, Thida was young then and I was writing about those times in early parenthood when nothing feels like it's in your control. You read a book on how to get a kid to sleep and you think if you follow that you can control her sleep . . . but, of course, you can't. A lot of the things I was writing about at the time were how angry I was at her. I was a short-tempered dad, constantly trying to control this tiny baby. And getting very upset when I couldn't.

JOURNALIST: Did the journalling help you see how deluded you were?

MAYOR: When I read back over it, sure. But it took a long time for the lessons to seep in and for me to really change. But this, writing it down, was the first step.

Smelling the omelette left cooking on the pan, the Mayor abruptly returned to the kitchen, leaving me with this treasure trove.

There was an opportunity to snoop—scan his journals, go through the drawers looking for photos, all great material for my article. But the old instincts for the kill had vanished. I left the study before I changed my mind and returned to our conversation in the kitchen.

Sitting back at the kitchen bench, I watched as the Mayor poured water into the teapot for another strong brew. Even though I was in a wretched state, even though I had been rude, had he thawed out, maybe even come to care for me?

MAYOR: I wonder—what might your diary look like over the last few weeks? Brimming with Stoicism, I'm sure of it! Courage in Davantown and on the journey upriver. Wisdom when picking your travel companions, and deciding when to go it alone or when to travel with a guide. Moderation in how far you pushed yourself each day. I hope you were making notes!

JOURNALIST: A reporter always makes notes. What about the meetings you have at the Stoa? All the community stuff? Surely they reinforce the philosophy? Or do you need to journal as well?

MAYOR: The meetings are great but not everyone can attend; people have other commitments. Or you might, as we discussed yesterday, find yourself alone in exile, or away from like-minded people in a big city. You can't rely on others to engage with Stoicism. It must primarily come from yourself. And self-reflection and keeping a diary are always within your control. You can reflect and write no matter where you are, setting aside some time each day. When Marcus was writing in his journal, he was in dialogue with himself, just as you and I are in dialogue now. In keeping a diary, say at night, you write down the Stoic principles and how they applied in your life that day, so that they might seep into your very being.

JOURNALIST: Like learning how to drive?

MAYOR: At the start, with learning any new skill, you need to commit to memory but then it becomes second nature. But each night, you don't sit down and make an inventory of how well you drove, and you don't necessarily have to replay the tricky three-point turn or the parallel park. Not after you've got your licence, surely? With Stoicism, even if you think you've mastered some of the basic principles, you must begin every day, and deal with each difficult person or encounter, as if you are a rookie.

Some days I'll encounter someone in a meeting or in my work as a Mayor whom I find to be really difficult, 'triggering' as you might say, and I'll get reactive, or I'll stew on something, and I must keep going back to the basic principles. Every day: begin again.

The Mayor folded the omelette onto my plate, took some naan from the oven, poured the tea and set out a jug of condensed milk.

JOURNALIST: You've always got naan on the go—I love it!

In the distance, I heard the sound of sirens again—another fire call—and startled.

MAYOR: Don't worry about it. There's another siren that goes off if we need to evacuate.

But the hangover made me anxious; the sirens unsettled me; and a dread descended, as it reliably does the morning after drinking.

I want to spend today talking about the passions. The body, really. Probably a good day to be doing it, as your hangover is talking loudly to you this morning.

JOURNALIST: Not so much talking as screaming.

MAYOR: As you are no doubt aware, any disturbance in the body tends to distract the mind. Sore head and that's all you think about. Even the smallest body part, when you have the slightest disturbance, pulls your focus away from where it needs to be. An itch on your foot, and you can't get to sleep.

True—even something as small as a hangnail on my thumb, or mild period cramps, would distract my attention until I did something about it. Let alone a raging hangover that seemed to infect the mind as much as it affected the body—anxiety and racing thoughts, recriminations and regrets, an all-round bad feeling.

Remember the goal is ataraxia: freedom from disturbance, being relaxed, being chilled, and this pertains as much to the body as it does to the mind.

JOURNALIST: And it's difficult to relax with a pounding headache and nausea.

MAYOR: Exactly. That's why the Stoics made a virtue of moderation: not because they were morally pure, but because they wanted to protect that state of ataraxia and keep their reason and rational thinking clear. Seneca wrote, 'The body should be treated more rigorously, that it may not be disobedient to the mind.' Your mind should be in control—not swayed by the animal passions of the body.

JOURNALIST: What do you mean when you talk about the passions? It seems to be a very old term, like your use of the word virtues.

MAYOR: Think about the things that carry you away from rational thinking. Love, desire, jealousy, envy, revenge, hatred, anger. All the strong stuff, emotions that have expressions in the body. They're the passions. Ancient Stoics saw humans as rational animals and violent emotions as the products of faulty thinking. Work done on fixing faulty judgements, work that we discussed yesterday, is helpful in taming the passions.

JOURNALIST: Love is good, surely.

And desire. Desire is wonderful. I had to suppress a smile—I was thinking about Dominic again. He just kept popping into my head. We had parted last night without making plans, but that was okay because I knew we would meet again.

MAYOR: Love is good . . . broadly speaking. We'll come to that later this morning. Because, of course, there are many different types of love and some excite the passions and other forms of love calm us.

JOURNALIST: Many of those passions you mentioned are drives that contain important information. To eradicate them seems stupid. Jealousy will tell you when you are attached to something. Envy will tell you what you want. And desire could be the most important drive of all. Without it our species would die out. And don't forget—anger will often arise as a result of an injustice.

Anger told me what stories to pursue. If something made me angry, I knew I should be writing about it. The school asbestos scandal, wage theft at the local cafe, services underfunded.

MAYOR: I agree; emotions can play a role in how we act or respond. They are not mindless or base instincts. But not all emotions are passions. Generally the passions are at the more extreme end of emotions and they are often excessive. Stoicism generally holds the passions in opposition to reason. When you become inflamed by something, whether it be a political issue or a love interest or a desire for revenge, reason is the first casualty. The passions cloud reason, and you end up making bad decisions. Often you don't even know what you're doing; you can't properly *see* yourself. Think about when you're arguing with someone and it gets really heated and they say, 'Stop yelling,' and you didn't even realise you'd raised your voice! You were just so carried away.

JOURNALIST: Why is that always so bad? It can be delightful to get carried away with a person, or a feeling or situation. A crush can transform a mundane day into something exciting—where you have something or somebody to look forward to seeing.

Dominic, again. Why was I so horny? I was here to work!

MAYOR: Because with that you become carried away on a chemical high, the sort of excitement that is very distinct from ataraxia, and leads to an oppositional state: the pain of withdrawal, the coming down. But there are a few more reasons to avoid the passions. They can distort reality. With a romantic infatuation, for example, you see someone or a situation as you want to see them, or you want to see the situation, not as it is.

Was it just my imagination or was that aimed specifically at me?

And we must deal only in reality, if we want to live fully and minimise suffering. The body and mind are always trying to get into homeostasis, where pleasure is counteracted with pain to bring things into equilibrium. And, of course, ataraxia, freedom from disturbance, being relaxed. That was highly prized by the Ancients. The passions were by their nature a disturbance, and they strived to be free from disturbance as much as possible.

JOURNALIST: Does sin come into play when you are talking about the passions? You know—lust, wrath, envy—and my favourite—sloth?

MAYOR: Not really. Traditional Stoics don't really believe in sin. They do believe in vice, but it's a different order of things. They didn't really have any word or concept that represented sinning, at least not in the way of the Christian tradition. But the Ancients did see the passions as leading people away from virtue, away from moderation, justice, courage and wisdom. How can you be wise if you are also envious? How can you be moderate if you are also gluttonous?

We both looked down at my plate at this. The omelette was gone. I'd wolfed it down.

JOURNALIST: Why is gluttony so bad? It seems like a victimless crime to be honest. And I don't think we should judge people on how much they eat.

MAYOR: Precisely. What other people eat is their business. You should be concerned with what *you* eat. Of course there'll be feasts and parties and events where there's a lot of delicious food. Live it up! Enjoy it. But remember that lavish food, rich food, gourmet food, food that you would get at a great restaurant is a preferred indifferent. Yes, it's preferable to have a good, tasty meal, but you should be indifferent to it. When the money is spent, or the invitations dry up because you're socially on the outer, or there is a famine or shortages of various kinds due to climate events, you won't be getting that food anymore. Imagine if you became accustomed to a steady supply of food, all kinds of meat, cream and cheese, vegetables and fruit flown in from all over the world no matter what the season, and then suddenly the supply stopped?

JOURNALIST: This is already happening where I live. In the last few months there has been no lettuce, no beans, no avocados, no eggs . . .

Shortages that seemed to come out of nowhere but seemed a portent to some larger catastrophe. And in the shortages, there was fear, there was also greed and stockpiling and anger in the supermarket aisles as people fought over the remaining items. Would an embrace of moderation stop people from being anxious and afraid about shortages?

MAYOR: So you know then that you would be suffering twice in that situation. The first time from the lack of supply but secondly from the panic, fear, from missing the things that you took for granted. Or you told yourself that you need a certain type of diet to survive. You could only eat organic food, farmed in a certain area. The ancient Stoics practised for this by fasting for days at a time, or totally simplifying their diet down to lentils and vegetables.

JOURNALIST: Were the ancient Stoics intermittent fasters? You mentioned Seneca was a part-time vegetarian?

MAYOR: If they had a food philosophy, it was to eat only according to what their body needed and stopping at that point. That way you eliminate food anxiety because you are not worried about overindulging. You just know when to stop.

The Mayor sighed.

Remember there are only four virtues, and moderation is one of them. Only four! There aren't hundreds of things you have to master. You must start trying before you say it's too hard. Moderation is not about ignoring appetite. If you have worked up a hunger, eat. If you're not hungry, don't eat.

JOURNALIST: Sounds like intuitive eating. I worked up a hunger just now. So I guess it's okay that I demolished that breakfast. Thank you. I feel better.

MAYOR: I was pleased to share it with you. Apart from when you're hungry, there are a few practical reasons for moderation around food and drink. One is how you feel in your body. Remember ataraxia, freedom from disturbance. You eat too much, how do you feel? I don't know about you but, when I eat and drink too much, I get reflux at night. It wakes me up! I can feel the acid in my stomach.

I felt my own stomach turning at this, and wished he would change the subject.

I have to sleep propped up on pillows. And, of course, I have a terrible night's sleep and my mood is compromised the next day. I need to really work to get my equilibrium back. Why? I overindulged and paid the price. It's all connected, all these Stoic principles. The body, like the mind and the spirit, is designed to be in a state of homeostasis. It means things balance out. Stable. Steady. Like blood sugar. Like temperature. Like our immune system. So many of our body's systems are designed to be in homeostasis. Just as in nature, there is also a perfect balance in the body. This homeostasis results in a finely tuned feeling inside and out. Things match; they are in step. Your body is not creating a disturbance for you, and neither is your mind. Both are serving you when you need to be served, leaving you to carry on and enjoy your life without constantly obsessing about it, or tending to them, or being anxious.

But how often did this happen? If I felt good in my body, my mind might be worried and ruminating about some issue, and if my mind felt calm, I might have had some ache or pain that was distracting me. Often, as I got older, both my body and mind were simultaneously complaining. And after the shooting, the pain was almost constant.

Think about the times when your body has felt great. It felt so good that you didn't even think about it—because it was giving you no complaints. How much easier is it in those circumstances to be relaxed and happy? To have clear thoughts? For everything to seem like it's flowing? You move from one event, one place, one task to the next. No friction. Exercise or movement has a role to play in this as well. Seneca advised short but strong workouts.

JOURNALIST: Like HIIT? You know—high-intensity stuff?

MAYOR: Yes. Seneca said, 'There are short and simple exercises which tire the body rapidly, and so save our time; and time is something of which we ought to keep strict account. These exercises are running, brandishing weights, and jumping . . .'

I groaned on the inside. Seneca seemed to have a hack for everything. If he were alive today, he would probably be a wellness influencer, with his own very successful podcast.

JOURNALIST: Diet and exercise are great but they don't solve everything. Do you believe in modern medicine? Taking pills?

MAYOR: Is taking pills what modern medicine is all about? Sounds like it hasn't changed much in fifty years. Medical treatment works sometimes, and it can work miracles. At other times, the whole shebang seems like a crutch, giving people something to lean on, a pill to take, a name to give their unhappiness and stress. In many ways I see doctors not so much as healers but more as namers: they make people feel better because they give their disease a name. I have *x*! I have *y*! It's not just me after all! And that lets them struggle on through another long day, another economic crisis.

Another controversial opinion. There was a lot the Mayor was saying that didn't chime with modern thinking.

JOURNALIST: I appreciate the elegance of the Greek idea of homeostasis but what if you go out of homeostasis—if you are injured and your body becomes unwell, like what happened to me? That's outside your control. So it goes to show that even this homeostasis is a preferred indifferent.

MAYOR: Correct. If you were poisoned last night by a bad oyster and felt unwell today, that would be outside your control. But you actually had control last night as to how many drinks you ordered, so that is within your control.

But now I could feel myself bristling at his crisp advice.

JOURNALIST: I meant when I became unwell after I was shot. I *know* last night was in my control.

MAYOR: Sorry, I thought we were still on your hangover. Yes, getting shot at . . . There is a tension in Stoicism, typical of this example, where you hold in your head two opposing thoughts. You can control what you put into your body and how you treat it but you also have no *ultimate* control over your body. They appear to contradict. But you must hold both positions. This tension is built in throughout the whole philosophy. You have to be able to hold this tension. Move with it.

JOURNALIST: What does that even mean in practice?

I tried to keep the edge out of my voice, but I could feel my face getting hot.

MAYOR: You couldn't control getting shot. You can only control how you *react* to getting shot. In the meantime, look after your body while you can, using the principles of moderation in everything including diet and exercise but be aware you are dealing with something fallible and vulnerable. Your body will age. It will get sick. It will get injured, as you got injured. People can hurt you, as *you got hurt*. And you will die. We all will. So we *must be* indifferent. We must control what we can and not worry when things outside our control happen. That is the tension. Epictetus said, 'I will expose its true nature by outdoing myself in calmness and serenity; I will neither beg the doctor's help, nor pray for death. What more could you ask? Everything, you see, that you throw at me I will transform into a blessing, a boon—something dignified, even enviable.'

JOURNALIST: I definitely cannot call being shot a blessing—or enviable. What rubbish.

MAYOR: But it led you here to me. Would that have happened otherwise?

JOURNALIST: No. I doubt it. But as interesting as this conversation is, I don't like the price of admission.

MAYOR: You may not like it, but this is where the journey is taking you—

JOURNALIST: So suck it up?

MAYOR: Find the joy. Find the purpose.

JOURNALIST: I'm not there yet. I don't think I ever will be. On some of my worst days, holding on to my hate and my anger for what happened to me seems to be the only thing giving me strength.

MAYOR: Perhaps you are here to let go of those things. Let go of the hate. Let go of the anger.

JOURNALIST: Don't tell me how to react. You weren't there.

I breathed deeply and thought of my inner citadel. What did it look like? It looked like my bedroom when I was a kid. I used to hide from the world there, safe and secure. I was back in my childhood bedroom, with all my toys and books, and felt myself calming.

Then there was ataraxia. I remembered that. Ataraxia was like an island I needed to swim to. I could see it. I was strong enough to get there. I just needed to build up the muscles, so I could get there, over and over again.

MAYOR: There is no other way. There is no world in which you did not get shot. There is only this world. This reality. Look it in the face!

JOURNALIST: It's a big deal what happened to me.

MAYOR: Oh my poor Goldfish . . .

I steeled myself for another blast but then the old man came over and raised a hand to my shoulder. It rested there for a moment, gentle. I could feel his thin fingers through the cotton of my T-shirt. Then his hand lifted, and he turned and invited me into the garden.

MAYOR: We must look to nature if we are talking about homeostasis. Nature is a blueprint for harmony, as long as we let Mother Nature do her thing.

To put it simply, it's a two-way street: us and nature. We're not separate from nature; we are not the masters of nature. And, I might say, nature is not the master of us either. We are *part* of nature, part of this beautiful world. Nature is rationally organised and provides everything we need; part of that bargain is that we look after nature. We get to know the ways nature works, including accepting danger and death, and we live with that reality.

JOURNALIST: Danger and death?

The air was heavy with the scent of fruit and blossoms, their perfume released into the air by the sun.

MAYOR: There have always been natural events that have overcome us: floods, fires and the like. And then there are animals. There is danger in living somewhere like this: predators—human and animal predators so close. It's predictable unpredictability: you may be killed by a tiger when you hunt or you may be hurt by a landslide near your home.

JOURNALIST: These natural events are becoming more frequent, and more devastating.

MAYOR: It certainly feels that way, and the best scientific information backs up this feeling. The feeling of doom people have? It's not new. The ancient Stoics saw the end of the world as a natural process that was part of the regular functioning of the cosmos. Their largely agreed position was that human development is limited, and that humanity and world catastrophe are inextricably linked. Nature has imposed fixed and inexorable limits to human growth and development.

Perhaps nothing really changes. We're always preparing for the end of the world, every single century. We're always in mourning for a past that only exists as an imagined idyll.

We walked in the shady orchard. The Mayor named the trees and stopped from time to time to turn over a leaf, put it to his nose, and trace a finger along its ridges.

MAYOR: We have more than 250 species of fruit trees in this region alone. And countless medicinal plants. It's our food, our shelter, our pharmacy.

JOURNALIST: When the Stoics talk about nature, is it human nature or the natural world?

MAYOR: Both. I think of them as inseparable. The Stoics believed that our individual human nature is part of a wider universal nature and that the nature of the universe around us governs all things. If you want to know how something will be for you, look at how it is in nature.

JOURNALIST: If nature is out of whack, then we are also out of whack—or as you call it, homeostasis?

MAYOR: Yes. Everything encoded in us is encoded in nature.

JOURNALIST [*sadly*]: But now we are fully separate from nature and see nature as something to either dominate or extract materials and fuel from.

MAYOR: You think we are separate from nature? That's not actually possible. No matter how many hours you spend inside, with the lights on, in the AC, looking at a screen, we are, as much as we ever were, part of nature. You can't escape it. You can only hide from it. You can only deceive yourself.

The Mayor pulled the ripe fruit easily off the branches and it tumbled into his open apron—bright red plums and soft pink apricots.

MAYOR: It's such a shame that people don't understand that. Two thousand years ago Marcus said, 'Nature does nothing in vain, and so, whatever is, is for the sake of something else.' That's speaking to the interconnectedness of all things. You think we have broken those links? Pure arrogance. We are not that powerful. We are not gods, although many people have convinced themselves otherwise, on all sides: industrialists and environmentalists!

JOURNALIST: So can we still say we are part of nature like the Stoics once did?

MAYOR: It doesn't matter what we say. We are natural. But if you know it, if you are aware of it, then you take more responsibility for the state of the world out there. Treat it with greater respect. We have a group of hunters in the village, descended from other hunters. They know the forest around here well and the animals. And yes, they kill animals but not on a mass industrial scale. They only kill what they need. There is no waste.

We turned back towards the house, the Mayor with an apron full of fruit. He passed me a plum, ripened almost to the point of decay.

MAYOR: You must eat that at this moment! It will be delicious but only for another hour. Its time is almost up. We get our cues from nature too. Just as things in the natural world grow, bloom and decay, so do we. Nature is change, and so are we. We cannot express surprise at growing old when we see flowers bloom and die. 'Everything that happens in the world happens in accordance with the nature of the whole, and this nature is a rational one,' said Epictetus.

Just as nature is always changing, moving towards death, so are you! You are still young but when I go and see old friends in other places, after some time has elapsed, say ten years, I get a shock when I see them. Who is this almost unrecognisable old person standing before me? Of course it is my friend, who wouldn't have had that shock, because he sees himself every day. But he'd certainly get the same shock looking at me. I too have changed. And I'm changing every day or, to paraphrase Seneca, I am dying every day.

I knew what it felt like to be dying every day. That's what it was like in the hospital. It was different from the luxury of slow dying over the normal passage of time that the Mayor was talking about.

MAYOR: You look tired. Do you want to take a break? Go into town?

JOURNALIST: What I'd really like to do—

I suddenly felt exhausted, weak with fatigue—and even though it was still morning, I needed some more sleep.

—is sleep.

MAYOR: That's fine. I'll drive you back to the inn. You're probably still tired from your journey and I have to do a bit of work anyway, a meeting about changing Bin Day. It just drags on and on . . .

JOURNALIST: I thought this was a utopia?

MAYOR: Not when it comes to rubbish collection.

ANGER, ONLINE ABUSE, MOB VIOLENCE AND MASCULINITY

SILVER SPRINGS, Thida's Inn, Friday, 2 pm—A couple of hours later, I woke up from my nap, still exhausted to the marrow. I'd been dreaming of the journey here, how at one point the wound in my head had started to flow with dark-coloured blood and they wouldn't let me continue because they said I was a health and safety risk. 'Any concussive symptoms need to be monitored, preferably by your medical team,' the driver said with finality.

As I was pleading with them, the blood was gushing from my head. I turned away, hoping they wouldn't notice the flow.

Waking in a panic, I instinctively put my hand to my head. The wound was closed and dry. It was just a dream, the sort one had during the day that felt more real and nightmarish than the ones that happen at night.

Awake, all seemed normal. It was sunny outside, and great big washes of sunlight fell over everything, giving the room a pale yellow glow.

The room was as neat and cosy as when I first checked in. Thida had filled the pitcher with fresh water and returned my washing cleaned and folded.

Propped up on the pillows, feeling the luxury of being in a comfortable bed in the middle of the day, reading, I picked up the book the Mayor had given me before I left him in the square.

De Ira. On Anger. Ha. Apt. It was a slim book by Seneca, more of an essay than anything, that dealt with the Stoic approach to anger.

It opens with Seneca addressing his brother, Novatus, about anger. He advises him that he is 'right to be especially fearful of this passion—which above all others is hideous and wild'.

The reason this passion was the worst, to be feared above all passions, was because of the havoc it created—not just for the angry person, but for everyone else around them.

Seneca believed, 'No plague has cost the human race more. We see all around us people being killed, poisoned, and sued; we see cities and nations ruined. And besides destroying cities and nations, anger can destroy us individually.'

There was nothing ambiguous about the essay. It was anti-anger and, flicking through it, provided practical solutions to overcome the ugly emotion. An easy read, before I knew it I was halfway through.

Anger was a topic that had become interesting to me in the last few years, not least because I was in the grip of anger myself. My fuse was becoming shorter—along with my tolerance for discomfort, disagreement and things not going my way. I was getting angrier, but so was everyone else.

Even before the shooting I saw it everywhere. Even if I hadn't been looking out for it, it seemed like anger had become the connective tissue for so many things I was reporting on in recent years—domestic violence, road rage, shootings, conspiracy theories and the increasingly violent street and campus protests.

Then there was the lower-level stuff. It was a year or so ago that the signs started popping up. I mean literal signs: in doctors' offices, in shops, at the ticket counter at airports and train stations, places where there was some sort of interaction between people about goods and services. The signs were all about anger: requesting customers not yell at, abuse or assault the service staff.

I remember my mum seeing them and getting indignant. 'I do not have to be told to be civil to the doctor's receptionist,' she said.

But she was angry too—angry at the signs telling her not to be angry.

The signs didn't make me indignant. They made me feel depressed. What is our society becoming? I wondered why we had to be told.

In the meantime, all this anger created its own atmosphere—a miasma of stress on my screen, in the streets, in the shops, on the road. It was only after a day or two in Silver Springs, and the journey up here without the internet, that the miasma seemed to clear.

I thought of my shooter. He was angry.

It was as if something 'hideous and wild' had taken him over, as Seneca had said all those years ago. And now it had taken over me.

His anger was all over the internet. It ran right through his manifesto. The anger was in his eyes. The anger was in his hands.

There was no pleading with him. He was unmoved by the carnage and moved easily around the newsroom, as if he were one of us.

In my more reflective moments, I wondered if there was ever any use for anger. Why are we so angry these days anyway? And what was underneath it?

Entitlement? Sadness? Depression?

De Ira was written in a compelling style but as much as I would have loved to have stayed in bed reading, I was going to be late to meet the Mayor.

He was waiting for me downstairs. There was a small room, a snug, off to one side, with a fireplace and a few rugs and armchairs scattered around. Thida's dog, Bourdain, lay sleeping in a weak pool of sun.

MAYOR: You look better.

I was wearing a clean dress, and that fact alone made me feel like a million dollars.

JOURNALIST: Sleep is nature's nurse. That's what my mum used to say to me when I was sick as a kid.

MAYOR: It really is. As for nature's scourge, that would be anger. The Stoics had no time for it, and neither do I. It's pointless and destructive—and leaves everyone feeling bad, including the person who got angry in the first place.

The Mayor's tone was even, neutral—not showing any emotion about anger.

JOURNALIST: But it can actually feel good to express anger, to let off some steam.

Like I did before, over breakfast, and the night before when I had too much to drink.

MAYOR: It can initially; there's a release. 'Whoa—how good do I feel? I'm back in control.' Anger is asserting yourself when you feel out of control or the victim of an injustice. So you lash out. But what often happens? Say if it's domestic violence, the man might be trying to control his wife: she's looking at other men, she's always on her phone, what's she doing? He feels like he can't control her, so he hits her, puts her in her place! He has control again; she's subdued. He feels triumphant. For about thirty seconds. Then what happens? Often regret, deep regret. He can't take it back. Something between them broke when he hit her. Say the kids are there. They're not going to forget seeing Dad do that! They'll remember sixty years later.

JOURNALIST: And anyway, you can't control another person—that's outside your sphere of influence.

MAYOR: Yes. Yet still anger is used to try to control people in our orbit. Often it comes with massive societal costs. Look at road rage. Someone cuts you off with a sudden swerve into your lane. How dare they! You pull up next to them at the lights. You're furious; you have your kid with you in the car, they could have caused an accident! The injustice of it terrifies you: that they could so carelessly hurt you and hurt your kid. You're provoked, so you lash out. Get out of your car. They get out of their car. Before you know it, you've hit them. They're on the ground. Oh no! They're bleeding. You wanted to teach them a lesson, but not that. What does your kid see? Something horrifying, but they see—okay, this is how the adults react when they need to work something out. Straight to the reptile brain. No reason. So, you've become angry. You've lost control. You're in big trouble now. Courts, gaol, a criminal record. Your family is looking at you like you're a thug. Do you have regrets about your moment of anger? You bet! If only you had waited a minute before getting out of the car.

JOURNALIST: I read *De Ira*. Or some of it. It holds up even now, two thousand years later. 'My anger is more likely to do me more harm than your wrong.'

MAYOR: This book should be given out in every courtroom, every school, every shop and prison. It's as relevant and useful now as it was when Seneca wrote it. Healthiest habit to learn: take nothing personally! Someone cuts you off, okay maybe they're an arsehole, but that's their problem. They don't know me, they may have directed their action towards me but nothing personal. It's a reflection of their consciousness state. You're a practising Stoic. You have ataraxia now as your baseline state. You've got inner peace all the time. It's harder to get worked up into anger. Nothing can really trigger you. Other people's opinions, their moods, their anger: they can't touch you.

JOURNALIST: So walk away?

MAYOR: That's always an option. Always. You can walk away. You can make a joke. You can choose not to react. You can hum a tune or sing a song or even distract yourself with your phone, if that helps. Anger is not a new problem, and philosophers have been grappling with it for a long, long time. It's in the writings of Aristotle, Plutarch, the Buddha, Confucius and St Augustine. Anger crosses cultural and historical boundaries. It's a human problem.

JOURNALIST: I suppose societies have always had to manage it—to ensure that people don't destroy each other. So that the angriest people aren't the most powerful.

MAYOR: Marcus said it was not in our nature to be angry; we are fundamentally creatures of community. Others saw anger as something more innate and harder to overcome. And some people, including more recent feminist, anti-colonial and Black Lives Matter activists, believe anger can be a tool used to prick consciousness awake when there's been an injustice. Anger is political. Aristotle also saw anger as a response to pain or injustice but he urged moderation in the expression of anger.

JOURNALIST: That's the Golden Mean, right?

MAYOR: Yes. He said, 'For in everything it is no easy task to find the middle . . . anyone can get angry—that is easy—or give or spend money; but to do this to the right person, to the right extent, at the right time, with the right motive, and in the right way, that is not for everyone, nor is it easy; wherefore goodness is both rare and laudable and noble.' The Stoics took it further. They wanted to eradicate anger. But, of course, the control test being what it is, they knew the only place that their actions could really take effect was in themselves.

I tried to imagine a world without anger. What would it look like? What would it *feel* like? Would it be boring—like heaven sounded boring? Or would removing anger be nothing short of transformational for the world?

JOURNALIST: So what was their solution for eradicating anger?

MAYOR: The first thing to examine is our nature. Humans are social creatures; we're meant to work together, and anger drives us apart. Stoics believed that our nature as humans is fundamentally good. People exist for one another, remember? Society thrives from alliances. Here in Silver Springs, we are very community focused, although no one goes around saying that. No one even uses the word 'community'; it is just how things are organised, and how they have always been organised.

JOURNALIST: Like what?

MAYOR: We care for people when they are sick; everyone looks after each other's children and checks in on the old people. I had two different visitors already today, just dropping in to say hello, check if I need anything. In addition, we try to do things as cooperatively as possible, including holding land in common for growing and distributing food. I share my wine with the community, for example. It's nothing radical. But it means it's hard to really have disputes with people or get angry for very long, because our lives are so intertwined, and we depend on one another. You can't stay angry at someone you depend on. The dependency and the connectedness force you to try to work things out.

JOURNALIST: It was like that in the early days of the pandemic. Suddenly everyone was applauding the essential workers, many of whom were poorly paid gig economy workers who had few rights. We were meeting our neighbours; we were bartering. Trumpeting virtues like kindness and community. Then, a few months in, it reverted back to whatever we are in now.

MAYOR: Atomisation? Individualism?

I nodded and found a quote I liked and read it to the Mayor.

JOURNALIST: Seneca wrote in *De Ira*: 'Mankind is born for mutual assistance, anger for mutual ruin: the former loves society, the latter estrangement. The one loves to do good, the other to do harm; the one to help even strangers, the other to attack even its dearest friends.'

MAYOR: Yes. Essentially, they believed, and I believe, that anger is anti-human. It goes against our nature. And while the release of it may provide a short-term buzz, the comedown is terrible. Better to forgo the release and not pay the larger cost down the line.

JOURNALIST: Maybe it's worth sorting it into good anger and bad anger. Good anger is the anger at inequality, injustice, corrupt politics and big business crushing progress on climate change and wage growth. Bad anger is the fury of the entitled, the spoilt, the unruly, the mob, the driver who acted like the highway was all his and smashed up and terrified anyone who got in his way.

I felt protective of this righteous anger—it wasn't just reptilian; it was rational anger that could change the course of society for the better.

MAYOR: Isn't this just a matter of perspective? Those indulging in 'bad anger' would probably say that an injustice had been done to *them.* That they were just as entitled to their anger as the political anger you experience on causes you agreed with. Maybe a small business owner is angry at the government telling her she must increase wages at a time when her profits are slim. Why is one anger good and another bad?

JOURNALIST: Maybe because I judge it so.

MAYOR: And using your rational mind, do such judgements hold up?

JOURNALIST: There are societal norms—not everything is relative. I think no one would dissuade me from the anger I feel towards the man who shot me and my colleagues.

MAYOR: Did your thinking on anger change after you were shot?

JOURNALIST: Since the shooting I've been much angrier. And I was already pretty angry! So much of the pain and distress that I experienced, that my family experienced, that my colleagues experienced, that Lou experienced, is because of some selfish arsehole with a gun. I mean the entitlement of it! I would say anger often feels natural because the emotions under it feel legitimate to the person experiencing them. Someone has caused us suffering and we are angry as a result.

After the shooting, I felt so alone. I wanted everyone to experience the pain and loss that I had suffered. Lashing out, getting angry, was a way of spreading the pain around, so I didn't feel so burdened and lonely with it.

MAYOR: That feeling of suffering, fear and vulnerability is legitimate, but the response of anger is not. The Stoics had systematised a response to anger. First thing: resist anger from the very beginning. When you are provoked, use reason to override anger and stop it before it starts.

Seneca understood it. They all did: that anger has the power to carry us away and destroy reason. It's the ultimate passion. Seneca wrote, 'for if once it begins to carry us away, it is hard to get back again into a healthy condition, because reason goes for nothing when once passion has been admitted to the mind, and has by our own free will been given a certain authority, it will for the future do as much as it chooses, not only as much as you will allow it'.

Seneca describes anger as 'the enemy' that 'must be met and driven back at the outermost frontier-line: for when he has once entered the city and passed its gates, he will not allow his prisoners to set bounds to his victory'.

JOURNALIST: So once anger starts . . .

MAYOR: It's really hard to stop. But if you don't think you have been harmed, then you will not react as if you have been harmed. So use reason to assess whether that has happened. And, of course, take into account the only thing, for a Stoic, that can harm you is if you compromise your character: if your reactions are anger-fuelled; if you are not meeting those virtues; and if you don't treat others well.

JOURNALIST: If you use that lens, the only thing that can harm you is yourself.

MAYOR: React angrily to something, and you are the one who is being injured.

I remembered Lou quoting Warren Buffett to his reporters when they were upset about people criticising them on social media. 'You will continue to suffer if you have an emotional reaction to everything that is said to you. True power is sitting back and observing things with logic. True power is restraint.'

JOURNALIST: I would say emotions and emotional reactions feel natural, though. At school, we were encouraged to feel our feelings, not to suppress them.

MAYOR: Unfortunately, that is very stupid. The implicit lesson is that your emotions cannot be wrong, and it places your whole self at their mercy. No one says that to toddlers! Why say it to older children? Some emotions should be suppressed! When you unleash them, others suffer. Who are you to unleash your toxic shit onto other people?

JOURNALIST: Wow. Toxic shit? You almost sound angry.

MAYOR: Yes. And if I was angry, who would I be hurting? Maybe you, anger is a very contagious emotion, but mostly me. So be selective in what you express and how you express it. Interrogate your judgements. Consider your words.

JOURNALIST: Any advice on exactly how to do that?

MAYOR: There was a sorting mechanism the Stoics used, and it's related to what we talked about yesterday when discussing judgements. They believed there are two major forms of emotion: those arising from 'impressions', and those arising from our judgements. Impressions are often not within our control; they are almost physiological in origin, like a shiver when you're cold or a blush when you're embarrassed. This is opposed to a judgement, which we can control. A Stoic would register the impression, say being frightened at a loud noise, but then discover it was just a firecracker going off—

But what if it was a gun?

—but then use reason to override it, should it disrupt your tranquillity or not serve you in some way. In relation to the firecracker, you adjust your reaction so you don't feel afraid. The impact of the impression is slight, and as a result there is no loss of ataraxia. You can't control impressions but you can't respond impulsively to them either. This helps tame anger.

JOURNALIST: Do you use the control test when you get angry—or is there just no time to make those calculations?

MAYOR: The control test is all about applying reason to a situation. Being in reality. Looking at something clearly. Create that air pocket of time, that shock absorber, between the provocation and the reaction, then apply reason; apply the control test. Work out what you can control, and focus on those areas, rather than try to control things outside your realm. It's when we have a false sense of how much we can control that we become frustrated and angry because we are scared by our lack of control. We need to use reason to cool down anger.

JOURNALIST: Sometimes I wonder if there's a portion of the population that lacks reason.

MAYOR: Almost everyone has reason, except for the most mentally ill or demented. It's just whether or not you use it. In the Stoic tradition, emotions derive from impressions or judgements of things. The key is to sift truthful impressions from untruthful; through sound reasoning, which must be trained with logic. By not attaching an emotion or judgement to an issue, or stalling or changing a judgement, you are changing or adjusting your perception of the issue. All this is within your power, as long as you are aware and examine the judgement you're applying to a situation. Stalling making a judgement is a cognitive trick; you just slow down your thinking so you become more aware of what judgements you make. Greek Stoic Chrysippus likened emotions to running too fast. The idea was to slow down your emotions, or at least become conscious of them as they're arising, and, in slowing them, recasting or reconfiguring your judgement. And all of this is in service of ataraxia. Lack of worry. Calm. Ataraxia is the goal. Stabilise. Achieve emotional homeostasis always. Don't be rocked. If you're not rocked, there's no anger.

JOURNALIST: There are a lot of studies around anger, contagion, mobs, that show the communal nature of humans also has a dark side. We can congregate and whip ourselves into a frenzy of anger, and we've done so throughout history. Look at the witch-hunts. You should see the swarm that emerges from the ether in an online shaming! It's frightening! And because it's online, we don't see the consequences, we don't see how it can destroy some people. At least out there in the world, if you're smashing someone with your fist and they're on their knees, you can see it. You can see the damage. You have to look it in the eye.

The Mayor laughed.

MAYOR: 'Smashing someone with your fist?' Goldfish, sometimes you really worry me. I agree though, from what I have heard of the internet, that it does make people less accountable for their anger. The Stoics saw anger as a contagion, meaning that someone else's anger could infect you if it spread in a mob-like setting. Stoics, of course, didn't have to deal with social media but they were social beings who thought deeply about how the mob could incite high emotions such as anger. After all, they were often the victims of mob rule, when Roman emperors did periodic clean-outs and purges of philosophers. Nero, after being trained in Stoic philosophy and having employed Stoic advisers such as Seneca, set about purging Rome of the Stoics.

JOURNALIST: Nero was meant to be a real arsehole, from what I've heard. Murdered everyone—including his mum and brother?

MAYOR: He is generally regarded as pretty sociopathic. But Seneca tried to persuade him, appeal to his reason, particularly when he was younger.

JOURNALIST: Today sociopaths are off the leash. People who once might have just thought vile things are now very relaxed about putting those things into words. They're not even ashamed or mortified by their behaviour. The trolling I've experienced by just being a woman online with an opinion is very distressing.

MAYOR: It's interesting the way you put it. Are you so sure it's 'just' because you're a woman with an opinion? Why not a journalist? Why not a human? Beware the word 'just'. It's the finger pointing outwards, away from yourself. Try instead to ask yourself another question: why do you choose to be distressed? Why torment yourself by reading the comments? Is there a part of you that is actually craving anger? The strong emotion? The rise?

JOURNALIST: Says someone who has never been a victim of a social media pile-on!

MAYOR: Seneca said in *On Anger*: 'The man who tries to find out what has been said against him, who seeks to unearth spiteful gossip, even when engaged privately, is destroying his own peace of mind.' And Marcus said, 'You always have the option of having no opinion.'

JOURNALIST: Stoicism is asking a lot of me here—

MAYOR: Stop! I know where you're going with this, and it's straight to victim mode. It's needing to be right. Of course, people shouldn't be writing vicious things about you online, but you can't control them! You can only control your response, and your own character!

As for those misogynistic trolls, Marcus Aurelius believed that a real man was someone who could control his anger. In *Meditations* he wrote, 'And when you do become angry, be ready to apply this thought, that to fly into a passion is not a sign of manliness, but rather to be kind and gentle. For insofar as these qualities are human, they are also more manly.'

JOURNALIST: It's different now with toxic masculinity being fuelled by anger. There are whole parts of the internet that serve up content that gives this distorted picture of what a real man is. And often they target women who they think shouldn't be in public spaces. It's a contagion and it's spreading.

MAYOR: These men could do worse than to look to Marcus as a model of manhood. He wasn't weak; he was commanding armies, running an empire, on the front, making decisions. He did it with a rational mind. In 175 CE, towards the end of his reign, Marcus faced a civil war when the governor-general of the eastern provinces, Avidius Cassius, had himself acclaimed as a rival emperor by the Egyptian legion. Cassius was a cruel general, known to torture his prisoners of war and deserters. He criticised Marcus for being a weak and unmanly ruler, calling him 'a philosophical old woman'. But after only three months, Marcus won the civil war when Cassius's own officers ambushed him and killed him, and sent his head to Marcus as proof. Marcus knew you don't win the long game through cruelty.

JOURNALIST: That sounds like a gory time to be alive. But his advice on how to be a good man is all through *Meditations* and I reckon you could apply it today.

MAYOR: Yes. Marcus thought deeply about what it was to be a man, a good man. And a good man was not an angry man. He wrote, 'And when you do become angry, be ready to apply this thought, that to fly into a passion is not a sign of manliness, but rather, to be kind and gentle. For insofar as these qualities are more human, they are also more manly. It is the man who possesses such virtues who has strength, nerve, and fortitude, and not one who is ill-humoured and discontented.'

To be a good man, you have to be able to stand upright, that is, not to be held by others. Be self-reliant! You do this by developing the virtues. I think if Marcus took a spin around the internet today, he wouldn't recognise a lot of those men as being examples of good men.

JOURNALIST: Stoicism has a reputation where I am from, as being very much for men. It's all over the manosphere.

MAYOR: Manosphere? That sounds like a grim place, the opposite of Silver Springs, ha ha. Stoicism is for everyone. As we were discussing earlier, even back in the Roman days it was recognised as such. Musonius Rufus said sons and daughters should receive the same education, since those who train horses and dogs train both the males and the females the same way. He rejected the view that there is one type of virtue for men and another for women.

Two thousand years on, Stoicism is still applicable to everyone who is alive and seeking some sort of ethical framework. Being ethical is not gender specific.

There was a knock at the door—the sound of a small hand tapping. A head peaked around—Septimus. He was fresh from a bath and his hair was as sleek as a swimming cap.

'Pa!'

The Mayor broke into a gooey, goofy grin. He opened his arms wide. 'Come up here.' Septimus jumped on his knee and settled against his shoulder.

MAYOR: How about we break? I did promise you time to absorb the lessons, and it's heavy going just to do a dump of all the main points of Stoic ethics in a couple of days. I can recommend a lovely spot for contemplation.

—

A chill wind was passing through the mountains and I shivered as I walked to the edge of the woods by the old colonial churchyard and a disused astronomy station. My path was dappled with shadows and delicate shafts of light. I seemed to be the only one on the path, so I took off my shoes and socks and felt the hard delight of stone, moss and rock beneath my feet. All the textures, all the sensations, all at once, flowing from the soles of my feet through the nerve endings of my body. Sharp and soft, cold and hard, pain and pleasure.

This was a Stoic experiment—to walk barefoot to endure discomfort—but it didn't really seem like a hardship. The temperature had dropped but was not unpleasant, and walking barefoot slowed me down and enabled me to notice more things: the way the breeze moved softly on my skin, the handfuls of butterflies with golden wings, the shafts of sun poking through the trees.

There was no one nearby, and my hearing became more attuned to the sounds of nature around me. It was loud! Cicadas? The koels again? Walking through the woods, I was struck by a new sensation—it was lightness. Something I wasn't even aware that I was carrying had lifted.

The Mayor had said to be curious about how I felt about Stoicism—not to prejudge or shut down any of the ideas, but to listen, absorb, let them settle—then ask: how's this feeling?

But what was this lightness? I was curious about it.

About twenty minutes later, I reached a clearing where a lake reflected the lilac sky above like a mirror. I had it to myself, but it was evidently a popular spot.

Making sure there was no one else around, I stripped right off and dived in. It was freezing—but in a good way that made me feel very alive. I felt an affinity with cold plunge man.

Was this Stoicism? I was doing things that made me physically uncomfortable. I was taking on some voluntary hardship. But I was also feeling more awake doing these things than if I had just sat by the lake, or walked with my shoes on, or had not gone into the woods at all.

I finished my swim, dressed and sat on the grass; the clouds had broken up and my hair dried in the patchy sunlight and the breeze. But my thoughts turned to a darker place. My bandage had come off in the water, and putting my hand to my head, I felt the hollow and softness of my wound, the changed shape of my skull.

A feeling flared so quickly it could not be stopped. I was so angry that I had been shot. I was disfigured! I took a breath. But it *had happened*. I couldn't change it. That was reality. Now I wondered—as I relived my trip, through the jungle and up the mountain, consumed by the fire of anger and sorrow—if I had been suffering twice?

The Mayor didn't talk about forgiveness. It didn't seem to be in the Stoic lexicon. You could only control your response. But all his teachings indicated the unnecessary pain of carrying hatred and anger long after the initiating event had passed.

Maybe this too needed a ritual—where the people who had been wronged and those who committed the wrong came together and some sort of exchange took place. It could be a violent exchange—a payback—or it could be an exchange of sorrow and forgiveness. And in this, a release could happen.

I collected the bandage from the lilac-coloured water and wrung it out. The sun settled full on me; the koels kept calling, the insects hummed and the tears that had started when I was swimming now threatened to never stop. Why cry over parts of life, when all of it calls for tears?

I realised there would be no reckoning; there would not be the release that I sought and desperately needed; there would not be revenge, retribution or a remedy. Whatever I needed lay within myself. I had to let go of my own anger in order to find peace. And I had to do it here, now.

DESIRE, LOVE, MARRIAGE, THE HEDONIC TREADMILL

SILVER SPRINGS, The Old Bar, Friday, 4 pm—I rushed back, exhilarated, an almost autumnal gust of fresh, bracing wind at my back. The oaks were heavy with leaves turning from green to orange, and many of them flew through the air, spiralling in bright columns.

Turning a corner, I found myself back in the town square. It was quiet this time—just two old men playing chess in the north-west corner and clouds across the sun throwing columns of shadow and light. I met the Mayor back at the Old Bar where, being more careful this time, I ordered a fresh lime cordial.

MAYOR: Still angry at the world after spending an hour in nature?

JOURNALIST: Ha. No.

MAYOR: Funny that. Get your mind right, reject anger and you can get on with enjoying your life. Society generally sees anger as a bad thing but, interestingly, desire is something modern society celebrates. To desire or, more importantly, to be desirable to others is very highly esteemed. Desire keeps the economic system ticking along, and in a society of love matches, desire is the thing that sparks the start of a relationship and a family. But is it all good?

JOURNALIST: Seriously? Who cares? Do we really have any option but to desire what's attractive to us? Aren't you the one preaching to only try to control things that are controllable? How can I control whether I find someone attractive?

MAYOR: Is that the way you want to live, a slave to desire?

JOURNALIST: Yes.

I'd been in a lovely daydream on my way back from the lake. In my daydream I return back home with a strong story about this Stoic, quasi-utopian community. Lou publishes it. It's a sensation and gets interest from publishers and streaming services. I finish up at *The Sentinel* but have lots of offers of other work on the back of my Silver Springs story. Dominic visits. We get to know each other and fall deeply in love. Maybe we start a family too? Perhaps it was time for me. They were my desires. Didn't our yearnings and desires show us the way? Before the Mayor could start on a long sermon, I wanted to get my point across.

JOURNALIST: It's not all superficial. When we get what we desire, there's the thrill of achievement, a dopamine hit of success, and then actually receiving the thing you want, the desired outcome. How can the Stoics be against this? It can feel really satisfying.

MAYOR: For a start, desire is insatiable. You get one thing then you feel good but that good feeling fades, and then you want something else, and, well, for most people this goes on forever. Their desires control them, leaving them constantly craving the next thing. It really never ends. Have you ever met someone who, after getting the thing he lusted after, said, 'Okay, that's it, I'm done: no more for me'?

JOURNALIST: In love, sometimes people find 'the one'.

I was scanning the square, in case Dominic walked across. The Mayor followed my gaze. It would be different if we both had phones; we could just text each other. But just waiting to bump into him was sending my nerves into a frenzy. Right now, I couldn't control whether I saw him or not this afternoon. I just had to leave it to chance.

When I turned back to the Mayor, I saw he had a broad grin on his face. Not his rare half-smile, but a big, blazing smile.

MAYOR: 'The one?' It's a notion so seductive because it promises you that when you find 'the one', this constant, maddening craving for the next thing will cease. It promises that desire will stop irritating and frustrating you because it only has one object—

JOURNALIST: The one?

MAYOR: Yes. And once that 'one' has been found, we can finally get some peace from the endless, annoying itch of looking for the so-called perfect partner.

JOURNALIST: Which is a good thing, right?

MAYOR: It is. But stopping the annoying itch doesn't happen by magic. It happens through your own character and actions. A wise person knows that 'the one' is not found, but decided. What feels like an almost supernatural fit between two people is the result of decisions from both of them to commit to one person. And both people have to commit! We all know it's out of your control to force someone to commit to you. But if both commit, it is here that the rational merges with the romantic. Anyone who has been in this situation knows that finding the love of your life is not the end of suffering or desire. There's always the next thing: a house to buy, babies, promotions at work. And sexual desire for others never entirely goes away but is ignored or subordinated by an ongoing commitment.

Suddenly I wanted what he had.

I have heard about these dating apps, and social media. They probably make things harder. They steer you away from commitment with the illusion of endless choice.

JOURNALIST: People end up paradoxically feeling empty. I know I did. Empty and used up, like a disposable coffee cup. But also like I was using other people. So how did the Stoics do love and marriage?

MAYOR: The ancient Stoics never wrote much about romantic love. It's a bit frustrating trying to guess. But their preference was for marriage, strong marriages where mutual support, companionship and family could flourish.

JOURNALIST: Pretty traditional.

I wondered if they had affairs. They had lived a long time ago, but they were flesh and blood, just like us.

MAYOR: Go back far enough and 'traditional' doesn't mean anything. The Ancients approached love and passion with caution. They saw how these things could throw you off balance, out of ataraxia, and leave you in turmoil. Reason goes out the window when you're in the grip of infatuation. If ataraxia is the key, if reason is of high importance, if the virtues are paramount, then becoming feverish and in the grip of infatuation or a crush is incompatible with all that. 'Not to display anger or other emotions; to be free of passion and yet full of love,' said Marcus. Once again, there's that tension. But it's achievable, you can walk that line.

JOURNALIST: To be free of passion and yet full of love . . . But doesn't passion lead to love? Without passion igniting between two people, how can there be passionate love?

MAYOR: Passionate love is essentially a preferred indifferent.

JOURNALIST: Love, an indifferent? Love is like oxygen. Without it we die!

MAYOR: That's the multi-trillion-dollar romance industrial complex talking. Think about it. You can't control if someone loves you back. Love is not a virtue. So what do you do with it? You would prefer to have love than not. Mutual commitment is not guaranteed to come your way, so you must be indifferent to it. Enjoy it and cherish it while it's there in your life. But don't expect it to be there forever.

JOURNALIST: So no long marriages for Stoics?

MAYOR: Why does that follow? The first flush of love can't last for any couple. Like everything, relationships change, mature. A person addicted to that rush, the breathless feeling of being in love, is a person condemned to a lonely life. I'm no expert on love and marriage—I only have my own, singular experience—but I would say a Stoic would be more likely to make a marriage work. Companionship, commitment, the happiness and the stability of children: these things are important. Passion is not all it's cracked up to be.

JOURNALIST [*sarcastically*]: Something to aspire to.

MAYOR: Actually, yes. Something to aspire to. That's what I had with Sandra. It was pure lust at the start and then it changed and became something else. Not better, not worse, just something else. And then she became ill. That was extremely hard to bear but I just had to keep reminding myself that I had no control over how long this thing would last. How long she would last. I would last. Our love would last. It was a real reminder to enjoy it while you have it. You know how we just talked about nature?

JOURNALIST: Yes.

MAYOR: Well, the Ancients said that love was analogous. Love, Epictetus said, 'has been given to you for the present, not that it should not be taken from you, nor has it been given to you for all time, but as a fig is given to you or a bunch of grapes at the appointed season of the year. But if you wish for these things in winter, you are a fool.'

JOURNALIST: So for everything there is a season? Even in love?

MAYOR: Love can endure but it changes over the years. Think of all the different types of love there are. If we're lucky, we get to experience them all. There's love in a long marriage, and there's love at first sight when you get a spark of attraction, and there's love of an object: a favourite dress or piece of furniture or even your drink of choice. Oh—I love that type of chocolate!

JOURNALIST [*with some bitterness*]: But tough luck if you don't meet the right person?

MAYOR: Do you want to know the secret to finding love?

Yes! I leant in.

Seneca said, 'I shall show you a love potion without a drug, without a herb; without the incantation of any sorceress: if you want to be loved, love.'

I grimaced. Easier said than done.

MAYOR: C'mon . . . what's on your mind? I can sense you are in the grip of something that's making you agitated.

I had seen the Mayor's stern side. I didn't want him to write me off as foolish, for becoming infatuated so quickly.

JOURNALIST: I am just having trouble with how unromantic this aspect of Stoicism is.

MAYOR: Be in romance or be in reality . . . that's the choice.

JOURNALIST: Maybe I choose to be in romance.

I looked around the square. A group of men walked past and sat on benches in the dappled sun. Was Dominic among them? No.

I have feelings for Dominic! They started as soon as I met him! I really like him—and it's killing me! It's hard to explain, but when you know, you know.

MAYOR [*smiling*]: Can you control if Dominic feels the same level of affection for you?

JOURNALIST: No.

MAYOR: So why compromise your ataraxia? Why become unbalanced?

JOURNALIST: Are you kidding? Do I have a choice?

MAYOR [*sighing*]: Don't get carried away. You've come so far in just a couple of days. But desire is the passion that really trips people up.

Epictetus states the Stoic position starkly: 'Freedom isn't secured by filling up on your heart's desire but by removing your desire.'

Aristotle called it '*appetence*', a longing or craving, and it was something shared with animals. It doesn't involve reason and deliberation. Epictetus says, 'If you want some good, get it from yourself.'

I found myself glowering. This was killing my buzz. Surely if desire was found in nature, if it felt good, if it enabled our species to continue, it was a good thing?

JOURNALIST: What about you? Obviously you were married to Sandra, but since she died—sorry if this is intrusive—have you been interested in anyone else? Or even just felt desire?

MAYOR: I try to desire only the things that are in my power to control.

It was a cold answer. I wondered if it were true.

JOURNALIST: Let me guess—your character, your actions and reactions and how you treat others.

MAYOR: Okay, I'll square with you. Yes, I desire. That's the sad thing about growing old! Always the same old desires. Maybe wrangling them gets easier over the years. But I don't become invested in these passing passions. I know I can only control certain things. And so I desire to be a better person, to develop my courage, to be more moderate, to not be so quick to anger, to respond to people with kindness. I can actually control all those things.

JOURNALIST: What if you meet a really attractive person—surely that's exciting? Surely you can let yourself desire them?

MAYOR: I can, of course, desire them but remember the tension in Stoicism. I can feel desire, but I should not expect the outcome that I desire.

JOURNALIST: Is that the secret to happiness—only wanting what you can control getting?

MAYOR: There is no secret to happiness. Except the open secret that anyone who chases happiness won't find it. If what you want instead is contentment—ataraxia—then remembering what you can control and what you can't is the key. And you can't control if someone loves you back. Or even likes you!

All the rejection came back to me, hitting me with wave after wave of shame.

JOURNALIST: That's happened to me, being ghosted. It's the pits.

MAYOR: Did you notice how quickly your happiness flipped to sadness when that happened?

JOURNALIST: Yes—it was like when you get a sudden shift in the weather—like this afternoon. As soon as I realise I'm being ghosted, I shift from elated to devastated. I know I'm kinda average looking, but it makes me paranoid that I'm not pretty, that I'm a monster!

MAYOR: You've fallen out of emotional homeostasis right there.

JOURNALIST: But I still struggle to see how I can control desire. I find the Stoic interpretation—or maybe it's your interpretation—troubling, possibly even wrong. I'm sure two thousand years ago the Ancients got a lot right about human nature but we have made so many more discoveries, particularly in the last hundred years, about what makes us tick. I think we have come a long way from the time when we saw managing desire via reason—and were able to use reason to turn desire on and off like a tap. People need to be loved—and loved by the person they have chosen. It's one of the greatest—if not *the* greatest—human drives.

I sighed and it all came out in a rush.

Then there's all this . . . yearning. You know how transformative love can be. If someone loves you, if you are special to just one other person, then it just makes the shit things in life easier to bear. You have someone by your side, someone on your team, someone to look forward to seeing when you go home at night. So much of what I have to bear in my job, with my family, with the uncertainties of life, is harder without someone by my side.

MAYOR [*softening*]: Goldy, this part of Stoicism is the most difficult to absorb. That, and the teachings on death and grief. Neuroscience, the subconscious, the role of trauma, we are beginning to understand how all these things interplay with desire. But what you are saying, when you divorce reason from desire, is that we have little or no control over desire, which I disagree with. Where I see Stoicism as having a place amid the modern knowledge we have around desire is that desire springs from strange places. Our urges can be inexplicable and weird, even to ourselves. Patterns are stamped on our psyche from past experiences; we can find it difficult to shift outside these patterns that limit us.

But in this, in how we act on desire, we always have a choice. We always have reason.

The temperature suddenly dropped again, and a new, nasty wind swept through the square, sending a chessboard flying and the old men scrambling for the pieces.

Remember, what I said earlier? Chrysippus talks about our reactions, specifically desire, as being like a dog tied to a cart that is rolling down a hill. Once it starts moving and you are tethered to it, you are helpless to its force. But you can stop it before it starts rolling. That's in your power.

JOURNALIST: Theoretically maybe. But who has that sort of presence of mind?

MAYOR: That's where Stoicism comes in and your Stoic training. Marcus was stripping desire and desirability back to its barest elements when he wrote 'as for sexual intercourse, it is the friction of a membrane and, following a sort of convulsion, the expulsion of some mucus'.

JOURNALIST: Oh my god, what? That's the opposite of erotica.

MAYOR: He was demystifying the things we claim to be desirable. What we should desire is to be good people. That is within our control.

JOURNALIST: Easy for him to write off desire. He had more power and wealth than pretty much anyone in the world. Every desire he had in life, he would have had the means of sating. These powerful men used to fuck their most gorgeous young slaves. I've read about it.

The Mayor raised an eyebrow.

MAYOR: All the more reason to listen to what he says. Marcus wrote about the temptations of beautiful slaves but said he never took sexual advantage of them, because such actions would have been damaging to his own character. You can be as rich as Seneca or Marcus Aurelius and be able to have everything you want, but ultimately that treadmill of desire, the hedonic treadmill as it's called, will run your life if you let it. As you know, you'll never be fully happy, as long as you are trapped in this cycle. The hedonic treadmill: where you never stop because as soon as you fulfil one desire, the next one pops up.

JOURNALIST: It's like whack-a-mole.

MAYOR: The Stoics distinguish between two forms of what they called 'eros', what we might call sexual desire. There is the passion built out of defective judgements that take over and warp your mind. This type of desire is characterised by possessiveness, jealousy, control and overheated emotions. That is a disturbed form of eros. But eros is natural as you say, and therefore cannot be bad, because it comes from nature. And so a Stoic would channel a positive form of eros that doesn't hold too tightly to an outcome.

JOURNALIST: An outcome?

MAYOR: The first lesson, go back to that, is that you can't control other people. And in this situation, you definitely can't control the object of your affection. So enjoy the eros, follow where it leads, but keep your reason and always remember where control lies.

JOURNALIST: That sounds sensible, which is the very opposite of eros. I love the instability of eros, the chaos, the mystery—the fact that it can come and hit you out of nowhere and reorder and destabilise your life.

MAYOR: A romantic viewpoint. Some people live for it. They love the drama.

JOURNALIST: It makes me feel alive. Connected! Excited! What is love, if not derangement? Love is a serious mental disease.

MAYOR: Ha—Plato! Beware, Goldfish. Remember everything we have discussed. Yes, it's fun. Like hunger, sexual desire builds. When you are hungry, eat. When you desire someone, go to them. Just don't pin too much on the outcome.

I couldn't help but smirk—was the Mayor advocating free love?

I was young in the sixties. I fed my hunger at every opportunity.

JOURNALIST: Were there a lot of opportunities? Or shouldn't I even ask?

MAYOR: There were a lot, for a while. Then things changed. As they always do. And, of course, I met Sandra. But enough about me. For you, the control test offers a way out of the derangement, if you want to take it. If you only desire what you can control, if you limit it right down to things that are up to you, not external to you, then you have a decent shot at fulfilling all desires. The benefit of realising where our control lies, which is in a tiny field, is the feeling of tranquillity or inner peace. Inner peace can come from realising that we don't really control much in life, so let the chips fall where they may. You can relax then; put down your weapons. You let life just unfold and you accept what occurs. How great would that be?

JOURNALIST: Maybe this is my near-death experience talking, but I want a passionate life. I want to lose myself in love. I want to lose myself in what pleasures are left. Anyway—it's a natural pleasure. It's not harming anyone.

MAYOR: Except yourself.

JOURNALIST: Maybe I choose passion instead of tranquillity . . .

MAYOR: I understand if you find it hard to swallow some of the teachings. Both Epictetus and Seneca wrote in many ways quite flippantly about love, saying you lose your love or lose your friend; it's okay, just replace them with another person. Epictetus said, 'With regard to whatever objects give you delight, are useful, or are deeply loved, remember to tell yourself of what general nature they are, beginning from the most insignificant things. If, for example, you are fond of a specific ceramic cup, remind yourself that it is only ceramic cups in general of which you are fond. Then, if it breaks, you will not be disturbed. If you kiss your child, or your wife, say that you only kiss things which are human, and thus you will not be disturbed if either of them dies.'

JOURNALIST: What? That's actually quite unhinged! How can you not be disturbed if your child or wife dies? Were you not disturbed when Sandra died?

The Mayor looked at me. In his green eyes I saw immense sadness.

MAYOR: What do you think?

I was silent for a moment. The resonant, regular note of the koel sounded across the valley.

JOURNALIST: I think you couldn't replace her as you would a ceramic cup.

MAYOR: That's right.

JOURNALIST: Because she's irreplaceable, right?

MAYOR: For me, yes. For a better Stoic than I, there are plenty more cups in the cupboard. Plenty more fish in the sea.

He said the last line with such resignation it almost broke my heart.

JOURNALIST: I don't believe you. And anyway, I'm here to tell you, there aren't. And don't tell me you don't think the same. I can see it in your eyes.

MAYOR: This is not about me.

JOURNALIST: Yes it is! I'm meant to be interviewing you!

The Mayor suddenly started laughing.

MAYOR: I had forgotten. All I would say on love and desire is that you can't control if someone else loves you. Or how passionately they love you. Or if they even think about you at all.

JOURNALIST: So love, but with the brakes on?

MAYOR: Love, but be in reality.

He glanced across the square, looking at the men looking at me.

Have fun with Dominic. He's a great person, although he's broken more than a few hearts around here. Funny, I knew him from when he was born, and now here he is, causing all sorts of interesting complications, all because of a sharp jawline! Just go into these things with a light heart, a good heart, the virtues, a sense of curiosity, no expectations of an outcome, no expectations that you will be able to control him or change him. Just love.

JOURNALIST: That's all?

MAYOR: That's all. Just love.

The Mayor sat back and I felt a surge of compassion for him. He had lived with and loved Sandra for almost half a century—longer than I had been alive and, in the end, he couldn't side with the Stoics and their ridiculous replaceable cups.

MAYOR: The things you value—justice, love, eros, friendship—are all beautiful things, compatible with the virtues. Exercise moderation, keep coming back to the control test. I know you struggle with this, and you are not the only one. It comes up a lot at the Stoa. Every week.

Oh no—do other women also talk about falling for Dominic?

This philosophy was and is not meant to be detached from life, and the emotions that come from being human, but is meant to work intimately with the things that cause us the most pain: grief, love, loss and our own mortality. The Stoics went right into the messiness of life, as opposed to this idea that they were standing remote from it.

The Mayor looked at his watch and startled.

Where did the time go? We're going to be late for the Stoa!

ON BEING BUSY, THE CONTROL TEST

SILVER SPRINGS, The Stoa, Friday, 5 pm—I promised the Mayor that our visit to the Stoa would be off the record, and so I turned my dictaphone off. But I did jot down a few notes and was thankful the meeting this week was held in English, as a courtesy to me.

In the centre of town, off the main square, there was a painted porch that had a faded sign nailed to the verandah: 'Stoa'. Under the porch was a door, which opened to a large, bare room, where meetings were held each week.

High-ceilinged, slightly dusty and with only one working light bulb that swung overhead, we could have been at an AA meeting, an adult education class or a parent–teacher conference. There was an urn and biscuits in the corner, wooden chairs and stools made from tree stumps. The famous Stoa! I was a bit disappointed about how drab it all seemed. The Mayor talked about it being the centrepiece of the town, the heart of this great Stoic experiment, but it was Quaker-level plain.

Three people ran the meeting—the Mayor, a young man I had seen at Adi's restaurant the night before and an officious woman who was carrying a copy of *Meditations* as if it were the Rosetta Stone. There were about forty people of various ages—men, women and some teenagers—sitting around flicking through their notebooks, marking up pages of Seneca's *Moral Letters*.

The meeting started with a short reading—this one a letter from Seneca, number 106, about being busy. It had been the set text the week before—and the group had spent the week mulling over it, what it meant and how it might apply to them.

The Mayor read aloud from *Moral Letters*: 'My tardiness in answering your letter was not due to the press of business. Do not listen to those sort of excuses; I am at liberty; and so is anyone else who wishes to be at liberty. No man is at the mercy of his affairs. He gets entangled in them of his own accord, and then flatters himself that being busy is the proof of happiness.'

Everyone shook their heads saying they knew many people like that—they may have even been like that themselves!

'Choose not to be busy. Make that your number one organising principle. Each day get up and say—today I will not be busy,' said the Mayor. 'Today I will not be busy: repeat after me.'

'Today I will not be busy.'

Until it rose to a shout 'TODAY I WILL NOT BE BUSY'—and the ice was broken as peals of laughter rang around the hall.

'How on earth do I get things done?' asked one anxious-looking man. 'Three children, a tea house to tend, hobbies!'

'Your day can be full: that is satisfying, to have a full day . . . but busy, that's not something you want to happen very often. Particularly not if you are using "busy" as a brag, to make yourself more important than those around you. Every time you say "I'm so sorry I haven't seen you, I've been so busy", you are just saying "I prioritise another task above seeing you",' said the Mayor. 'We actually do have time, so much more time than those in the rich world, who must keep toiling in order to pay their housing debts or their car loans.'

The week's work was to journal about how busy we thought we were versus how busy we were in reality.

'You will not be as busy as you think,' said the Mayor. 'But write in your journal about it this week, and make note of how much free time you have and then do what you can, what is in your power to do, to increase that free time.'

'And what should we do with that free time?' asked one woman.

'Why, Kyi, read philosophy, of course,' said the Mayor. 'Spend time with your friends, your husband, your children. Ride your bike up to the square and have a tea, watch the world pass by. Lie under a tree and see the clouds race above you. Those are wonderful uses of time.'

Each person at the meeting was a student of Stoicism but also was facing a variety of problems that people anywhere might face. For two days now the Mayor had been telling me that Silver Springs wasn't a utopia, and listening to people's very universal (even banal!) problems that evening made me realise the truth of that.

In the Q and A session, one man who farmed tea in the nearby hills wanted to know how philosophy could help him survive the stress and uncertainty of wild weather patterns that threatened his crops. There was a woman who was worried about money and the mental health of her sick and out-of-work husband, and there was a crying woman who was coming to terms with her husband leaving her for another man.

The Mayor, using the principles of Stoicism, attempted to answer them.

'Everything we face, the Ancients have faced, but without technology. Every answer we seek, they can provide. There is nothing new under the sun,' the Mayor said. 'Think of the philosophy as medicine. And as a community, we are all learning to apply the remedy to one another.'

I cornered the Mayor during the break. 'But surely a woman having lost her husband to another man—that's not a problem the Ancients would have faced? How on earth do you help her?'

The Mayor laughed. 'You think this kind of situation is a new thing? Now people have a lot more freedom to pursue their sexuality, to live openly, but the problem is age-old, and that is: my spouse no longer loves me in the way he used to. Apply the Stoicism to that—go on.'

'Okay—so first the control test.'

'Yes. And she can't control him, can she?'

'No. She can only control her response. She can act with virtue—probably using wisdom and courage. And she has to realise that all things change.'

'Precisely.'

'It sounds like she has to bear the burden of a shitty situation though—when you put it that way.'

'She can only control herself and her responses, and that burden is hers alone. But she is resilient. Once the shock wears off, she will be okay; I know it.'

'Plenty more cups in the cupboard,' I said and the Mayor laughed.

For the second half of the meeting, Thida, helping her father, divided the participants into groups of three.

'These are sharing circles,' Thida explained to me. 'Each person talks about a challenge they faced that week, and the others in the group advise and apply Stoicism to that particular situation. The whole point is to support each other, but also think critically about how problems could be tackled, solved or simply accepted.'

I moved around the groups, observing.

'If I can't control something, then I don't worry about it, especially if the class I'm teaching is being difficult,' said one man. 'And I've found that kids thrive in homes and schools where the adults are emotionally robust and even-tempered.'

A man dressed in heavy hunting boots said that visitors often noticed in the tea house how people were pleasant and relaxed with each other, even when things went awry: the generator not working, or food shortages. No one got angry or upset.

The woman whose husband left her for another man was running her situation through the control test. I could see it frustrated her—that she wanted him to change, to be sorry, to come back to her. But as she admitted, all these wants were out of her control.

Stoicism could be harsh medicine. I knew that now, well.

But after two hours together, there was a lightness in the room—a warmth they all shared. I sat on the edges of the circles, before they spilled out into the cold night and around the corner for supper—and wanted to be part of the discussion, not just sitting on the outside, reporting.

ACCEPTING REALITY

SILVER SPRINGS, Town Square, Friday, 7 pm—But, as interesting as the discussion was, there was only one thing on my mind. I had a plan—and felt optimistic and energised by it. I would stay. What was waiting for me back at home? No job. My friends had been killed. Others had moved on. Yes, I had my mum, Caroline and now Hannie, but I felt the future was here.

Staying, getting this future, was—of course—out of my control. But like the archer, I could aim my arrow in the right direction and hope for favourable conditions. After the meeting was over, the Mayor and I walked out together, and I seized my moment.

JOURNALIST: Do you think—I hate to ask—but do you think you could extend my visa? I mean, what I saw back there, the model for how people support each other, solve disputes, come to solutions. I think if I had more time, it's a model I could bring back down the mountains, to my own country. As you know—things are broken where I'm from.

I was excited by what I saw at the Stoa—people helping people, but in a framework of ancient philosophy. Maybe I could apprentice myself to the Mayor for a bit? Then, if I had to return, roll out the model in communities back home, just like the Mayor had suggested the previous night. Forget just writing about it—we could build Silver Springs all over the world!

The Mayor looked at me with immense sympathy—as if there was nothing he would like to do more, but . . . but. He didn't reply but his face told me everything.

JOURNALIST: C'mon. Three days is not very long at all! I'm still tired from the journey—you've seen it, sleeping during the day, the exhaustion—I . . . and there are other people I'd like to speak to for the story. Plus I need other voices for the podcast.

MAYOR: That wasn't part of the original deal. Reality, Goldfish.

We walked up an unpaved street by the cliffs, back towards the square—the sky a dark navy blue, the mountain ridges tinged with gold in the dusk, and all around flew flocks of birds, heading to their evening shelter. The moment was shot through with a sublime beauty—all the more so because it was fleeting. Soon it would be fully dark.

As if he were reading my mind, the Mayor turned to me.

MAYOR: It's very beautiful here. That's what I thought when I got here. It's too beautiful to leave. And if I left, I knew it would haunt me forever. I'd never stop thinking about it, and about the life I could have led here.

JOURNALIST: Yep. That's how I feel—so how about it? Just another week? What would another week hurt?

I was reduced to pleading but wasn't it the Romans who taught the art of rhetoric and persuasion alongside philosophy? You might come up against the limits of control, but you could always make a case for yourself.

MAYOR: Isn't that what everyone wants? Just a little more time? But when they realise they are running out of time, when they realise how precious and unique it all is, it's usually too late.

JOURNALIST: What do you mean?

MAYOR: Tomorrow morning is our final interview. We talked about the mind on Day One, Thursday. Today was the body. Tomorrow, Saturday—the spirit.

JOURNALIST: So I must go tomorrow?

MAYOR: I'm afraid so. You can't overstay your visa.

I bristled.

JOURNALIST: Why not?

MAYOR: The visa rules are very strict. They have to be. Otherwise we'd be overrun, and we're simply not big enough to cope with extra people. It only works if we're able to carefully manage visitor numbers.

JOURNALIST [*becoming irritated*]: The rest of the world deals with immigration—I don't see why that's something you can't do here. Why can't you grow?

MAYOR: Oh, I'm sorry, Goldy. Don't look so crestfallen. Reality. Reality. Look at things with clear eyes. You always knew it was three nights and three days. You applied for the visa. You signed the paperwork. You *lined up* for the paperwork. This was always the deal.

JOURNALIST: But you got to stay.

MAYOR: I fell in love. I had to stay.

JOURNALIST [*clinging*]: What if this is love? With Dominic? Doesn't that count? And don't say it's only been two days! How long before you knew with Sandra? I bet you knew straight away.

MAYOR: I knew. How does Dominic feel about you?

JOURNALIST: I don't know yet . . . but maybe . . .?

MAYOR: Goldfish . . .

I felt frustrated and not a little despondent by the time we got to the town square. Adi had set up long trestle tables, lit with lanterns, near his restaurant for everyone from the Stoa and placed steaming plates of pickles, rice, tofu, pork and vegetables along the tables. But despite it looking and smelling delicious, my appetite was gone. Pleading a headache, I left the square determined to find Dominic, to see—or even to ask—how he felt about me. The answer could change everything. Looking back, I noticed the Mayor's eyes were on me, as I slipped down a side street.

—

The twilight had ended as suddenly as a slammed door, and it was now dark. The outlines of the mountains that ringed the town could still be seen in the distance—looking like a cardboard stage set, while the famous stars were covered by clouds.

Dominic had mentioned a house party in one of the old British officers' holiday quarters. I wandered the dark streets until I came to some flimsy huts blazing with candlelight, and an old Union Jack flag depicted in faded and cracked paint on the side of the main building.

Pushing open the door, a girl whom I recognised from Adi's the night before shrieked, dragged me in and gave me a large cup of straight rum. Yum. It was the good stuff. The walls were a stage for our shadows, moving shapes around the creeping mildew and runaway vines. An old portrait of the girlish Queen askew on the wall, a crisscross of wooden oars, a sepia print of some long dead young British men with guns, astride a magnificent tiger that was freshly killed. It hit me as hard as the rum: look deep into the eyes of those young British men—and you will see the past, with its changing empires that rose and fell, and then you can foresee the future too.

I realised Stoicism had me looking at everything differently.

There was a young guy I recognised from the group in the square, playing ragtime on the piano while people were swaying. I was brought into a huddle, when he started playing Simon and Garfunkel's 'The Boxer'. It was the wrong tempo but no one seemed to notice and everyone sang too quickly and I swayed and went from feeling like an outsider to part of some glorious and silly fellowship. The last time I felt that way was a spontaneous night out with colleagues. It had been another awards night when we'd come back empty-handed. But instead of making our own separate ways back home, we'd found ourselves at a karaoke bar in Chinatown—all singing Aretha Franklin, screaming the words at the top of our lungs. And before that—the school choir. And before even that—me, my mum and my sister singing harmonies of songs we heard on the car radio, tuned to my mother's favourite easy listening station that repeated the songs of the sixties and seventies.

Now—in Silver Springs, another song in and calling for another cup of rum, I felt a surge of love and affection, and even compassion, for my fellow choristers. We were all in this thing called life together. We would all have our own sufferings and all of us would die. How could I not have compassion for my fellow humans? After all, we were destined to experience the same hardships, but to go through them all alone.

I stayed with the singers a bit longer. People seemed to know my name, kept passing me more cups of the sweet rum, and the pianist sang 'Moon River' and we swayed some more.

In a piercing moment of clarity—and insight that almost brought me to my knees—I saw it so clearly now. The exquisite preciousness of everything and interconnectedness of everyone and everything. All separation fell away. Our differences were only cosmetic. After all, we were built of the same matter, fragments of the same stars, brought together at this brief moment in time. It was a miracle really when you consider the vast span of history and space. As soon as I felt this, I got excited, tried to grab it, but then it slipped away. What did Lou call that fleeting, precious moment? Sartori!

Then from the corner of my eye—Dominic. He was sitting across the room, grinning right at me, and I moved towards him, and started dancing.

'I didn't think you'd come,' he said.

'I got so lost.'

'Oh man, how can you get lost here—there's only three streets in the whole town . . .'

'C'mon, let's get out of here,' I said to Dominic. He grabbed my hand and we slipped out the back door, where his motorbike was resting up against the fence.

—

'Why didn't you talk to me when you brought me up to Silver Springs? I thought you resented coming to get me,' I asked. It felt like months ago, but it had only been two nights.

Dominic sighed. 'It's a pain in the arse to be ferrying people up and down the mountain. They all want to know the same thing: what's it like in Silver Springs? What's the Mayor like? Are we really the happiest place on Earth? Am I happy? And if I'm happy, why don't I smile more? It's annoying. I feel like an animal in the zoo, being studied for clues.'

'So are you happy?' I asked.

'Sometimes. But there's no great secret to be found. If you want to be happy, just be happy. Just live—and experience life and have a good time. Don't worry too much about anything. I don't get how you people complicate things and make it so much harder,' said Dominic with a shrug.

We were sitting in the hollow of a tree's branches at the edge of what Dominic called the Black Lake. Like the night before, he held my hand.

My heart was beating so fast, I thought I might go into cardiac arrest. In profile, up close it was Paul—just as I remembered him, a little bit older, but if I squinted a little—it was Paul.

How had we got from the basement to the bedroom? How did we get from the party to the lake? How could it be so easy just to take another person's hand and be led to a quiet place that promised intimacy and pleasure?

Or maybe the question was—how, in the intervening years, had it become so difficult, so awkward? When did everything become so cold and everyone so untrusting? When did I become so cold and untrusting—maybe the better question.

Dominic smiled in a sweet, lopsided way, moved closer and put a hand on my leg. Then he moved a bit closer. Such simple pleasures, available to us since the dawn of time. Another body, touching someone else's skin, friction and release. Easy smiles, sighs in the dark, and the deep calming sleep after that felt like a hospital coma.

I took off my shoes. The air was still in the forest, paused—as though it was holding in a breath. My feet felt the moss, I sunk my toes in. My feet felt the carpet as Paul led me up the stairs.

Gently stoned, a roar subsiding in my ears, someone playing Pearl Jam from another bedroom. He lay me down, pulled down my jeans and then my pants and then quickly took off his top and jeans as if we didn't have much time, as if he knew we had to hurry. His skin was hot to touch. He smiled, and whispered my name in my ear and then called me baby, and we were ready, we were ready to go . . .

'What are you thinking about?' asked Dominic. 'You've suddenly gone far away.'

'My mother.'

'Ugh—why?'

'Do you know you remind me of a boy I used to know? So much. It's like you're him.'

'But I'm me. And you're . . .' He bent his head to mine and whispered my name in my ear and we started kissing deeply and I knew then that I never wanted to go home.

The infinite sea of yearning that was always inside me started to recede, and the relief of letting go was physical.

Suddenly—it came over me. It was that familiar feeling that I had coming up the goat track with Dominic two days ago. It was like the resolution of unconscious longing, a coming back to something that I never had but we all need. Tonight there was nothing more I wanted than what I had.

Dominic shifted and lay above me, removing clothing as he went, and whispered that I was more than just pretty, I was *beautiful.* By now, I was drowning in anticipatory pleasure that was more than just the effects of the rum.

When I first heard the sounds, I thought they were my moans, then I thought they were cicadas, loud and incessant. Then when

Dominic stopped, moved off me and turned his head to listen with a worried frown—I knew it well enough to recognise it now.

'Fire call.'

Standing up, we could see the black sky in the distance lit with red tongues of fire, the smoke like nighttime clouds filling the air and obscuring the stars.

The sirens kept their rhythm, and I struggled to find my pants and pull on my boots.

'Do we have to go?'

'Yes—fire call, and I need to be out there with my group,' said Dominic, pointing towards the trees. He promised to get me safely back to the inn before he went into the fire.

THE SPIRIT

THE POWER OF NEGATIVE THINKING, MORTALITY, THE SHORTNESS OF LIFE, GRIEF

SILVER SPRINGS, No-man's-land, Saturday, 12.30 am—I don't know what time Thida woke me but I was deep asleep, lost in some strange dream. I was swimming but found myself under a long, underwater shelf with not enough oxygen to get to the surface. In the dream I didn't panic even though a part of me knew that I would soon run out of breath, and instead I just turned back and swam as far and as fast as I could—

'Wake up, Dad's outside—' said Thida, pressing on my shoulder.

'Dad is gone—' I garbled. 'Long gone.'

'My dad! The Mayor! Get dressed. I have a hot drink to take with you.'

Take with me where?

I didn't want a hot drink. I wanted more time in bed. Surely I had only just fallen asleep. It was in this half-asleep, half-awake state, where nothing seemed real and everything possible, that

Thida took me out to a car—the first I'd seen in Silver Springs—and helped me in.

Was this a dream too? It was bitterly cold out and the moon was partially obscured by smoke. The Mayor turned on the heating and I felt warm, even drowsy, as we drove along the main road in town—and that's when I saw him, or thought I did, illuminated by the headlights. A tall, thin man with a moustache, walking on the side of the road, dead hand tucked behind his back, cigarette ember glowing in the other. He turned to look straight at me, and I shivered and felt suddenly awake and very afraid.

'That man . . .' I said.

'What man?' replied the Mayor.

We were driving fast now, past his vineyard and down a rough road into a valley, east towards the military zone, in the direction of China.

MAYOR: You're dreaming of men, sleepyhead.

Maybe the man was a fragment of a nightmare, made manifest by the blur of the car along the road? I shook him off, as one shakes off a bad dream.

JOURNALIST: Why am I up so early? Or is it late?

MAYOR: Because you don't have much time left before your visa runs out.

My heart ached at this. Why was he still talking of visas and time running out?

Let's recap. Day One was about the mind, and how we are able to control how we frame things. Day Two was about the body, and how to keep the passions in check, and Day Three is about the shortness of life, mortality and beyond. Body. Mind. Spirit. All the things that make the self.

JOURNALIST: All the mysteries.

MAYOR: The spirit is the most mysterious of all. Science can't reach it. Language isn't adequate for it. There are things that can only be felt to be known.

JOURNALIST: What are we doing out here? Why are we here in the middle of the night? What happened with the fire last night? Is Dominic okay?

MAYOR: Everything is okay. Everyone is safe. I'm going to take you down the alternative Southern Silk Road, the old connector between East and West. Yes, I know it's dangerous, but we should be okay at this time of night. From there, I want to take you somewhere quite different from the other places you've been. Damn, I can't get a radio signal. Sometimes out here we pick up the stations from the next province.

It was warm in the car, and I must have nodded off—because when I woke the landscape had completely altered.

Look up at the sky! You see why we're famous in the astronomy world, why we get all the stargazers.

The heavens were so dense and bright with stars that it looked like a lake in the sky. Under the sky's dome, the clarity and concentration of points of light were so startling and different, it was as if we had entered another realm. The Mayor pointed out the Milky Way, looming just above us, more accessible here than it was back home. I felt if only I were a bit closer, I could reach my hand in and grab a creamy slice.

We kept driving through the sparkling night, shooting stars overhead, a comfortable silence between us, like you sometimes get when you're in a car, on a highway, late at night. I felt so good, my body loose and responsive, the vivid nightmare of the moustached man, receding.

MAYOR: I thought I'd bring you out of town for our morning meditation.

JOURNALIST: I'm already in a meditative state because I've had barely any sleep.

The Mayor looked sideways at me and smiled.

I felt changed in the last few hours. Just thinking about Dominic seemed to melt everything hard inside. And he wasn't distant like a star. He was real. I had touched him.

MAYOR: How's Dominic?

JOURNALIST: More divine and beautiful than this sky.

The Mayor laughed.

MAYOR: Don't get too carried away. He's not in your control, right?

JOURNALIST: Sure. I know—he's not in my control.

Could desire and rational thinking be elements that ever commingled? I would find out.

So what type of meditation are we doing?

MAYOR: It's called the 'premeditation of evils' or negative visualisation.

JOURNALIST: I was hoping for something more Zen. That sounds terrifying. What is it?

MAYOR: Thinking deliberately about worst-case scenarios; asking yourself how badly a given choice or event could work out, rather than trying to persuade yourself everything will be all right.

JOURNALIST: Hmm—give me an example?

MAYOR: So, say I go to the doctor to get a small lump looked at; I imagine she says that the lump is cancerous and the cancer has spread.

I looked down at my hand. Would it heal again? Would I be able to write without pain again?

JOURNALIST: What's the point of doing that? That's a recipe for anxiety.

In the distance, a low fire burned. The headlights illuminated piles of rubbish, boulders, yellow dirt and skeletal trees. It was no pristine wilderness—rubbish was blown around; old tyres and the hulls of burnt-out trucks, mountains of trash had been dumped over the border by the Chinese trucks that used the alternative Southern Silk Route to get to India, the Mayor explained.

Flying from a stick in the ground, like a flag, I saw the Corpus brand jumper—so hot in the stores last year, now ragged and discarded. Winds shook the car, and outside there was a howl—whether from the winds or an animal, I didn't know.

The static from the radio sounded like white noise, stations came in and out, snatches of languages I didn't understand. I thought of how only a few hours ago, I was running my hands through Dominic's hair and he moaned, and how much I adored making him make that sound.

MAYOR: The point of doing this meditation is almost as an inoculation. You imagine the worst, and, if or when that situation happens, you've already run through a simulation in your head. It can't take you by surprise if you've already prepared for it.

Right now I could think of just one worst-case scenario—being kicked out of Silver Springs when my visa lapsed at the end of the day and not seeing Dominic again. But maybe that's why the Mayor was taking me out here—to discuss the possibility of immigration? Amazing how, in an instant, the future could be transformed from something miserable, small and vaguely terrifying to something exciting and sweet. Something that made me tingle with anticipation. After all, wasn't an exception made for the Mayor when he fell in love?

JOURNALIST: I would say being shot *was* my worst-case scenario. But the worst has actually happened and I survived it. So my negative visualisation might be that I didn't survive the shooting. That I died either at my desk or soon after in hospital.
MAYOR: Okay, so you were shot but don't survive.

I didn't want to do this.

MAYOR: Go on . . .

I looked out the window at the darkness and took a deep breath. I heard the screams—I'd never forget them . . .

JOURNALIST: The shooter was spraying bullets around—and most of my colleagues were killed. Bullets to the front of the head, the chest. Eight of us died straight away. Two of us were injured, then Joe died in the ambulance. It turns out it was a 3D-printed gun. A ghost gun. Did I tell you that? Homemade but pretty effective, unfortunately.

My voice was shaking. I slowed down, trying to get control back—where was I? What did I see, touch, smell and feel?

The bullet hit me in the head but missed my brain by millimetres. I was still alive when they took me to hospital but in a bad way.

They had to get the bullet out. It was lodged not far from my brain. Too close to my brain, really. Placed in an induced coma, I was there for a long time—drifting in and out. People gathered around my bedside, held my hand, told me stories. That's when I first heard about Silver Springs from Lou. This magical place far, far away, not like the fucked-up place I was in.

In Silver Springs there wasn't random violence, they worked things out by talking them through. By reason. And compromise.

The Mayor was nodding and looking straight ahead at the road. His expression was hard to read.

MAYOR: Don't forget you are negatively visualising something terrible that could happen, not something that has *already* happened. So, what is it?

Deep breath. I remembered the music of Laurel Canyon coming from the hospital radio—the warmth of my mother's hand, Caroline's baby being placed gently on my chest and people taking photos. Then at night, so alone. My eyes rolling back, the rush of chemical beauty and oblivion just when I thought pain might overwhelm me.

JOURNALIST: So there's a shooting in my workplace. I don't survive. The operation isn't a success. They've opened my skull, they're trying to remove the bullet without damaging my brain, but it's too close to the major operational centres, the places that create and hold memories, the things that govern how I move, think, write, talk. The risk of permanent brain damage is too great. Part of my head is shaved and wired. I sense the fear coming from my mum and sister in the waiting room. My mum would be doing that thing with her hands, wringing them, like a wet cloth. The doctor would be coming out to consult with them, get their view—risk the operation but with permanent brain damage, or retreat?

My voice was thick and speech strangely clotted. Suddenly I was icy with terror. It was like a shadow had come over me and there was new knowledge that had settled into my very core and I felt extra fretful, like a small child. I thought I had courage but now I could feel it leave me, as specifically as a loved one leaving a room.

JOURNALIST: I don't want to go back home.

I was falling for Dominic, I was here.

I am here.

MAYOR [*putting his hand on my arm*]: Time to come out of it.

JOURNALIST: Out of what?

MAYOR: Your negative visualisation. You were going too deep. It's not meant to cause distress. It's meant to be a short exercise that gives you a tiny taste of the worst-case scenario. You tap into it, get a picture, then tap off. Don't dwell in there; you'll end up getting anxiety. Think of Dominic or something pleasant, like my garden.

JOURNALIST [*shakily*]: It was like it was real. Now I don't know what's real and what's pretend.

The Mayor swerved to avoid a burst bag of clothes, illuminated by our headlights, on the side of the road—sleeves flapping in the wind like a dumped headless torso.

MAYOR: You need to be able to come out of it and back to the present moment with an appreciation of what you have, rather than anxiety about what could be. You okay? You look rattled.

I took a few deep breaths and, instead of thinking of Dominic, I thought of an artist I had interviewed once. He worked with the blackest colour known to humans: Vantablack. Black so dark that it had depth, like if you stood too close to it, it might swallow you. The sky was Vantablack. That's what it felt like right now, that we were driving into darkness and being absorbed by it. The dread realm of absolute truth.

MAYOR: This task can initially be unpleasant, but it gets better. I enjoy it, because when I finish the short meditation and open my eyes, the thing that was the worst thing for me hasn't happened yet. And so I feel relieved.

JOURNALIST: But it could happen.

I was still back there, in my head, where the worst was happening.

MAYOR: It's just an exercise. Remember, Goldy—reality, reality, reality. And remember ataraxia. If your equilibrium is strong and secure you should be able to go in and out of negative visualisation without being disturbed.

JOURNALIST: Why do it at all?

MAYOR: Negative visualisation is actually many people's default mode. Without them realising it, so many people skew negative, they always think the worst. It's just how we're designed. But many people don't know how to channel the power of thinking negatively; they don't know how to come out of it and back into reality. If used properly, negative visualisation is helpful in preparing you to face calamity, death, suffering and illness calmly, rationally and without suffering more than necessary. Then there are the other benefits to the exercise, like gratitude. When you come out of your operation and the doctor says 'All clear', you have a renewed appreciation of life, because you got a taste of how finite it is when you did your negative visualisation.

JOURNALIST: So that old saying—expect the worst and hope for the best.

MAYOR: Something like that, although hope is not a Stoic emotion, because, after all, you don't have control over much of what happens to you. I actually see negative visualisation as working best in the context of time.

JOURNALIST: How so?

I trembled even though the heating was on, blowing hot air on my knees.

MAYOR: Seneca wrote a great essay on the shortness of life. He, and the other Stoics, believed that we act as if we have a limitless amount of time, when we, in fact, squander the very resources that are finite. Instead we are much more miserly with things such as money, which are not so nearly as valuable. Seneca wrote, 'You are living as if destined to live forever; your own frailty never occurs to you; you don't notice how much time has already passed, but squander it as though you had a full and overflowing supply—though all the while that very day you are devoting to somebody or something may be your last.'

That hit hard. How many days and nights had I frittered away doom scrolling, wasting my life on a meaningless stream of scary posts on X.com? Or been filled with envy at the lives of others, as I lost hours on Instagram?

JOURNALIST: But how do you know if a day will be your last? I think we would go insane if we were aware of how long we had, if we knew the moment of our death.

MAYOR: Maybe we would go insane. Or maybe we would be shocked by how we squander time and finally come to our senses. 'When a man knows he is to be hanged in a fortnight, it concentrates his mind wonderfully,' said Samuel Johnson.

JOURNALIST: When I was in the hospital my mind kept focusing on regrets. I vowed I would do a lot of it differently if I had my time again—and I remember praying, even though I'm not religious, because I now had this knowledge. I prayed for more time. I wanted the chance to start again and make other choices.

My face was wet with tears. I'd do it all differently. I only had one life, and I hadn't known what to do with it. But now I knew.

MAYOR: What was this knowledge?

JOURNALIST: That time is so short. That life is short! And if I was given more time, I would do things differently. I really wanted that—more time, and a chance to begin again.

MAYOR: What would you do differently?

JOURNALIST: Before, I felt as if I was just moving through time, like I was going on a road trip somewhere, but the trip itself wasn't important, and I was in a hurry to get where I was going, to the destination . . . So I was always wanting time to pass, because I didn't want to be where I was. I wanted to be at the next place. And I'd try to make it pass by working a lot, or drinking a lot, watching a lot, scrolling a lot, or sleeping a lot, just willing time away to get *there.*

MAYOR: Where was the destination? Where were you in such a hurry to get to?

JOURNALIST: That's the crazy thing. I don't know! Or I know now—there was no destination. No terminus. It's such a cliché but I realised the whole point of the journey was the journey. And I was trying to rush it because it was boring or something. But where *was* I going?

MAYOR: 'So many direct their purposes with an eye to a distant future. But putting things off is the biggest waste of life: it snatches away each day as it comes, and denies us the present by promising the future. The greatest obstacle to living is expectancy, which hangs upon tomorrow and loses today.' So, knowing what you know now, what would you do differently?

JOURNALIST: Oh god—just enjoy it. That's all I'd do—just enjoy myself, appreciate nature and the world, and other people. There were all these small moments that I didn't clock, because I was in a hurry to *be* somewhere else, to *get* somewhere.

MAYOR: 'You were arranging what lies in Fortune's control, and abandoning what lies in yours. What are you looking at? To what goal are you straining? The whole future lies in uncertainty: live immediately.'

JOURNALIST: That's got to be a quote! Seneca?

MAYOR: You got me. Guilty.

JOURNALIST: Live immediately. Yes. I think living happens in the moments when we are just hanging out, when we aren't striving for some future thing. At work we had this ritual—actually Lou started it—called the coffee train. After the morning conference, every morning, we'd all go across the road to the Mountain Cafe and sit at the big table, and have a coffee together. There were enough of us that when we went across to the cafe, it was like a road train. Ha ha. And so we called ourselves the coffee train. We'd talk about what stories we were working on, tricky stories or stories that were going well, people we were about to interview, share tips and advice. It wasn't always work. We'd talk about what we'd cooked for dinner the night before, or what we were doing on the weekend, show pictures of our pets or kids. What we watched. Good TV shows to binge. Nothing profound. Sometimes I missed it because I was making calls. It didn't matter because I'd just catch the coffee train the next day. Every day at 11 am.

But that will never happen again. The newspaper will shut. Many of those people are dead—

I was all choked up.

MAYOR: Go on.

JOURNALIST: I didn't appreciate it when it was happening because I thought it would never end. Just a stupid coffee train. It would always be there—as regular as the commuter trains. But . . .

MAYOR: Everything is finite. Everything ends. The Stoics said we should do this: remember that we will die. Be ruthless with the things that don't matter. Value your time more than money. Pursue the virtues each day, and review how you went each night. Make sure you rest, but rest properly: make it enriching.

JOURNALIST: What's enriching rest?

MAYOR: Well, it's not scrolling on your phone. It's not numbing yourself with drugs, alcohol, streaming, gaming, tweeting. It's not passive. Seneca actually said the most enriching thing you can do with your time is to study philosophy.

JOURNALIST: At university?

MAYOR: No. How we're doing it now, you and I and the last two days. And how we do it at the Stoa. Seneca wrote that 'of all people, only those are at leisure who make time for philosophy, only those are really alive'.

The whole project of the Stoa, and of Silver Springs in general, was making more sense to me. It was, in its own way, deeply countercultural. Residents had resisted the drift to passivity, of letting life (and the algorithm) just wash over them, or worse—like I did—try to hurry through it, trying to get to a destination that, if pressed, they were never actually able to name or conceptualise. Instead they had formed a deliberate community that was dedicated to reducing, or at least supporting, each person's load of suffering, and increasing their enjoyment in life. Crazy now to think we could just muddle through on our own.

MAYOR: Seneca was saying that philosophy was above all else a guide to how to live a good life. And a good life also includes contemplation of death. They are two sides of the same coin. Death is a recurring theme in Stoic teaching. And it's a great leveller. We are all going to die, so we need to get busy planning for it. Or at least mentally prepared by acknowledging it. You know, when coming back from battles, Roman generals would have someone whisper to them '*memento mori*'—remember you will die. It reminded the general that, as he was coming back triumphant and feeling like a god, he was a mortal. A mere mortal.

The road we were on was straight as we drove into Vantablack. Headlights on, the flicker of moths on the windscreen. That low buzz of static from the car radio.

JOURNALIST: We definitely don't mentally prepare for death in modern society. We always think there's more time.

MAYOR: That is unsurprising. It's always been that way. Two thousand years ago, Seneca was talking about how people can waste their lives at work. They work too hard! Why??! People put off learning philosophy, leisure, time with friends and family in order to work more. What's changed? He wrote, 'You will hear many people saying: "When I am fifty I shall retire into leisure; when I am sixty I shall give up public duties." And what guarantee do you have of a longer life? Who will allow your course to proceed as you arrange it? Aren't you ashamed to keep for yourself just the remnants of your life, and to devote to wisdom only that time which cannot be spent on any business? How late it is to begin really to live just when life must end!'

'How late it is to begin really to live just when life must end.' True.

JOURNALIST: Do the Stoics make an argument for not working, that work is a waste of life?

MAYOR: No. Work, your duty, was also incredibly important. It had its place among the other things of life. Marcus refers to nature, or what the Buddhists might call dharma, when he asks, 'For what task were you yourself created? A man's true delight is to do the things he was made for.' For some, that task is parenthood, for others it's teaching, or storytelling, for building houses. There is a satisfaction in doing the thing that feels natural to you, being part of nature, part of a community and contributing. To not work if you can work, that is not good.

But, as we've seen, all things in moderation, including work. My parents used to quote the old union movement slogan all the time in our house: eight hours work, eight hours rest, eight hours for doing what you will.

It felt like a hundred years ago that the Mayor had given me my first lecture on moderation.

JOURNALIST: What about people who die young? That's tragic, right?

MAYOR: What's tragic is a ninety-year-old dying without ever having properly lived. What matters is not the years someone is alive, but what they have *done* with their years. There is no reason for you to think that any man has lived long because he has grey hairs or wrinkles; he has not lived long, he has *existed* long.

You can live without purpose for ninety years but you haven't really lived; you've just been tossed about, passive, wasteful. But thirty purposeful years are a far better use of a life. Is it really a tragedy if you die at thirty and in that time you have *properly* lived? I mean, look at Jesus of Nazareth—thirty-three years! He was a revolutionary. Whether you are Christian or not, he changed the course of history in a brief period.

JOURNALIST: I still think it's a tragedy if someone dies young, particularly if they were brilliant and could have gone on contributing to society. Jesus might have achieved even more if he lived to sixty or seventy.

MAYOR: Yet he was fated to die, it seems—sent by God, his Father, to die for our sins, in the most gruesome way imaginable. It's interesting how Seneca frames death. He talks about fate. Because in the cosmic web of cause and effect, there is only one timeline: you are going to live for exactly as long as you are going to live; there is no longer or shorter version. No one dies before their time.

JOURNALIST: I don't know if I can accept the notion of fate in that way. Life and death seem more random.

What if I had gone to the bathroom a few minutes before the gunman came in?

MAYOR: That's okay but what you must believe is that our time on Earth is limited. It's a bit of a design flaw that we keep forgetting.

JOURNALIST: Or maybe it's design genius. To live without thinking of the shadow that dogs everyone . . .

MAYOR: But in order to fully live, we have to keep on reminding ourselves. *Memento homo*: remember you are only a man, or a woman.

JOURNALIST—Or non-binary . . .

The Mayor smiled.

MAYOR: *Whoever* you are, and whatever beliefs you have, you *will* die. And if you keep this front of mind, a strange thing happens—you actually become more involved in your life.

JOURNALIST: I don't see how being more involved in your life, and the lives of others, makes dying easier. Or the deaths of others easier? Surely detachment is the key.

MAYOR: Detachment about death; involvement in life.

JOURNALIST: That sounds like one of those mysterious Zen koans.

MAYOR: There's nothing mysterious about it. If you can work out how to deal with death, your own and others, before it hits you, you end up appreciating your life more. And the people in your life.

The mountains seemed to be getting closer. It was still dark but above us were bright stars. I thought of Marcus writing in his journal, all those centuries ago, 'Dwell on the beauty of life. Watch the stars, and see yourself running with them.'

JOURNALIST: How can we be both detached and involved?

MAYOR: Epictetus told a story about a man whose daughter became ill, and instead of staying by her bedside, he fled because he was so upset. He believed the feeling of being overwhelmed by suffering was a natural thing that any father would experience. But Epictetus said the father had control over whether he went or stayed, and, in leaving, he left the thing he loved the most to suffer alone.

Those hospital weeks—my mother to my right hand, my sister to my left. This I understood even when swimming in the darkest reaches, out of range, out of contact, brain and body largely offline.

This is in contrast to a second father who stayed with his child through her terrible illness.

Epictetus reasoned that if both children died, the first father would be suffering twice, because in the time that his daughter had on Earth, he had not used his time with her wisely. Instead he had run away. The second father stayed with his daughter. He would have known after she died that he made the most of her short life, did not abandon her and that he acted with courage in facing up to reality. In these situations, both fathers suffer but the first father is going to suffer more intensely, because he will have more regrets.

JOURNALIST: He'll suffer twice.

MAYOR: Yes. Look at how many lessons this story contains. And how true it is today. Were there people who didn't come and see you in the hospital? People you thought would have been there for you?

JOURNALIST [*a wave of sadness moved through me*]: Yes.

MAYOR: So what Epictetus is saying is do your duty to your family and friends, even if it is hard. That it is our nature to be communal and care for other people. Make the most of each moment. Realise that we are all going to die. And front up to that reality with your eyes wide open. Don't run away! Be there for the sick. Be there for the dying. Not only is that doing your duty as a friend, as a person, but it will make *you* feel better. If your friend dies, not only would you miss them, but you'd feel guilt and regret for not spending time with them while they were still alive. So spend the time with them while you can! You also need to be there for *yourself* when you're dying. Don't abandon reality just because you don't like it. Face up to it!

I felt the chill again, and once more regressed into a child who needed comfort.

JOURNALIST: I don't want to die.

MAYOR: That's out of your control, so why not accept it? Fearing it is useless. Fear won't stop you from dying, and it won't make dying any easier. For the ancient Stoics, death was a natural part of life, and seen as a process, a return to the universal source of all things. It's the cycle of life. What is terror? Terror is when you haven't squared up to death. Terror is of your own making.

I realised how much I would miss the Mayor if I had to leave. Even though we antagonised each other, I had come to realise that under his harsh exterior lay sympathy and a latent gentleness. I wanted to stay near him, for just a little bit longer. He reminded me of Lou in that way.

JOURNALIST: How do you feel about your own death? And, say, the death of your child?

MAYOR: I think about it all the time. I feel sad when I think about Thida's inevitable death. My own . . . I am now habituated to thoughts of my own death.

JOURNALIST: And Septimus?

MAYOR: I don't like to think of that, but think of that, I do.

We were quiet for a while, lost in our own thoughts of death.

We're coming up to the best place to see the stars. If you're lucky there might even be the hint of an aurora.

The road had been straight for the longest time, but suddenly there was a bend and a small rise. Mountains surrounded us, but in the distance. We came upon what would have once been a river mouth, but it was all dried out and hollow like the imprint of a giant spoon.

The Mayor stopped the car. Reeds whispered secrets in the wind, and the air was scented with incoming rain. Even though this stretch of earth was desolate compared with Silver Springs, the world was a beautiful place, and for a moment I adored it with a force that felt physical, that might break my heart. Breathe and hold steady. Then I thought of Dominic and relaxed.

MAYOR: Are you up for talking about grief now?

We were silent for a long time.

GRIEF

SILVER SPRINGS, The Dead River, Saturday, 4 am—The Mayor and I got out of the car and sat on a log in the immense darkness. It was cold. He brought some wood out from the back of the car and set to building a fire on the hard mudflats.

JOURNALIST: I don't want to go back home. I'm frightened.

MAYOR: I know. But part of the work you need to do next is grieve the friends and colleagues you lost.

I nodded and swallowed hard. My lungs hurt, up so high.

JOURNALIST: So what's the Stoic take on grief? Harden up? Take it on the chin? Death is a part of life, etc. etc.

The Mayor looked a little stung. He poked the fire a bit and didn't answer me.

JOURNALIST: I'm sorry.

MAYOR: It's okay. Do you want to talk about those you have lost?

Silence. I was crying. The air smelt like rain and fire, but even by the flames it was cold. The sky was still dark but I felt a sense of something approaching—light from a dead star, particles from a stellar remnant, in the great cosmic graveyard of space.

Julie was 51, Pete 29, Rachel 43, Sonya 22, Mel 63, Pat 30, Alex 30, Vin 27, Joe 35. I would talk about them one day. But not today.

MAYOR: I'll go first, shall I?

He took a deep breath and suddenly looked defenceless and alone.

I had a tough time of it when my wife died. The grief came at unexpected moments. It woke me in the night and I couldn't fall back to sleep. Or I'd be at the market and I'd see the bread she always liked to buy on a Saturday morning—bread and wildflowers—and that would be enough to stop me dead in my tracks. I leant hard on Stoicism and it didn't let me down. I took consolation in Seneca's *Letter to Marcia*. The letter itself was called a consolation. And you know what? It really was. Just like Seneca's teachings on anger, it's full of nuggets of wisdom that are sublimely practical today.

JOURNALIST: What's the letter about?

MAYOR: It's really more of an essay. The *Consolatione ad Marciam* is a work by Seneca written around 40 CE. I must warn you: it's not a particularly warm essay. I don't know if Marcia, whose son Metilius died young, would have felt particularly consoled reading it. But it might have helped her become more resilient. It quite logically sets out the arguments for her to stop grieving the death of her son, because she was suffering twice. The first suffering, of course, was the loss of her son, three years prior, and the second was her prolonged and chronic grief. My own loss was quite fresh when I re-read it and I took it as a warning about not going down the chronic path.

The Mayor took some sheafs of paper from his rucksack. Exhaustion was hitting me like a brick. I was depleted. The night with Dominic in the woods felt like a dream. Everything since the shooting was adrenaline, but I was finally coming down. Suddenly light shot through the blackness, and between one instant and the next the sky was transformed into a swirl of colours—purple and gold.

MAYOR: Oh look! Isn't it wonderful? An aurora! The colour of imperial robes!

There were no words—just wonder. The sky was being painted, as if by an unseen hand, before our eyes and the colours swirled and settled around us like a benediction or an epic psychedelic trip.

JOURNALIST: You know there was a year—the year before last—when things were really bad in my part of the world, worse than usual. There was a terrible war in the Middle East and weather all around the world became intense and disordered. Loads of flooding. Wildfires. Mass extinction events. Elections everywhere that shook up world politics. The rise of authoritarianism. But the skies that year were insane, stunning. Auroras keep popping up in the most unlikely places. Every second night it seemed the sky was turning colours like I'd never seen. No one could explain it. My feeds—the whole of Instagram—were all war and auroras. Darkness and light.

MAYOR: Ahh, another mystery. But beauty and horror have always coexisted. That is reality.

We sat for a while in silence. The fire cast shadows that skipped across the ground. And as the colours in the sky deepened and moved around us, a feeling of peace and contentment crept up on me again. The feeling was so strange and good that I became anxious it would leave me soon. Was this the much-famed ataraxia? Then—just like the good feeling—without warning, the night's colours faded and we were left once again in the almost tactile darkness. The Mayor pulled out his torch and read from Seneca's *Letter to Marcia*.

MAYOR: 'Let others use soft measures and caresses; I have determined to do battle with your grief, and I will dry those weary and exhausted eyes, which already, to tell you the truth, are weeping more from habit than from sorrow.'

He's saying to Marcia that her grief had become a habit, which was now inappropriate.

JOURNALIST: He's calling her out.

MAYOR: I know! Bold claim, but a compelling one. Seneca writes that, although it's been three years, 'still your grief has lost none of its first poignancy, but renews and strengthens itself day by day, and has now dwelt so long with you that it has acquired a domicile in your mind, and actually thinks that it would be base to leave it'. In other words, he's saying yes she's still feeling grief, but it's habitual now and it must be broken like any bad habit. What she thinks is grief is misplaced loyalty and she needs to change that.

Seneca also addresses the shock of death. It's a common thing we don't really interrogate: that when someone dies we suffer from shock, or we are in disbelief. When Sandra died of cancer, some of her friends were really shocked, really disbelieving. But she had been sick for almost ten years and, towards the end, looked very ill. When she died, it was quite sudden and it *felt* shocking. Unexpected. But her friends probably should have been expecting it.

JOURNALIST: Were you expecting it?

MAYOR: Yes. But did it make it easier? Theoretically. I had spent years training to be Stoic, taking out an emotional insurance policy.

JOURNALIST: Did it pay off?

MAYOR: The shock of her death was lessened with preparation, I suppose. Part of the unnecessary suffering that the Stoics were hoping to eliminate is the shock that someone has died. The shock can really disorder our senses and mess with our capacity to feel ataraxia and therefore to reason.

But shouldn't the death of someone we love disorder our senses and mess with our reason? Isn't grief the price we pay for love?

Seneca wrote: 'So many funeral processions go past our houses, but we don't think about death.' So we see it all around, we go to funerals, we see death happen to others, but this strange magical thinking takes place where we believe we are immune from what others experience.

JOURNALIST: But it was different with the murder of so many of my colleagues. We were at work. We were well. Coffee train that morning, everyone was talking about Vin's upcoming birthday party. We were all making plans. Discussing costume ideas. That afternoon . . . it really was shocking. I still can't believe it.

MAYOR: You've read and maybe even covered these acts of violence: in shopping malls, in movie theatres, in nightclubs, at political rallies, at concerts. No one wakes up that day, goes to the mall for a new pair of shoes, and expects to be stabbed, for example. But it has happened. And it's not just death. It's any misfortune. Any accident or illness. 'Who ever looked at his property thinking he was going to lose it?' And who among us would ever dare to think about exile, poverty or grief? We would not do it even if someone asked us to. Our imaginations limit us.

You've spent a lot of time since the shooting thinking 'why me?' haven't you?

JOURNALIST: Some time, yes. I thought it was unfair that people older than me, or in some way—and I hate to admit thinking it—less talented than me, were not killed that day. People were away or had ducked out to the bathroom or were out on a story or working from home, or the bullets just missed them. I could spend years asking 'why me?'

MAYOR: Let me read you this: 'When, therefore, misfortune befalls us, we cannot help collapsing all the more completely, because we are struck as it were unawares: a blow which has long been foreseen falls much less heavily upon us.'

In that last line—there is the key. *A blow which has long been foreseen falls much less heavily upon us.*

That death is foreseen. Here they are trying to reduce your suffering. That was the point of all this. So, the Stoic way of preparing for death, doing exercises such as negative visualisation and the like, is a way of preparing for death. The blow still falls, but it doesn't fall as hard.

JOURNALIST: So basically Seneca is saying 'you can do this the easy way or the hard way'—and that is within your control.

MAYOR: Yes. Although I know from firsthand experience, there's no easy way with grief. When someone you love dies, it's going to be hard. It's going to be *really hard.* I did negative visualisation exercises a lot when my wife was sick. It was painful because there she was in front of me, so sick, and I was imagining her funeral.

That felt disrespectful to her, in some weird way. I didn't want to go to that place in my mind. I wanted the sugar pill of hope.

The fire was consuming all our fuel fast up here, and the aurora was similarly exhausted. We made our way back to the car and starting driving.

JOURNALIST: But you had obviously been practising Stoicism for a long time?

MAYOR: Yes, both of us had. So we knew what we had to do, what we had to get down to immediately, that the business of dying and grief was our immediate task. It was work. That's what her dying and my grieving felt like—work. Hard work. Seneca wrote in his letter to Marcia, 'This companion at your side will soon be lost.' Either I would die first or Sandra would die first but, unless we both died at once, one of us would be dead and the other would be grieving. There was no way around it. 'This companion at your side will soon be lost.'

JOURNALIST: So how should we grieve? What way do they think is correct?

But was there a correct way?

MAYOR: Seneca told Lucilius, who had lost a friend, that it's to be expected that one will feel some grief, and even express it, but that it is possible to do so in a way that remains within some rational limits. Extravagant gestures, words and wailing, those don't serve the person who has died, the person feeling grief or anyone else for that matter. Many people mistakenly assume that, if you cared for a person, you show it by the amount and intensity of grief you display, but a Stoic would easily recognise that as a mistake.

What if you do find yourself overcome by sadness and grief? Pay attention to what you are feeling, and, using your rational mind, shift through the surges of feeling, and apply logic. You miss that person a lot? Be with the reality that they are gone forever, but you had the privilege of knowing them. And you now have the capacity to remember them. Also know also that nothing is forever.

Much of life hurts, not just grief, which we reserve a special place for in the pantheon of misery. As Seneca says, 'Why need we weep over parts of our life? The whole of it calls for tears: new miseries assail us before we have freed ourselves from the old ones.' Misery after misery. So why get too upset about one misery? Why elevate one misery? Why elevate grief?

JOURNALIST: Because the misery of the loss of someone you love—or even your own life—is final. It's a misery that cannot be redeemed.

MAYOR: Well, it can be redeemed by virtue of the fact that you had that relationship in the first place. You have memories. You have been changed by that person. 'I am a part of all that I have met,' wrote the poet Tennyson.

Seneca asks us to consider something important when a loved one dies. 'Has it then all been for nothing that you have had such a friend? During so many years, amid such close associations, after such intimate communion of personal interests, has nothing been accomplished? Do you bury friendship along with a friend?'

JOURNALIST: So he's saying, the friend is dead, but the friendship—or the effect of it, the memory of it, and the impact it had—is still there?

MAYOR: Yes. We can be so devastated by the death of a friend that this death has a blinding effect and we forget all the good times. Seneca is saying that death should not nullify that person's life or impact. Even when the death is dramatic and shocking, like a suicide, it shouldn't retrospectively colour and cancel out the whole life that preceded the death. In addition, Seneca throws a lot of arguments, very logical arguments, at Marcia, advocating for a short, sharp grief. So it allows you to properly feel all those painful and deep feelings associated with loss, but in a timeframe that doesn't inflict prolonged suffering on you.

JOURNALIST: That's all good in theory but—

MAYOR: I know. But remember the Stoics were attempting to minimise suffering. We can't stop living because there is death in our midst. Death is always in our midst. My life today, even without my wife, is full of surprises, pleasure, purpose, meaning and joy. Her death has not stopped me from living a good life, from being a good person. And I think that's the root of what Seneca was trying to get at in his *Letter to Marcia*.

JOURNALIST: And I guess Seneca might also argue that it's better to have loved and lost than not loved at all. But what if it's something horrible, like your child dying?

I thought of Hannie and if something happened to her—and I could not imagine anything less than total devastation. Not just for Caroline and her husband, but for me, Mum, everyone who ever held her or looked at her, and all those who didn't.

MAYOR: That is horrible. But once again, Seneca is not offering false sympathy. He's being quite hardheaded, and reminds readers of the bargain they made with nature when they chose to have children. Basically, you don't know what you're going to get. Children don't come with a guarantee that they'll be the people you want them to be, or that they'll outlive you. 'To everyone Nature says: 'I do not deceive any person. If you choose to have children, they may be handsome, or they may be deformed; perhaps they will be born dumb. One of them may perhaps prove the saviour of his country, or perhaps its betrayer . . . If you still choose to rear children, after I have explained these conditions to you, you render yourself incapable of blaming the gods, for they never guaranteed anything to you.'

JOURNALIST: Reality.

MAYOR: Yes, that is reality.

JOURNALIST: Where's Sandra buried?

MAYOR: Not far from here. Out in the desert. Not really a burial. More a return to nature.

JOURNALIST [*shuddering*]: One day, it ends. It just ends abruptly. Your parents die, your teachers die—

MAYOR: And you must strike out on your own.

JOURNALIST: I'm not ready to strike out on my own yet. I still need Lou. If he hadn't given me his watch, I couldn't have traded it to be guided away from landmines. He's constantly either enlarging my world or saving my life.

MAYOR: I think you're ready to make it on your own. Look at your journey here. You did it all alone. The trauma and violence of the mass shooting, the loss of your job and your newspaper, the death of your colleagues, leaving your mother, sister and niece behind, carrying the pain and disfigurement of your injuries, carrying the grief. So much grief!

Every day since the shooting—waking distressed and gripped by a deep sadness that never went away.

You survived the dangers of Davantown and the perils of the journey across the river, through contested territory, deep jungle, and up those mountains, the lurching, exciting and terrifying sensations of desire and lust. Now the final test: the shadow that has been hanging over it all . . .

JOURNALIST: What's that?

I was afraid.

MAYOR: Letting it all go.

I felt resistance. I wasn't ready.

JOURNALIST: I don't like it up here. It's pretty forlorn.

I was trembling all over, like something foreign was occupying my body.

MAYOR: We call it no-man's-land. Now that the sun is about to rise, our safety is not guaranteed here: bandit country. But not even the bandits spend too long here. They get spooked. I suppose I should tell you, it's where we dispose of the dead.

. . . the town had these macabre burial rites. The bodies would be driven on a road out of town—a real no-man's-land—and placed on a mountain to be devoured by wild animals.

JOURNALIST: A hippie I spoke to before I left told me about this. He advised me not to travel here.

MAYOR: Many visitors think it barbaric—so we don't talk about it much, but it's an old pagan tradition and it's also something, personally, that best fits the philosophy. And anyway, you wanted the full experience, the full story, right?

JOURNALIST: I think so. What's the story?

MAYOR: It may seem harsh to moderns, who hide death away or seal the body in a box, but the idea of a body returning to nature is also deeply Stoic. Marcus wrote in *Meditations*: 'That which has died falls not out of the universe. If it stays here, it also changes here, and is dissolved into its proper parts, which are elements of the universe and of thyself. And these too change, and they murmur not.'

In the distance, there was a small, rocky rise—and there was a committee of vultures flying in. Was it to feed? Was there a body left there? A Stoic burial?

There's this section in Seneca's *Letter to Marcia* where Seneca says that everything we have has been lent to us. Not as a gift, but as something we'll need to return. Certain things sooner, others later, and only a few we can keep till the end. And when we get 'asked' to return something, we shall not argue. 'It's the worst kind of borrower who insults the lender. We should, therefore, love our dear ones . . . as if their permanence was never promised to us . . . not even a day with them was promised.' We should remind ourselves that what we love will leave, because we were given these things by Fortune without a guarantee.

JOURNALIST: Stop the car! Let me out!

MAYOR: Everything okay?

I had to escape. I tried to open the door but it was locked. There wasn't enough air. A mortal panic flooded every cell. I had to get out of the car. We had to turn around. I didn't want to go where we were going. The Mayor kept driving but slowed down. He didn't look at me.

MAYOR: This was always the last place, the final destination. Not just for you, Goldy, but for all of us.

It had suddenly hit me where we were going, where I was going. I'd been going there all along. I had been going there when I set off with a map and a mission. I had been going there when I got to Dav. When I got my visa. When I crossed the river and climbed the mountain. I had been going there every day since the shooting—waking in the afternoon, face wet with tears, gripped by a deep grief. I had been going there every day of my life.

JOURNALIST: Are you fucking kidding? Please no! Please no! Drive me back to Silver Springs! I need to see Dominic. I don't want to be left out here!

MAYOR: It doesn't matter, when you are dead, what happens to your body. You'll have no consciousness to feel upset by it. 'The body and its parts are a river, the soul a dream and mist, life is warfare and a journey far from home, lasting reputation is oblivion.' Marcus—of course.

JOURNALIST: No. No. *No! NO!*

I couldn't breathe. Headlights illuminated the bleak road ahead.

MAYOR: Do you realise how lucky you were to even get the last three days here? To prepare for what was always ahead? Hardly anyone prepares; hardly anyone gets this chance and so the end is horrible for them. It's pure chaos and terror. People refuse death! They struggle against the inevitable. They cry out 'No!' at the end. And they are always defeated.

I knew where we were going. Towards death, and that death was my own.

JOURNALIST: I'm not ready to go now! I'm too young! I'm discovering new things, rediscovering old things, the beauty of the world, the preciousness of places and people—I'm not done with life yet! I've just started. And I'm—in love! What about Dominic?

Did he even love me? I never found out. Maybe it didn't matter. 'If you wish to be loved, love.'

MAYOR: You don't get to choose. Marcus also said, 'In short, know this: Human lives are brief and trivial. Yesterday a blob of semen; tomorrow embalming fluid, ash. To pass through this brief life as nature demands. To give it up without complaint. Like an olive that ripens and falls. Praising its mother, thanking the tree it grew on.'

We were driving across the flat, empty plains. The ground beneath us was cracked and blowing up dust. The sky was huge and the sun rising, not gently but harsh and blown out, like a flare from a rocket taking off. Small, treeless rises—looking more like ossified anthills—dotted the landscape. Old bits of fast fashion, escaped from their garbage bags. A wake of vultures in the distance, coming in to feed.

JOURNALIST: When I was shot, I didn't survive, did I?

MAYOR: You hung on for a while in hospital. All those conversations with Lou, the planning the trip here, the story—that was a place you went to in your head. But the doctors couldn't save you. You settled into a vegetative state, fated never to recover. Your mother had to make a hard decision.

My mother! I was pierced with a sudden heartbreak that I would not get to see her, or talk with her, or have her hold me and brush my hair. I would never again see my sister. I would never see my niece grow up. Why cry over parts of life when all of it calls for tears?

MAYOR: She's had to learn to let go, too. They all have. It's not been easy for anyone. Everyone's put up a fight. Everyone is struggling. Everyone's crying out 'No!'

It was cold by the sea, but I only remembered sunny days. Barefoot and walking on the soft grass with my sister—her plump baby hand in mine, the light in columns of pale gold shining through the slats of the fences we walked past. I was under a spell. Then older—in our best dresses, the smell of seagrass and the ocean, and the trees a vivid green, deep and alive, humming with birds, insects, cicadas . . . life . . . And it all seemed so achingly beautiful that to depart would be unbearable . . .

JOURNALIST: So what is this place? What is Silver Springs?

I was filled with wonder and awe. I was flooded with fear and terror.

MAYOR: This is the realm of absolute truth. Everything you have been through here is real.

JOURNALIST: It feels real.

MAYOR: It is. It's not some random, liminal space, although it's not of this world either. Be okay with the mystery! This is a place where you need to come to face all you must face. All the living you were yet to do, all the things you needed to do before you go, all the lessons you needed to learn. All the love you needed to give, all the love you needed to get, all the pain you needed to feel. All the grief, all the wonder. And finally, at the end, to let it all go.

JOURNALIST: But it feels so real—the smell, the sounds, the birds, the people—all of it. Is it real?

I wanted it to be real.

MAYOR: Yes, although elements from both realms have commingled. The fire calls?

JOURNALIST: Yes. There was another one last night.

MAYOR: They are the sounds of the alarms going off in the ICU. The highland koel that emits that haunting, regular call?

JOURNALIST: Yes, everywhere in Silver Springs.

MAYOR: Everywhere because it's the sound of your heart monitor, and it was constantly humming.

I remembered becoming anxious if suddenly it stopped.

The hospital came back into focus. It was such a noisy place, even at night; medical alarms going off on equipment. IV pumps, heart monitors. But so much easier to bear if I could transform them into the deafening choir of cicadas. And the pain was so much easier to bear if I was high. The fentanyl going straight into my veins, was that the heavenly rum? The drink that I wanted more of, every time?

The Mayor confirmed it.

MAYOR: That special rum, made with the silty river water? That night you had too much? You've had it several times now, and you find it makes you feel really good: numbs the psychic and physical pain and gives you vivid dreams. You were always wanting more.

I looked at my hand and unwrapped the bandage. I tried to recall what had happened. It had been that night in Dav, right? I got fucked up in the bar and had some sort of psychotic break in the room. When I woke up later, my hand was bleeding, my phone was broken, but now it was obvious. My phone never even came to hospital with me after the shooting. As soon as I was admitted, an IV cannula was inserted in my hand, and it left my skin sore and black with bruises.

I felt heartsick. The pine smell that was everywhere in Silver Springs was obviously the smell of antiseptic cleaning products used to clean the wards. And I knew without having to ask that the man with the handlebar moustache was death himself, appearing three times, a warning and a beckoning: *'Come with me.'*

JOURNALIST: Was the shooting real? Was I shot at work?

MAYOR: That, sadly, is all too real.

JOURNALIST [*full of wonder but also distress*]: And the songs I kept hearing—they were all songs that my mum had on in the car all the time when I was young? They are my memories, right?

MAYOR: Yes. The songs you heard at the parties were the soundtrack of your youth, and the other songs—the Laurel Canyon songs, as you call them—they are what the nurses listen to on the overnight shift. Easy listening.

I heard the music again, coming in through the car radio—the Mayor had been trying to get a signal. We were still driving, although the landscape was changing. More trees, mist drifting in from the forest, down a slip road, deer running fast alongside the car, eyes shining, a satin blur of brown. The Doors were singing 'The Crystal Ship'.

JOURNALIST: I'm so afraid. I know you said not to be. But . . .

The DJ was promising hits and memories. The Doors rolled into The Beatles. 'Dear Prudence' was playing. Light fell like broken bits of a Christian heaven through the canopy of trees, and everything was quiet—idyllic even. This was nature, pure and untouched by humans, ancient nature.

JOURNALIST: Can we just keep driving?

Fleetwood Mac was singing 'Silver Springs'. We passed through all the seasons that I had lived in and loved. All the weather I had dressed for, starting from when I couldn't even dress myself, and my mother helped my tiny arms into my first coat.

Then—all the quiet mornings and peaceful, anticipatory moments of sipping that first coffee. The choir. All of us singing in parts in the cold school hall, and how the music made me feel so good. Plunging into a cold sea on a hot day. The day we finished school and drove out of town, got high in the forest, and lay on the soft moss—speakers playing Rihanna and feeling free. Riding a CitiBike, at night, the lights of the 7-Eleven, the lamps lit around the gardens, the deserted carparks, the wide streets, laughing our heads off, believing we were immortal. All the journeys. All the planes landing at night, staring out the window at the city's grid lit up—a pulsating string of jewels as we flew along the coast. The first time I saw my name on a page one story. The baby on my chest, my heart expanding in my body. Lou at my side. Caroline at my side. Paul at my side. Mum at my side. Rachel and Sonya and Mel and Pat and Alex and Vin and Pete and Julie and Joe at my side. The Mayor at my side. Dominic at my side. Snow and sun and night and day—all the weather. Things growing fast like they do on double speed. Dying every day. Living every day. So much beauty, I was ready to explode like a dying star. All of it had been wonderful, even when it felt bad.

The Mayor had the car in cruise control. The sun was high, the day was getting hot; through the enchanted forest we drove, the sun was setting, all was dark. I was so, so tired. The journey was long and beautiful and full of strange things. I saw animals and plants I had never seen. Things I thought had become extinct.

Things that had to be seen to be believed. My head was spinning with wonder; my jaw hurt from smiling. The Mayor was driving by my side.

I might go now. I could go now.

A GUIDE TO THE LESSONS

THE MIND

THE BODY

THE SPIRIT

ACKNOWLEDGEMENTS

Many friends suffered through my first Stoic journey, and I want to thank them all again for being guinea pigs as I tested my latest project on them.

This time around, the challenge was broadened by incorporating fiction into the mix. For a steer on making a story compelling—but not so compelling that the theory takes a back seat—I'd like to thank Robbie Arnott for his advice, Zoe Coyle for her help with the character's psychology, and Michael Safi for his feedback on the final draft.

Thanks to my publisher, Cate Paterson, who was able to trust me that this wild idea could be pulled off and who gave me the extra time I needed when political life got in the way.

I'd also like to thank the team that worked on this book with Cate—Angela Handley, Susan Keogh and Dannielle Viera, and Josh Durham for his stunning cover design.

Thanks to my long-time agent, Pippa Masson, for her support.

Thanks also to Maximilian Horsley, for taking me off the beaten track and right up into northern Myanmar when it was still possible to travel there; Michelle Jana Chan, an extraordinary travel writer and friend whose own adventures inspired the opening scenes of this book; Kelly Fagan, for initiating my Stoic journey many years ago and publishing *Reasons Not to Worry*; and Andrew Charlton, for discussions on Stoicism and how it might be explored through fiction.

Thanks to Adam Wesselinoff, for his help with the conceptual framework of this book and introducing me to the work of Pierre Hadot, whose 'joyful yes' can be found in these pages, and to my mother, Mary Delaney, for suggesting I read a 1933 novel by James Hilton, *Lost Horizon*, and study *Brigadoon* for story inspiration.

I want to acknowledge the work of Ryan Holiday in *The Daily Stoic*, Martha Nussbaum's *Therapy of Desire*, and the philosophy of Byung-Chul Han, particularly around the loss of ritual (speaking of, thanks to KG's office, from which I borrowed the ritual of the Coffee Train).

Thanks to my friends who have read portions of this book or helped me as I tried to talk through these ideas, including Jenny Valentish, Sharon Verghis, Lee Glendinning, Melissa Fyfe, Bonnie Malkin and Paul Farrell.

And thanks to Carl Massy, for coaching me on how to be more Stoic.

Finally—the insightful and generous assistance given by Hal Crawford has elevated this book to a new level. Hal spent many hours carefully reading versions of this book and, without his honest feedback and brilliant suggestions, it would have been a lesser work. Hal—*you* are the Sage.